DEAR READER

Celebrating
30 Years of Publishing
in India

DEAR READER

A WRITER'S MEMOIR

SANKAR

TRANSLATED FROM THE BENGALI BY ARUNAVA SINHA

HarperCollins *Publishers* India

First published in India by HarperCollins *Publishers* 2023
4th Floor, Tower A, Building No 10, DLF Cyber City,
DLF Phase II, Gurugram, Haryana – 122002
www.harpercollins.co.in

2 4 6 8 10 9 7 5 3 1

Originally published in Bengali as *Eka Eka Ekashi* by Dey's Publishing, Kolkata

P-ISBN: 978-93-5629-535-3
E-ISBN: 978-93-5629-536-0

Typeset in 11.5/15.7 Bembo Std at
Manipal Technologies Limited, Manipal

Printed and bound at
Thomson Press (India) Ltd.

MIX
Paper
FSC FSC® C010615

This book is produced from independently certified FSC® paper to ensure responsible forest management.

Contents

Introduction

THE NUMBER OF AUTOBIOGRAPHICAL PIECES I HAVE ATTEMPTED at various points of time is not a small one. Some have said that if curated properly, they can add up to something like a memoir. But others have also cautioned me, 'Almost all your books are illuminated by your own memories—your novels, short stories, belle lettres, travelogues, even your enquiries into Vivekananda, none of them is exempt.'

Having hit eighty-one despite all obstacles, I am sometimes entertained by the things that have happened in my life. It seems not to be a bad idea to offer these stories to a new generation of readers. If they arouse some curiosity, the writer in me might be rediscovered.

It did not seem appropriate to arrange these pieces according to the strict demand of chronology. And so the stories jump back and forth in time, as the storytelling demands. In my defence, I can state that I am wholly and personally involved in the making of this whimsical collection.

A Bangaal from Bongram

I WAS BORN ON 7 DECEMBER 1933. BONGRAM IN JESSORE DISTRICT was my birthplace. India had not yet been partitioned. We were getting by as a middle-class family, but then one day in my adolescence I saw grown-ups cutting my country into pieces. For a few hours my birthplace became a part of Pakistan—they even raised its flag. Then some people found serious mistakes in Radcliffe's map, and we were turned back into Indians from Pakistanis.

The new district in which Bongram was placed was named 24 Parganas. I do not know why we couldn't stay on there, but the entire family had to move to Howrah, on the west bank of the river Hooghly. I enrolled in a school. On my very first day, the other students surrounded me and asked where I was from. Bongram, I said. That was it, they began a clamour, 'We have a Bangaal in the school, we have a Bangaal.' A Bangaal is someone from East Bengal (present-day Bangladesh). I tried to explain it was only forty-eight miles away, but who was listening? Their reasoning was that since I'd got off the train at Sealdah Station with my luggage I had to be a Bangaal.

I was ostracized at that early age. Taking advantage of the well-known Bangla expression 'Bangaal ke High Court dekhano'—

showing a Bangaal where the High Court is—my classmates would try to make me lose my temper by pointing at every dilapidated building and saying, 'There, look at the High Court.'

It was painful to listen to their constant taunts. I had vowed that if I were indeed a Bangaal, I would show them the High Court instead one day.

In school I was terrible at mathematics, but I still managed to pass my matriculation examination in 1948. The credit goes entirely to Mahatma Gandhi and Muhammad Ali Jinnah, for those who took their examinations in the year after the Partition were given an endless supply of grace marks so that large numbers of them could pass. Thank heavens I was among the candidates in that first year after Independence, for that was how I escaped the spectre of mathematics. Who knows what might have happened otherwise!

My father died in 1947. My mother took up the responsibility for our family of eight children. We lived in a rented house. The little money that came from Baba's insurance was deposited into a bank in Bengal, which collapsed in due course. It was a dreadful situation; penniless, with so many mouths to feed. Still a teenager, I was forced to wander Calcutta's streets in search of work. Some people said learning shorthand and typing would help me get a job, so I did. But no one would hire me because I was not yet eighteen.

From vending wares on the road to other adventures and misadventures, I have lost count of all the things I did to earn money. I had enrolled at Surendranath College near Sealdah at this time. The teachers here loved their students. I worked, I studied, and when I found the time, I read novels and books of short stories. I even wrote a little, whatever I wanted to. One day I read out a satirical story I had written at the college literary meet.

P.K. Guha, the vice principal, heard me—I became one of his favourite students. When he learnt of the situation at my home, he made arrangements to waive my tuition fees. For the first time I realized that even something as useless as writing could bear fruit in some way. But free tuition did not mean no household expenses. And so I had no choice but to leave college.

I simply had to earn more, but I had no idea how. That was when a friend's brother took me to Mr Noel Barwell, the barrister. A new chapter in my life began that day. I was hired as a stenographer-typist in the Englishman's office—and as a schoolteacher. This meant toiling day and night, but I had no option given the size of the family. It was Mr Barwell who changed my life, teaching me to live afresh in an old world.

Only Mr Barwell knew what qualities he saw in me, but he used to say I was a genius, that I would go a long way in the race that was life, that I was extraordinarily gifted. This made me laugh. Imagine being extraordinary yet being unable to get two square meals a day.

While Mr Barwell was at the High Court, I would read the numerous books from India and abroad stuffed into his shelves. Hours would go by, and I would lose all sense of time. My employer's affection for me and his books brought me news of a different world.

Then, one day, Mr Barwell went to Madras for a case and never came back. He died there, leaving me fatherless once again. I felt lost; it was as if the ground beneath my feet had been taken away. Who would give me so much love and affection ever again, who would teach me the philosophy of life the way he had?

I did find another job to make ends meet, but I was growing restless every day. Was there nothing I could do for the man to whom I owed so much? I hadn't been able to do anything for him while he was alive—now that he was gone I wished to do something as a mark of respect. But what? I told one of my friends, 'I would like very much to put up a statue of Mr Barwell's.' He chuckled. 'How much have you saved for the statue?' My total savings at the time amounted to Rs 57. When I told him he burst out laughing. Forget a statue, this money wouldn't even pay for a watermark of one. I would need at least a lakh. Then I thought of commissioning a portrait in oil, but I discovered that too involved great expenditure.

Was there nothing I could do?

I was having tea at a roadside shop. In the course of the conversation I asked an acquaintance, 'How can one show one's respect for someone in this city at very low cost?'

After much thought he said, 'There's something you *can* do. Many roads in Calcutta are named after famous people. I believe it doesn't cost any money. You could consider having a road named after Mr Barwell.'

I was astonished. I had assumed that the descendants of the people after whom these roads were named had to pay a fat rent every month. Galvanized, I went to meet a councillor in his house to present my request.

But luck was not in my favour. He flew into a rage when I mentioned Mr Barwell. Scolding me roundly, he said, 'So many years have passed since we gained independence, and yet you want to petition for a road to be named after an Englishman? Shame on you for not discarding your slavish mentality yet.'

Not knowing how to respond to this, I stared at him in consternation.

He said, 'What was so special about this Britisher?'

I said, 'Sir, he was someone who told an average person like me that I am exceptionally talented and will go far in life. To me he was next only to god.'

I don't know what the councillor concluded from this, but he practically threw me out of his house.

Out on the street I asked myself: Is there really nothing I can do for Mr Barwell? All my memories of him would fade slowly—how could I hold on to them? Then it struck me. Why don't I write about him? That would be my homage. I started writing as soon as the idea occurred to me, making quick progress.

One day I was introduced to the journalist and writer Gour Kishore Ghosh. As we chatted I humbly told him of my writing project. With great enthusiasm he suggested I meet Sagarmoy Ghosh, the editor of *Desh* magazine, with what I had written thus far. The *Anandabazar* office was in Chitpore at the time. With great trepidation I submitted my manuscript, which was about half its eventual length then. Sagar Babu said grimly, 'Leave your piece with me, but don't bother telephoning over the next two or three months to find out its fate.' I nodded mutely and left, my eyes fixed on the floor.

When three months had passed, I thought it might be worth enquiring. Just as I arrived at the *Desh* office everyone there burst out, 'Ah the missing person is here at last! Go, meet Sagar Da, he's been looking for you for days.'

Looking for me? Surprised, I entered his cabin. He reproached me, 'What a strange fellow you are! How can you submit a manuscript without an address? I had no idea how to reach you. Anyway, I like what you have written, I will publish it. Finish it quickly.'

I was overcome with joy. I said, 'Will you give the manuscript back, Sagar Da? I want to repair it a little.' He shot back immediately, 'Never, I'm not letting this out of my sight. Finish it, then we'll see.' So I did. It was serialized in *Desh* magazine as *Kato Ajanare*. The year was 1954. I had begun to earn from writing.

After this I began writing regularly for all the Bengali dailies—*Basumati*, *Jugantar*, *Anandabazar*. My earnings from literature began to grow slowly. One day *Jugantar* asked me to interview a famous person of my choice. But was anyone famous likely to grant me an interview? No one knew me, they wouldn't even give me the time of day. One morning I found several bulls wandering about happily in Burrabazar. Why not interview them, I asked myself, no one knows anything about them after all.

I returned to Harrison Road early the next day. Picking one from the herd of bulls, I followed him about all day, swiftly taking notes. A most gentlemanly creature, he walked along the side of the road, never crossing it until the signal turned red, and ate at the same shop every day. I titled the piece 'Bull Culture'. It was published in *Jugantar*. Parimal Goswami was in charge of the section at the time. He was full of praise. 'How did you get this idea?' he asked. 'None of the hotshots of the city has time for me, so …' I explained.

And so life continued with all its unpredictability. I had never imagined being a writer or anything remotely like one; I didn't have the leisure for such fancies. I could barely do enough to survive.

I began writing very young, but no more than one or two persons encouraged me and said, 'Here's a new writer, he should be given a chance.'

In fact, it was just the opposite. I was worn down by the tyranny of those in charge. But then I have always been impossibly obstinate, with more than my fair share of the reckless impudence of the lower middle class. I may have been forced to compromise, but I made no promises of subservience. The sycophants who controlled the share market of Bengali literature had declared that I would never amount to anything, least of all a writer. Apparently I was a 'one-book author'—my book was a fluke, there wouldn't be another. (My books were never reviewed anywhere. This would break my heart, but I never spoke up.) I had neither the time nor the inclination to get into a confrontation. Once, the power supply to our rented home was cut off because I couldn't pay the bill on time. I had earned Rs 400 in all for my serialized story in *Desh* and wanted very much to buy my mother a Benarasi silk sari with the money, but when I told her, she said, 'No need, get the power reconnected instead, darkness is awful.' I obeyed her.

There was a great regret I carried in my heart—that was being labelled a one-book author. My mother would tell me not to be upset. 'If what you have written is truly worthy, one book is enough. How many works did Valmiki or Krittibash produce? Yet everyone knows their names even after all these centuries.' What she said comforted me, but it didn't ease the pain. I would often go to a Kali temple nearby and pray: 'Whatever else you may do with me, Ma, don't make me a one-book author.'

Some time passed this way. One day, I was sheltering from torrential rain in front of K.C. Das's famous sweetshop in Dharmatala. A shop nearby was selling second-hand books. You could deposit one rupee and bring home any book of your choice; you'd get seventy-five paise back on returning it. I got myself a book to read.

When I opened it, I found an English poem on the first page, which said all of us are sitting in a plush hotel on a winter day, some of us will leave after breakfast, some will linger till lunch, and others will stay on till dinner. So don't be upset, everyone has to leave eventually. And the longer you stay, the higher your bill.

The rain had let up a bit, and I could see the Grand Hotel clearly. Suddenly it struck me that I could write about a hotel. Mr Barwell used to stay in one, and I'd been inside several times with him. I knew a lot of things that went on in hotels, why not write about them?

I went to Sagar Babu again and expressed my desire.

'Go on, write,' he said encouragingly.

That was all I needed to get down to it. After a few years my novel *Chowringhee* began to be serialized in *Desh*.

This time too I was the object of many people's ire. Some said I had no right to write about a hotel when I didn't even know how to pronounce the word 'restaurant' correctly; I should immediately stop publishing my weekly instalments. A well-known writer of the time expressed her resentment in a letter to Sagar Da: How could someone who didn't know the difference between bed-and-breakfast and bread-and-breakfast dare set his book in a hotel? Not that the mistake was mine, it was a printing error. But I had to bear the brunt of it. Still, Sagar Da said, 'No need to pay attention to what people are saying. Keep writing.'

And so it went on apace. Meanwhile I ran into Amiya Chakraborty, someone Mr Barwell had been extremely fond of. He was the collector of excise for the state government at the time. He took me to his office, where, in the course of the conversation, I told him about *Chowringhee* and that I had never got the chance to see the bars and hotels of Calcutta for myself. At this he sent for an inspector and told him to quietly arrange for me to spend as much time as I wanted at any hotel or bar in the city.

A new vista seemed to open up for me. Till midnight I would sit in various bars, observing and taking notes. When I went back home in the early hours of the morning, I would write. Calcutta had a colourful nightlife. I saw many bar girls. The pimps and their clients negotiated in code. The rule was that if a girl had to be picked up from the bar, she would first have to be given dinner. The bottom line was that the men had to spend some money; if they just disappeared with the girls quickly the hotels and bars had nothing to gain. Hence these arrangements.

I saw a great deal, without which I might never have been able to write *Chowringhee*. Now that the book has been translated into so many languages around the world, many foreigners tell me that reading it makes them want to see Calcutta for themselves, and I am reminded of those days.

In any event, I have received a great deal from life, especially the love of people, both known to me and strangers. Life's currents have swept away all the agony and the filth that had gathered. Many say I am a corporate storyteller. I am amused to hear this. I am the same clerk that I was at twenty, there's been no change. I would dress in a dhuti then, I wear shirts and trousers now—that's the only difference. There's no distinction between the writer Sankar and a corporate Sankar. A decent human can only be a single person. I am neither corporate nor a writer. Somerset Maugham used to say you are either a full-time writer or you are not a writer. I believe this too. But because it is not possible to make a living writing in Bangla, I couldn't become just a writer. When I am exhausted by work, I come back home and enter the life of a writer, and when I get tired of writing I go back to my job. This is how it has been, But there is a fundamental difference between other professions and writing. The job of a manager in an organization is to engage the right people for the right tasks and get them to do everything. But as a writer there is no question of getting anyone to do things for you. Here everything is your responsibility, and getting someone else to do your work amounts to plagiarism.

The reader's is the last word for me, the reader is the lord of my life. I don't care to get into squabbles over what I've received and what I've been denied. I have said already that I'm not a writer, so everything that has come my way in the field of literature has been an unexpected gain. Rabindranath Tagore once said on the artist Nandalal Bose's birthday, 'Nandalal may have been cheated by the marketplace, but he never cheated himself.' It's the same with me. I may have been cheated in the marketplace, but I have never deceived myself. Nor have I persecuted myself.

A thought has occurred to me often during this long journey: Everyone has an extinguished lamp within themselves waiting to be lit. It is the job of literature to light it. The greater the writer, the more lamps they can light to dispel the darkness within readers. I don't know how many I have succeeded in lighting, but it is what I have tried to do all my life—and wish to keep doing for the rest of my years as well.

May Your Family Be Perfect

BE HAPPY, MAY YOUR FAMILY BE PERFECT. THESE ARE THE WORDS of benediction with which my mother's mother would bless her daughters and everyone else in the world.

Images from that time swim up before my eyes after all these years and I am filled with regret at not having understood my grandmother despite having seen her up close.

She was a true beauty. Her name was Amritabala—and she was indeed an embodiment of sweetness. I can recall the appearance of my grandfather Khirode Bandyopadhyay clearly—tall, tending towards fair, not an ounce of extra fat on his body, a permanent smile on his face. The man himself was reckless and audacious, but we'll come to that later. Although I remember him well, I cannot recollect my grandmother's appearance as a married woman; I can only picture her as a widow, in white with closely cropped hair. Her face was one of god's unique works of art.

She used to live in Calcutta's Shyampukur area. When I was nine, my mother packed me off to stay with her after my final examinations. 'Be a good boy, don't make any demands, and never ask about Bogola Mama,' Ma instructed.

My grandmother's joy knew no bounds when I turned up at the small house on Keshta Kundu Street. Dipping into the emergency funds she had squirrelled away, she made sure to get fish for her favourite grandson's meals. Then she took me to the Kashi Mitra Ghat on the Ganga for a bath. The crematorium was next to it. Here she sprinkled water on the spot where my grandfather's body had been laid on the pyre a few years earlier, muttering, 'Om shanti, shanti, shanti.'

Always a precocious child, I asked her, 'What does shanti mean, Didima?'

Flummoxed by this unexpected question, she calmly answered, 'You'll know when you grow up.'

But I wasn't one to give up. Now that I had asked the question I needed an answer. After her bath, Didima bought 250 grams of assorted fish from the road next to the ghat, along with some potatoes and vegetables which she bundled up in the anchol of her sari. Needless to say, we had no shopping bag. She handed me the fish in a paper packet. As a Brahmin's widow she must have been loath to give off the smell of fish from her clothes immediately after a bath in the holy river, but with her favourite grandchild—her second daughter's eldest son—staying with her, what was she to do?

Back in the house on Keshta Kundu Street, I began to wonder how such a meagre quantity of fish would do for the two of us. There were other reasons for concern too. The first: it wasn't enough to buy the fish, you needed mustard oil to fry it—my grandmother may not have had enough in stock since it was close to the end of the month, she had to make what little oil she had last five days more. She had a special arrangement for conquering the family finances at month-end—this was to boil the rice with potato, dal and seasonal vegetables like radishes, and then add some salt from a little bundle. The country hadn't been partitioned yet, so Himalayan pink salt was still available. Didima used to call it 'shonduk noon'. Mustard oil in boiled rice and vegetables was a luxury, its absence didn't matter.

Satiating me as much as she could with two different preparations, my grandmother would get down to her own meal of boiled rice and vegetables. She was seated on one of the two low wooden platforms, or pidis, and I, on the other. Like a fool, I asked, 'What about your fish?' She smiled. 'I left it behind at Kashi Mitra Ghat for your grandfather.'

That no one came back from Kashi Mitra Ghat, or that that was the reason my grandmother had given up onions, garlic, fish and mooshur dal was not something I was able to grasp. 'This is the way of the world,' she said affectionately, 'you'll understand when you grow up.'

The sheer number of things I would have to understand when I grew up was beginning to give me immense anxiety.

Instead of explaining further, Didima added, 'There'll be many things in this world you'll have to think about when you're a grown-up. Didn't your grandfather tell your mother you'll be a great scholar, another Ashutosh Mukherjee?' My beautiful grandmother often bolstered her fair-skinned daughter's confidence by hinting at a correlation between dark skin and high intelligence.

One of the things Didima did tell me was that eating fish and wearing colourful clothes after one's husband's death would invite harm on the family.

I pressed her to explain what this meant. Finishing her frugal meal, she said, 'Everyone in the family should prosper and be happy. How will that be possible if we invite harm on them?'

I used to think she was foolish for choosing austere food and attire simply to ensure no harm befell others. She didn't even have a line of vermilion in her hair like my mother did. When I mentioned this, she said, 'You mustn't say that, it will bring harm on the family, there won't be peace.'

In the evening Didima lit an incense stick in the tiny room, and touched the images of gods and goddesses, and finally, two framed photographs standing in a niche in the wall, with them. Both photographs looked blurred behind the profusion of sandalwood paste smeared on them. My grandmother was constantly concerned about the welfare of not just those who were alive but also those who had died. Unlike the photographs though, her memory was as sharp as ever, as her daily rituals revealed.

It's best to share some facts about Didima at this stage. She was born with a silver spoon in her mouth. She was married to a mid-level assistant in a British company in Calcutta. Hers was what you might call the perfect family, complete with husband, sons and daughters. My grandfather worked at Fairlie Place or some such area in a company whose name is lost to history. Once, a young Englishman planted his booted foot on Dadu's chair. My grandfather's self-respect asserted itself instantly, and without giving any thought to the consequences, he chose the medium of a slap to convey his outrage. It was an unprecedented affair: An Englishman had been struck by an Indian employee in full view of everyone. Dadu walked out of the office immediately afterwards and never returned. He might have been in greater trouble had he gone back, for when it comes to slapping legal cases on employees the English have no match.

Patriotism and pride had won, but financial ruin stared my now unemployed grandfather in the face. He returned to his village with his daughters of marriageable age and his sons to fight the last phase of the battle of life. He spent most of his time in Calcutta, however, in search of work, and earned some money sporadically—like Harihar in Bibhutibhushan Bandyopadhyay's novel *Pather Panchali*. All the responsibilities rested on the shoulders of the Sarbajaya-like Amritabala, except Sarbajaya had two children to look after, while in Amritabala's family there were seven mouths to feed.

My grandmother did not visit our house in Howrah too many times. But whenever she did, she would bless my mother with these words: Be happy, may your family be perfect. My mother would listen to her own mother's benediction with bowed head. There was no doubt that she would try her best to fulfil Didima's wishes. But it must be remembered that the lack of money and fear of social censure had led her to wed someone who had been married once before. With the wedding my beautiful mother had to sacrifice two things—her wish for a young husband, and the name she had been given at birth.

I am not going to add to my readers' burden of sadness by providing an elaborate account of my battle-scarred grandmother's sufferings. Two other daughters had even more cheerless married lives and a third was relieved of all earthly pain through an early death. And of Bogola Mama, whom my mother had expressly warned me not to bring up? I've been told he was a lively, talented and popular young man, with extraordinary abilities both in sports and studies. But one day he fell ill while playing football, and thereafter ran up a high fever. His mother threw herself into nursing him, but she wasn't able to get him treated medically. The god of death took full advantage of this and made Didima suffer the loss of a son in his prime. She didn't even get the time to grieve—eventually she tried to forget the agony of losing her son by moving to Calcutta. Meanwhile the home back in the village was lost to debt. It was only when my nationalist, courageous and spirited grandmother finally surrendered to death that she was freed of the anguish of failing at life.

During the days that I spent with her, she would bathe and feed me, make me lie down on a rush mat in the pigeonhole that was her house, and run her fingers through my hair. Her touch was so delightful that even today my body thrills to its memory. And through all of this she would shower blessings on me. 'May you be a king, may you be the apple of your mother's eye, may you make her a queen. You will, won't you?' I would answer, 'I will make her, you, and my wife queens.' She would laugh loudly and say, 'You'll have to order three gold crowns at the same time then.'

Not understanding the implications, I would say, 'Of course I will, Didima. I'll have diamonds and emeralds set in yours.' She would say, 'Give the crown with diamonds in it to your mother. I couldn't give her any gold jewellery when she got married. She wore the neighbour's ornaments for the wedding, and even those were removed and replaced with imitation gold jewellery before she left for her husband's house.'

'Did you also wear imitation gold ornaments to your husband's house, Didima?' My grandmother was a trifle disconcerted by the question, for who would believe she had come to her husband's house with over a kilogram of gold jewellery? Amritabala's father was affluent, with a cowshed full of cows, a granary full of rice, and a safe full of gold and silver.

Why did my grandmother wear no ornaments then? She explained to me that a woman's happiness didn't flow from her father's wealth but from her husband's fate. Then she told me something that seemed strange at my tender age: A woman's life is sustained by three different fortunes—her father's, her husband's, and her son's. 'You'll see how happy your mother will be when you put a crown on her head and make her a queen.'

'I'll make you a queen too,' I told Didima. Possibly because she knew that this wouldn't be possible, that one cannot become a queen after death, she kissed me, ruffled my hair, and said, 'Your saying so is enough to make me a queen right now.'

Today I think back in wonder at how my grandmother told me so many funny stories to make me laugh regardless of all her suffering. Despite the way my grandfather's nationalistic fervour had hurt the family's fortunes, her sense of humour was laced with her love for her country as she sang and danced to patriotic songs. Some of the lines from her songs have survived my forgetfulness: *You may talk about your land but it isn't really yours, if it was then why would English ships with foreign goods sail along these rivers?*

I should mention that Didima would pray to god every day for the emergence of the perfect family for her only living son, whose income was quite meagre. Her home consisted of a small room on the first floor of a house, and an even tinier kitchen on the terrace. She had to share a bathroom and a toilet with the other tenants. My uncle—Didima's son—and I slept in the tiny room, while she would go up to the terrace after feeding us and lie down on a mat outside the kitchen beneath the open sky. The difficulty arose when it rained, for then she would have to roll up her mat and go into the kitchen, which wasn't large enough for her to even stretch out her legs. If it rained harder, the water would get in through the broken door and tile roof and flood the kitchen.

Once, Didima spent the entire night on the stairs because of an onslaught of unseasonal rain. In the morning I asked her why she hadn't woken us up. She had no grievance against anyone in the world—not the British, not her husband, not even fate. She was from a highly regarded family; waking her son and grandson in the middle of the night was not her style.

~

After sprinkling holy water in the Kashi Mitra crematorium with the words 'Om shanti', in response to her talkative grandson's question—'What is peace?'—Didima had answered, 'You'll know when you grow up.'

Every time I have thought about her in the years since, I have realized she was right. The truth is that peace is accessible even without happiness—as was the case with my long-suffering grandmother despite all her travails. She had no complaints against anyone in the whole wide world; all she wanted was for her son, her daughter, her grandson to have perfect families and live happily. Their happiness meant her happiness. She made being happy at another's happiness even when you had none of your own look easy.

A Remarkable Battle

My pitiful grandmother's prayers for the future generation did not, however, reach the arbiter of our fates. But at least her bones had been reduced to ashes at the Kashi Mitra crematorium by the time misfortune struck us in Howrah. All that was inevitable in my mother Abhaya's life finally materialized, starting with my father's untimely death late one night.

Thereafter my mother embarked on a remarkable battle, with nothing by way of resources except a few thousand rupees of life insurance and a body capable of toiling round the clock. She cooked four meals a day for eight children, did the dishes, washed the clothes, packed everyone off to school. When our power was cut off because we hadn't paid the bill, she cleaned the glass chimney of the lantern after all her chores were done.

Although she was not an atheist, I didn't notice my mother being as devoted to religious rituals as my grandmother had been. Her devotion was limited to going to the Kali temple on new moon nights, offering hibiscus flowers to the goddess and praying for a perfect family and happiness for her children.

The deity in the temple heard her prayers but did not comply. Her children would fall ill frequently. Abhaya would stay up nights taking care of them and read Bengali novels meanwhile. She was extremely fond of Saratchandra Chattopadhyay's works. Not a rebel herself, she sought solace in the stories of women who rebelled.

Matters became worse during the monsoon. Advance preparations were made. All the buckets and mugs, pots and pans at home were gathered in a corner to combat the misbehaviour of the rain. Anyone severely ill was packed off to the south-east end of the room, where the roof would begin leaking last.

Ma would be up and about within minutes of the downpour beginning, busy positioning the vessels in various parts of the room to collect the rainwater and protect the ancient mattresses from complete destruction. She didn't have a mattress for herself, making do instead with a mat woven with thin sticks. On the nights when she did manage to get some sleep, the sticks would leave triangular patterns on her soft skin.

My father once brought a clock for the house. It created problems for us by stopping one day, for everything went haywire unless my mother left her bed at dawn and completed the cooking in a timely manner. I remember she overslept one day, and when she jumped out of bed eventually and hurriedly tried to light the unoon, she failed because the cow dung cakes used as fuel were wet. How upset she was at having to send her children to school on meals of nothing but muri. Later in the day she brought some batasha from the grocer's on credit so that she could serve them with water to cool her children's overheated bodies when they came back from school.

It was a prison cell for continuous punishment: our kitchen, affectionately named 'Roshoboti'—the room of flavours by happy affluent poets. Far from being a room of flavours, it is a torture chamber for women. Had the Maker possessed a clear understanding of what it is like to light an unoon two times a day, he would have been magnanimous enough to send my mother and my grandmother LPG cylinders instead of compelling them to cook on these. The ashes from the previous day's flames had to be raked before lighting the unoon, especially in winter. Venomous scorpions would often seek shelter in the warmth of the ashes after the fire had been put out. One of them had attempted to sting my mother, though according to her version of the story, it had not succeeded. In an effort to mitigate her agony I fetched some antidote from a neighbour. She bore the pain without a word, for she knew that informing the doctor would mean paying not only his fees but also for the medicine and the compounder who would administer the injections.

I often marvel at how she steered the massive boat that was our household across the turbulent ocean to the safety of the shore. And yet she made no proud announcements, no demands—she had no complaints against anyone. I never saw my mother envy anyone either. Her only weaknesses were reading novels borrowed from Binapani Library and visiting the Kali temple with hibiscus flowers on new moon nights. She didn't wear widow's whites, for one of her younger children had asked her innocently but fearfully, 'Ma, are you a widow?' Several of my siblings were convinced our father had gone somewhere distant to recover from his illness; it was taking time because it was serious.

Only I, the precocious one, knew that he wouldn't return, that we'd have to stand on our own feet regardless.

Ma had long wanted to own an alarm clock. I fulfilled her wish by winning an essay competition. When the organizers asked what books I wanted as a prize, I shamelessly said, 'May I get an alarm clock instead? Don't tell my mother though.' This was my first gift to the woman engaged in constant battle to keep her family alive.

At times she seemed impatient, expecting me to beat time and accelerate on the path to adulthood. If only I'd been eighteen and not thirteen when my father died, Ma wouldn't have had to suffer so! But of course, she had no grievances. Holding the flowers from the Kali temple close to my forehead she would say, 'Bless you, be good.'

In the temple too they would sprinkle holy water—'shanti' jol—after the rituals. My mother would bow her head and make me follow suit, nudging me forward so that at least a drop of this water would fall on me.

I asked her the same question I had asked my grandmother earlier, 'What is shanti?'

And—how strange!—she gave the same reply. 'You'll know once you grow up.'

Much later, my mother looked up from a novel she was reading to tell me, 'See what it says here. Pleasure and peace of mind are not the same. Pleasure doesn't imply peace of mind.'

In other words, we can find peace even if we cannot experience bliss—as my suffering grandmother had, as my fearless mother did.

Many years later, when the storm clouds cleared somewhat, my mother could finally read her novels tranquilly, as though there had been no turbulence in her life. And even if there had been, it was as though women like her habitually appeared on earth to dispel all dangers and create happy families. Sometimes they were named Amritabala, and sometimes Abhaya.

Although she didn't say anything, did my mother have no questions at all of life? Though our family experienced little joy, my mother must have had immense reserves of peace, else it would have been impossible for her to battle on as our sole provider.

I recall two episodes. There were no photographs of my father at home. From an old trunk my mother extracted a group photograph, taken at the day-and-night studio of the Nimtola Crematorium, of my father sitting sadly, with several others, beside the dead body of his first wife. Despite our poverty, Ma sent for the jeweller and sold a bangle for Rs 21, with which she sent me to the Electric Photo Studio on Khurut Road, where they were experts at making hand-drawn portraits from hazy photographs. Ma came along too. When they asked, 'Should we add a palace or a hut to the background?' my mother replied, 'Draw a marble mansion with pillars.' This would cost Rs 3 more. 'Don't waste money, Ma,' I told her, but she ignored me. A few days later, having paid Rs 18 in cash, I came home from the shop with a portrait of my father sitting proudly in front of a grand mansion. Ma gazed at it for a long time before propping it up in the niche where the idols of deities were kept. When people die they are elevated to godly status in Bengali families.

Even today, when I recall those days of joys and sorrows, I regret asking my mother not to waste money on getting a mansion drawn into my father's portrait—I regret not giving her the courage to ask for an even bigger mansion at twice the cost.

The other scene that comes back to me, with or without reason, involves a small embroidery carpet that my grandfather had bought at a stationery shop and given to my mother as a gift. This was the practice at that time. Lines from poems would be written on jute carpets for womenfolk to bring to life beautifully with needle and thread. The artist's name would be embroidered in a corner too. The carpet that Abhaya had brought to her husband's house, embellished with her patient needlework, read:

> O master, your sport you do repeat
> Your compassion makes sorrows retreat.
> This world is a prison, a broken fleet,
> May I, a sinner, drown at your feet.

From infancy I would read the words on this framed artwork every morning, and tremble with an unknown disquiet because my mother's name was embroidered in a corner. Why should my mother drown? Anyone who tried to drown her would have to deal with me, whether they were a god or not.

Worried when I told her as much, she said, 'No, you mustn't say that. When you grow up you'll understand.'

When I grew up I began to understand many people, but my grandmother and mother weren't among them. Why are such women born in Bengali families? Why haven't we been able to conquer the world despite having them in our ranks?

During a trip abroad I was introduced to a Canadian professor who had married a Bengali woman. He said, 'You are a fortunate race—God himself has taken mercy on you and granted you women who are incomparable in the entire world.' Following this up with a most unusual suggestion, he said, 'Instead of monopolizing this gift of God's, you should share it with the West, this will make the world a better place to live in in the future.'

Initially I considered him nothing but a gushing devotee, and did not respond. But I have often wondered what power it was that enabled my grandmother and my mother to emerge victorious in the face of such adversity. How did they rise above the joys and sorrows of the world to remain calm and composed?

At first I used to think they were unique. But I realized my mistake over time. Anywhere I went, in every family I would find an Amritabala or an Abhaya; my mother was clearly one among many.

At one point in my life I met the artist Bikash Bhattacharjee. I greatly admired his mother, who had lost her husband young. When Bikash began to paint middle-aged Bengali women, it seemed to me from the early drafts that he was ignoring their physical attractiveness and possibly hurting his own interests. But later, during a visit to his studio, I discovered how the ordinary housewives he painted had been transformed: He had drawn a third eye on each of their foreheads.

Bikash Bhattacharjee's insight finally made clear to me what all my analyses and pondering had not revealed. I left in a trance-like state. All the women I had met in Bengal, on the streets or in their homes, in happiness and in misery, had a third eye on their brows. They were all trinayanis. It is to worship this power that people run desperately to temples and organize Durga Puja festivities. And yet all these women live in our own homes with their third eye and ten arms, without expecting to be worshipped. Only, we don't realize this.

Where would we be without them? It does not need me to point out that despite all the poverty and suffering in the world, the happiness and peace that suffuse Bengali households are not to be found in too many places on earth—those who are aware of the goings-on in the great global marketplace will be the first to substantiate this claim.

Mrs Mukherjee and Mrs Jennings

Another extraordinary pair of women was my other Dida and Mrs Jennings.

During my visit to America, Mrs Jennings was one of the people with whom I formed long-standing relationships. She had taken the responsibility of showing me around Seattle. That brief meeting drew us to each other, and we grew very close. One of the reasons for this was that Mrs Jennings reminded me of my other Dida—my great-aunt.

Many years ago, in 1905 to be precise, two lovely baby girls were born at about the same time, one in Jougram in Bardhaman district, and the other in Omaha in the American Midwest. One was named Golapsundari, and the other Rosalind.

Golapsundari's family found a husband for her at the appropriate age of fourteen with the help of a matchmaker in Bhadrakali. The groom was my mother's uncle, her father's younger brother, Kalipada Bandyopadhyay. Didima, a staunch devotee of the goddess Kali, grumbles even now, 'My luck was so wretched that I couldn't utter her name after I turned fourteen,' for she couldn't possibly speak her husband's name. Whenever she wanted to visit Kalighat, she would thrust her tongue out like the goddess to indicate her destination!

When I told Mrs Jennings this, she didn't believe it. 'You must be joking!' she said. 'Their husbands' names mean everything to married women, why would your granny cut it out?' Her surmise: 'There must have been some trouble in their married life.'

I didn't report this suspicion to Didima. I knew only too well how she would explode. But I did ask her why married women couldn't utter their husbands' names.

'It's easy for you to talk,' she said, 'but do you want me to utter my husband's name and fry in hell as a result?'

I smiled. 'But what about all the names you call him?'

Didima sat up on her bed in agitation. 'What else am I to do? Shameless man! Pushed off, leaving me here, helpless. How does it matter to you, you're revelling in the joys of heaven, and here I am, draped in widow's whites, living on boiled vegetables and burning in the fire of life.'

My great-aunt had lost her husband early in life and was left with two daughters and two sons to raise. A blurred photograph of my great-uncle hung on the wall. Sometimes she looked at it and said, 'Just you wait, your happy days are about to end. Once I arrive there I'll fry you up in a cauldron of oil.'

Mrs Jennings was confused when I told her this story. 'Didima believes a marriage is for all lives,' I explained. 'Kalipada Bandyopadhyay will fall into Golapsundari's clutches again in their next life, and she will exact revenge on him.'

I told Mrs Jennings of the austere widow's life Didima led—the clothes, the meals, the fasting. 'Poor Golap Shundaari!' she said regretfully. 'Why does she have to deprive herself of the everyday pleasures of life?'

Mrs Jennings didn't do any such thing. She had her share of boyfriends till the age of eighteen and then settled down with one of them. 'We had some morals still back then,' she told me, 'we hadn't turned sex into a snack like boys and girls now. My granddaughter cannot believe I didn't sleep with John before our engagement.'

When I told Didima this on returning home, she began to slap her forehead. 'Have all the women in those countries become whores then? But Krishna was born there with the name of Jesus Christ, wasn't he!'

It proved difficult to calm her down. 'Please Didima, why should everyone have become whores? It's just a matter of the culture there.'

'But sleeping with your husband before marriage? I'd die of shame!'

'I told Mrs Jennings about your chaste marriage, Didima. She was about to faint when she heard the details.'

'Why?' Didima asked with great interest. She was on her way to the bathroom, wrapped in a bright red gamchha, one of those homespun towels she favoured.

'Mrs Jennings was terrified. "A complete stranger whom I've never even spoken to will come into my bedroom and lock the door behind him on the strength of some religious rituals. Don't mind my asking, but doesn't this seem obscene to you? No girl here would stand for such a thing," she said.'

Didima's response was prompt. 'Oh please, what's obscene about spending the wedding night with your husband?'

Both Rosalind and Golapsundari had eventful married lives, details of which need not be recounted after all these years. Didima had children, and so did Mrs Jennings. The difference was that my grandmother married once, and Mrs Jennings twice. She became Rosalind Brown upon her first marriage. And after she had been a widow for some time, Mrs Brown married Mr Jennings.

'Two marriages! My god!' This was Didima from her bed.

Everyone knew she was my grandfather's second wife. 'If there's nothing wrong with remarrying after your wife dies,' I said, 'what's wrong with remarrying after the death of one's husband?'

'You cannot compare women with men on everything,' Didima answered. 'If this kind of competitiveness continues one day women might say why don't men have babies, why should we be the only ones to bear labour pains?'

At this Mrs Jennings said, 'The women in your country are human beings too. Are you trying to tell me your granny never wanted to return to married bliss after her husband's death?'

I asked Didima this question directly. She made me wait a little before replying, 'Of course I wanted to marry again. I will too. All of you will be there, there will be celebrations and a grand feast. My sons will be there as well—just that their heads will be shaven. I'll be marrying the god of death.'

Mrs Jennings told me, 'I have enjoyed life as much as possible. I've travelled in Canada, in Europe, in Australia, in Africa. My only regret is not having visited the Taj Mahal in India. I still want to taste the tandoori chicken in Delhi's Moti Mahal.'

I asked my great-aunt whether she had enjoyed life.

'What on earth is that? I don't understand the questions you children ask nowadays.'

'Having fun to your heart's content,' I explained to her. 'Mrs Jennings says you'll regret it on your deathbed if you haven't enjoyed life. Even death won't bring peace.'

Didima flared up in outrage. 'I suffered a widow's life for my sins! And now you want me to ensure I burn in hell. Do you think the god of death will escort me to heaven personally if he hears I've been having fun despite being a widow?'

'But have all your wishes been fulfilled, Didima?' I asked.

Didima proceeded to tally up the accounts. 'I went to Kashi while your grandfather was alive. I won't lie. My son has taken me on pilgrimages to Gaya and Vrindavan and Hardwar. I've been to Tarakeshwar too. I've been to "his" temple in Calcutta too. My only unfulfilled wish is to bathe Baba Pashupatinath's idol.'

Mrs Jennings and Didima have not met each other, I'm the only link between them. They know each other through me, but they cannot understand one another.

Didima is my mother's aunt, not her mother. But with my own grandmother having died long ago, this is the great-aunt who cared for me. Both her daughters were married. And Khoka Mama, her son, Kiran Chandra Banerjee, took care of his mother. His job with the railways meant constant transfers; he had now been given quarters near our home in Howrah. Every so often I met Didima and our conversation flowed comfortably.

As for Mrs Jennings, I would never have met her had I not visited America. In that distant land I was fortunate enough to receive her genuine affection. She drew me in effortlessly, as though I really was her grandson. We have exchanged letters ever since. She writes long letters, complete with photos and all manner of news; I reply to the best of my abilities.

I may have spoken about Mrs Jennings a little too much to Didima, for one day she smiled slyly and asked, 'You haven't fallen in love or something, have you?'

'You were my only girlfriend all this time,' I said. 'Now I've got another.'

'And which one do you like more?' Didima asked.

'They're different from each other,' I said. 'You're in bed all the time, or you sit around, at most you come out of your room to the head of the stairs. Mrs Jennings is out and about, on her feet all day, her house is usually locked.'

Didima grimaced. 'Oh please, this widow hussy of yours is like my daughter-in-law, must visit every house in the neighbourhood every day. Never mind the household chores, never mind the mother-in-law's needs.'

There was no stopping Didima once she began criticizing her son's wife. To change the subject I said, 'You don't wear anything but white; Mrs Jennings wears such colourful skirts.'

'How dreadful!' Didima was thunderstruck. 'God has decreed that husband-eaters must dress in white.'

'Mrs Jennings wore white gowns for her wedding—I've seen the photographs,' I tried to explain to Didima.

'What! Dressed like a widow for her wedding? Do they kill and crunch up their husbands' heads between their teeth that very day?' Didima was furious.

I had extensive discussions about Didima's attire with Mrs Jennings. She was deeply interested in such matters. She herself was always well turned out in immaculate clothes, stockings, shoes and hat. As for my grandmother, she was practically bare-bodied these days. With her bile rising, she felt too hot to even keep her blouse on much of the time. And given her obsession with what must not be touched, she ended up spending most of the day in a gamchha that was about as short as Mrs Jennings's skirt.

I probably shouldn't have disclosed any of this to Mrs Jennings, for she nearly fainted upon hearing this. 'If aged women in their right minds are doing such things in your country,' she remarked, 'how can I blame my granddaughters! No wonder they go braless.' Then she grew serious. 'It may not be right for me to say this since Golap Shundaari is your great-aunt, but she's not setting a good example for young girls.'

I didn't report this back to Didima. It does not behove a gentleman to unnecessarily instigate a quarrel between two women of similar age.

However, I did give Didima a complete account of Mrs Jennings's beauty routine. Even if she was just going shopping, Mrs Jennings spent three-quarters of an hour on her make-up, using various creams, lotions, powders, perfumes, lipsticks, and so on.

Visibly annoyed, Didima said, 'Only whores dress up that way.'

Mrs Jennings had learnt that good lipsticks were expensive in India. She put me in a quandary the day I was leaving. 'Give these three lipsticks to your grandmother with my best wishes.'

I would be delighted to convey the wishes, I told her, but my grandmother didn't use lipstick. Mrs Jennings was astonished. To stop her from wondering about this, I said, 'Even Didima shuts herself up in her room for an hour and uses cosmetics, but not for herself. She bathes the idols of our Lord Krishna and his beloved Radha and then anoints them with sandalwood paste.'

These days foreigners know more than Indians about Krishna. Mrs Jennings blushed when I mentioned him. 'Lord Krishna is the finest of your lovers, isn't he? Your Don Juan? He had an affair with a married woman named Radha Ghosh, didn't he?'

I didn't protest, for she would immediately open a book to show me the references. With great regret she said, 'I wish your granny wouldn't encourage this immoral behaviour and adultery.'

Back home, the next time I visited her, Didima said with a big smile, 'Now that I'm an old woman you don't care for me any more. Remember you'd promised to take me to your Dadu's temple?'

Mrs Jennings flew around the world by herself with two suitcases. Poor Didima had never been anywhere on her own. Even to go next door she took her six-year-old grandson as an escort. She didn't even know her way around the city. I had to appease her with a promise to take her to Kalighat, as she had asked, within the week. Then I brought up Mrs Jennings and told her, 'She's sent you her best wishes.'

Didima gave me an impish but probing glance, much like a detective. Then her interrogation began. 'Can you tell me why, instead of the mountains and forests and gods and goddesses of that land, you keep talking about that woman?'

I laughed. 'Mrs Jennings is your age, Didima.'

'Don't try to laugh it off. I've heard these older foreign women like marrying boys.'

I continued laughing without protesting.

Didima said, 'And how did my rival trap you?'

I explained everything. Here Didima couldn't take a step out of the house unless she was accompanied by someone, and there Mrs Jennings showed strangers around town. Not for money; she simply enjoyed it. She had registered to be a guide for foreigners, spending her own time and money on fuel for her car. And she grew so fond of me while driving me around that she insisted I check out of my hotel and stay with her instead.

'And then?' Didima's interrogation continued.

'Mrs Jennings said, "Call me Rosalind, Sankar." I didn't agree. "I have a great-aunt your age back home, I call her Didima," I told her. "I'll call you Gran too."'

Obviously she wasn't pleased, no one abroad wanted to be thought of as old. 'You'd better call me Didima too,' she said.

Buckling under the pressure of Didima's grilling, I showed her a colour photograph of Mrs Jennings. Scanning it carefully for a long time she said, 'What is this? How will anyone know whether she's married or a widow?'

'You cannot tell over there,' I said.

This didn't please my great-aunt at all. 'No wonder the scriptures say it's a land of heathens,' she said.

Didima discovered more reasons to be furious. She practically fell off the bed at the next photograph: Mrs Jennings was lighting a cigarette. 'Oh lord, did I have to see this too? A woman smoking! The end of the world is nigh,' she wailed—and promptly put a dollop of chewing tobacco in her mouth. I stared at her. Didima said, 'I don't care how Western your ways are, don't you encourage your wife to start smoking.'

'Her cigarettes and your tobacco are the same, Didima,' I submitted deferentially.

'Did the hussy tell you this? Oh my god, has anyone heard such a thing? Are milk and liquor the same thing too then?'

Arguments were pointless after this.

But I noticed that she was gradually beginning to accept Mrs Jennings, who, on her part, kept enquiring about Didima in her letters. They were becoming friends in a sense.

Whenever she saw me Didima would ask, 'How's that foreign lady of yours? I bet the hussy still strolls around town in rouge and lipstick.'

'That's what reports say,' I told her. 'Mrs Jennings has been asking after you too and has a question for you: What desires do you still have?'

'Desire? What's that?'

'Your wishes,' I tried to explain.

'Tell her I have just one desire—to get out of here as soon as possible holding Death's hand.'

Didima's health took a turn for the worse. And according to reports, she was growing proportionately irritable.

The next time I visited, she sent for me as soon as I arrived, gesturing to me to close the door behind me. I realized she had been stockpiling complaints against her family.

'The end of the world is nigh,' she said. 'Aged parents are worthless today.'

'What's the matter, Didima?' I asked.

'What do you suppose! A woman has no one but her husband. Do you imagine I would have had to suffer such terrible joint pain if your Dadu had been alive? One time, I had a pounding headache—I still cannot forget how he massaged my head half the night. But who cares for an ancient widow now! No one here even has the time to give me an oil massage for this rheumatism.'

I spotted a bottle of medicine near her head. 'I see your pills there.'

Didima sneered. 'That's just for show. A bottle of pills from the doctor so people think they're taking care of me. Tablets don't help rheumatism; you need hot oil massages. But do I have a maid to do these things for me?' After a pause she continued, 'Khoka goes to work. Bouma is busy with the household and the kitchen. My grandsons have their football.'

'Let me talk to Mamima,' I said. I knew Didima's daughter-in-law looked after Didima to the best of her ability.

'It's no use.' Didima stopped me. 'She'll give me an oil massage for show, and after that everyone in the country will hear about how the cooking got delayed, her husband got to work late, the children were scolded at school ... all because of this.'

'You mustn't stand for it,' I advised. 'Tell Mama everything when he's home from work.'

'You think I don't? I do, every single day, but who's listening! The end of the world is nigh. The sages said long ago that the wife would be more important than the mother in this period.'

'Mami has so many things to do, the maid hasn't been coming for a couple of days. Why can't you order your grandsons to give you a massage?' I tried to pacify Didima.

'Wait till you grow old, then you'll know those who pretend to care are even worse. I can't tell you how horrible rheumatism is. Even labour pains can be endured, but this is far worse. One day

I did ask the elder grandson very nicely to massage my joints. He did it but with such force I was shrieking in agony. Deliberately.'

Holding her arm out, Didima said, 'People will say I'm exaggerating. But see for yourself, it's still swollen. There'd be a criminal case if I informed the police.'

'You didn't tell Mama?' I asked.

'Of course I did. But the scolding he gave his son was just for show. The boy said he didn't realize, and his father believed him at once. Dhritarashtra, blind with love for his son.'

Popping a paan into her mouth, Didima continued, 'Those days when children worshipped their parents like gods and goddesses are gone.'

I ran into my aunt on the way out. Theirs was an ordinary household; Mami somehow managed to run everything smoothly. And she took care of her mother-in-law with great dedication. 'What was the discussion about?' she asked.

'Top secret,' I said, suppressing a smile.

'Not secret at all, she complains about us to anyone she meets. She won't let us massage her though. It's not like kneading dough, she says.'

A letter from Mrs Jennings arrived around the same time by airmail. It said her rheumatic pain had flared up so she was now exercising for half an hour at the clinic every day on the doctor's advice. This had produced good results. Praising her son, she had written, 'It was touching how anxious John and my daughter-in-law have been.'

The next time I met Didima she was on the verge of tears. Asking me to shut the door, she grasped my hands and said, 'No matter what you do, never bring a girl from Hooghly Raghunathpur into your home as your bride. My decision to wed my son to a girl from that neighbourhood has proven to be disastrous.'

'What are you saying, Didima?' I asked. 'That's where you're from too.'

'Doesn't mean I won't tell the truth,' she said, all but crying.

'What's the matter?' I tried to console her.

'At first they would just beat me up, but now they're rationing my food. I'm a widow, what do I eat anyway but plain vegetables? Now she says she won't add sugar to my tea. What are they going to gain by saving four spoons of sugar a day?'

'But the doctor's forbidden sugar for you,' I explained to her.

'That's what they tell everyone. Imagine cutting off the roots and watering the leaves. What joys do widows have anyway? No need to prolong my life by cutting off sugar.'

'Have you told Mama?' I asked.

'I have, but he pays no attention. His wife's word is supreme.'

'Complain about her to him,' I advised.

'Hah! Do you really think he will say anything to her?'

Didima went on to air a litany of complaints against today's young men. The only relationship with them was one of giving—give birth, clean their shit and piss to raise them, spend money on their education, then hand them over to someone else's daughter and live like a maid, doing all the housework in return for your meals and clothes.

I recalled that Mrs Jennings didn't criticize her son at all. On the contrary, she wrote reams in praise of him and his wife.

Suddenly Didima asked, 'Is that my friend's letter there in your pocket?' Her antipathy to Mrs Jennings had dissipated, she now referred to Rosalind as her friend.

'Your friend has rheumatism too,' I said, 'but she's better now after exercising.'

'Has she written about her children?' Didima asked.

'She's praised her son and daughter-in-law profusely, they're very good to her, love her dearly. The daughter-in-law is very sweet and caring.'

'Fate!' Didima sighed. 'Not everyone is as lucky.'

'Why do you say that?' I asked.

'These memsahib hussies do nothing for their children. They give birth to them, that's about it. They don't nurse them, don't let them sleep in the same bed, don't stay up nights, don't wash their sheets; they teach their children to be independent from the age of three. Just look at all the trouble we go to! Yet she's the one who can't stop praising her son and daughter-in-law.'

An image of Mrs Jennings's family in distant America floated up before my eyes. Her son lived near his mother even though he was married; he owned a barbershop.

Didima was so irked she said, 'You've seen for yourself how things are here. Teach them how one should treat one's mother.'

'It's true, Didima,' I said. 'Mrs Jennings always says, "There's no one like Bob, I'm so proud of Bob."'

'So he's the kind of son who makes the mother who gave birth to him proud,' commented Didima.

'His visits were a sight to behold,' I said. 'He'd run up to his mother and hug and kiss her.'

'Even hearing about it makes me happy.' Didima sighed. 'Never mind a hug, your Mama couldn't even be bothered to ask how I am.'

I had to tell her more. 'Bob never visits Mrs Jennings without a gift, Didima. Sometimes he brings flowers. He and his wife ask her together, "How are you, Mother darling? Any problems? Tell us if there are, don't hold back."'

'Instead of me, tell your uncle these things. He comes to me only on the days I fast, doing his duty with a handful of fruits. And a perfunctory enquiry every day: Is the rheumatism better? That's all.'

'Mrs Jennings is truly happy with her son,' I had no choice but to tell Didima.

'I'd have been happy too if I were treated as sweetly,' Didima rued.

'But Didima, remember when you were so ill you kept losing consciousness? Mama took a loan from his Provident Fund for your treatment. He hasn't managed to pay it back yet. Mamima never left the house during that time so she could look after you.'

'Oh please, it was all for public consumption,' Didima retorted glumly. 'Only done because they wouldn't know how to face people if their mother died without being treated.'

Lying back in her bed, Didima instructed me, 'Write to my friend that fate has been very kind to her to provide such a son and daughter-in-law.'

I recalled that Mrs Jennings had admitted as much. I was her guest at the time, and she was reeling off Bob's qualities as she served me breakfast—how smart he was, how his business enterprise was flourishing, how much he loved his mother, and so on.

It was after breakfast. Mrs Jennings was examining her face in her vanity mirror. 'I have to go out for half an hour,' she told me. 'I have an appointment at Bob's salon.'

On her way out she added, 'I can't tell you what a good boy he is. He will cut my hair himself with great care and give me a wonderful massage. And he won't charge full price, he'll give me a twenty per cent discount. Who gives up twenty per cent these days? As a son he's one in a million.'

This information had hit me like a bolt of lightning. Charging your own mother for a haircut—what sort of civilization was this? But I was hesitant to burden Mrs Jennings with such questions. Nor could I bring myself to tell Didima, if she felt some peace of mind at the thought of Bob's love for Mrs Jennings, why should I come in the way?

I Remember My Father

There was a time when I would join an adda with friends whenever possible. There would be frequent and long sessions with familiar faces in the Ramakrishna–Vivekananda Ashram in Kasundia. Later on, though, I withdrew from these; I felt that I didn't know myself well enough and ought to spend some time on introspection. When a seemingly extroverted person becomes an introvert without notice, it can lead to a lot of misunderstandings. People whose affection and indulgence I had grown up with complained that I was changing, that I was drunk on success and was no longer accessible to those I knew.

But that is not it at all! The truth is that having spent much of the leisure in my life without putting any thought to it, I want to be a little thrifty now, I do not have enough time left to say spending it in one way is as good as spending it in another.

I want to immerse myself in writing for some time, without seeking even a moment's respite. My only objective is to close the study door, stop the clock from glaring at me, open the window of my mind and shamelessly seek inspiration from the goddess of learning. Even after all these decades, I have not been able to solve this mystery of literature—sometimes a story will pop up in one's head unbidden, on other occasions not all of one's entreaties to the goddess will yield anything! Like a disinterested idol, the goddess, Saraswati is wrapped up in herself.

These moments of seeking alms but not receiving any are discomfiting. I begin to lose faith in myself, even though self-confidence is the foundation of all creation. The finest creator is one who can keep faith in themselves and yet lose themselves. As for the unfortunate like me, who are employed as casual labourers in the goddess of learning's factory, we are entirely dependent on her daily handouts. All's well if we get them, but there's nothing to be done if we don't.

It is in the nature of the heart to retreat rather than advance when these alms are not available. Victory implies progress, while defeat leads to a backward journey. And that in turn means recalling those who were with us once but aren't any more.

I know there might be a reunion with all of them in my heart during this period of leisure. They do not care for crowds, they are shy and retiring even after crossing over, unwilling to bother me unless I have endless time at my disposal. I will have to invite them loudly. *Ihagachha, ihagachha, ihatishtho, ihatishtho,* come and take your seat here, please, I am longing for your company. Too many details of these reunions cannot be shared, for even the writer, who is a slave to the reader, needs privacy at times. That is when they have to humbly submit, 'I have left my pen elsewhere, it is only your company that I seek. Make a little room for me in your joyous world of unexpressed feelings, I shall not disrespect you.'

Those who return thus, secretly, do not sign my visitors' book; they seem to exist beyond the relationships I once had with them. This is a peculiar situation. These days I often feel death is a kind of divorce. My father, my mother, my brother are all separated from me by death—they are now my former father, former mother, former brother, they have obtained divorces from the court of God and severed their relationships with me. They have tasted freedom.

As Durga Puja nears, I wonder who is stationed on memory lane for a silent rendezvous with me. The number of divorces in the form of death keeps growing—there are so many people in this world I know, so many whose love made my unbearable suffering bearable, so many whose debts I have not paid, who did not wait for the accounts to be settled, who left on their own, issuing ex-parte decrees of eternal separation. All year long, I am completely immersed in my work, forgetting I am the victim of hundreds, even thousands, of divorces. Trouble strikes when the music of reunion floats through the air during the festive season of Durga Puja.

This time when they visit, I'm considering not letting them leave so soon. I'll interview them in the manner of an experienced journalist. I mean to get answers to the questions I couldn't ask them when they were alive, to settle the doubts that fester in my mind even today. I will find out what can be done about the debts I have not paid back. For instance, I will ask my father, 'What about that money?'

My father was a grave man, perpetually occupied with the compulsions of earning a living. A huge family, no savings, and additional responsibilities. There were many temptations too—after all, he had control over the property and assets of other people temporarily. Still, he tried his utmost not to be tainted. Lawyers had a bad reputation anyway—even when someone was honest, no one believed it.

I had asked Baba for money once. Not a paisa or two, an entire eight annas. He was in the drawing room, counting out some money with the cashier's help. He had been appointed the court receiver of a jomidar's assets at that time.

He was counting out thousands in currency notes and coins and arranging them neatly, but he didn't give me the eight annas I asked for. 'When I have some money,' he said.

This made no sense to me. There was so much money that even two persons were finding it difficult to count, and yet he had just said 'when I have some money'.

I considered asking the cashier for the eight annas, but that was out of the question. He had given me a four-paise coin once, which had led to mayhem at home. My father had returned the money to him on that occasion, and a new rule was established: There would be no monetary transactions with visitors.

I was both upset and angry now, but Baba paid no attention, he was busy counting. 'Go and do your sums,' he said. 'Don't waste time here.'

I was too young then to understand the value of time. What happened next gave me great joy. I wanted my father to be in trouble because he had not given me the eight annas I had asked for. And that was exactly what happened. The cashier and he could not tally the amount.

They counted the loose change obsessively but it turned out to be a rupee short every time. It made no difference how many times they counted. 'You can't have brought the entire money from Joynagar,' Baba scolded the cashier.

'I counted three times, it was the right amount down to the last paisa when I left.'

They began counting again, but the outcome was the same.

The cashier got to his feet, shook his clothes out, checked his own bag, all to no avail. 'No one has taken it, have they?' he said finally. My father was irked at this. 'What do you think you're saying, Bara Da? There's no one here besides you, me, the clerk and Sankar. Surely you don't suspect my son?'

The cashier was contrite. 'Suspect your son? May I never commit such folly in my entire life.'

My father agreed. He had deep faith in his son. The boy didn't study nearly enough, but there was no question of his being dishonest.

'Let it be, we'll square up later,' the cashier said eventually. My father was unwilling. Sending for my mother, he said, 'Give me a rupee out of the shopping money.' A rupee was not a small sum in those days, it would put pressure on the household finances. But despite her reluctance, Ma had no choice. 'I don't need so much milk this month,' my father told her. 'Integrity is more important than a glass of milk.'

Time rushed by. My father was still a young man when he left us for the place where children's pleas for money could not be heard. In my childhood I pondered a great deal over why we became fatherless so early. I had read somewhere that the sins of children are visited upon their parents.

When I asked my mother, she replied confidently, 'My children are gems, each and every one of them. They have done no wrong. It must be my sins from my past life.' I had no response to that; we were never particularly frank with each other.

If I get the chance, I will try to settle the accounts with my father for that one rupee. Such a small amount! Now, in the afterlife, perhaps he is not bothered by such trifles any more. But I am. 'Help me shed my guilt, Baba,' I will say. 'It was I who took a rupee in rage that day. You'd have found it if only you had searched me, but you chose to trust me instead—Haripada Mukherjee's son is nothing if not honest.'

I still feel afraid at the thought of the dangerous turn my life might have taken had I been caught with the money that day. Your faith in me has saved me every time I have come face to face with temptation since then, I have reminded myself that Haripada Mukherjee's son is nothing if not honest.

I didn't spend the money, but I didn't have the courage to return it either. I threw it into the drain through the window.

I do not know why, but I spent my entire childhood in deep agony over this. Was it because of my wrongdoing that Baba left us abruptly? It was all so long ago, but I am desperate to settle the account of this rupee. If I ever get the chance, I will bring it up with my father, albeit with great trepidation.

Shoe Shopping

I HAVE COME TO KNOW COUNTLESS MEN AND WOMEN OVER THE years, but even today, when it's time for Durga Puja, there are two people whom I think about the most. My father, and the writer Saradindu Bandyopadhyay.

Separated by many years, the two did not know each other, yet they are connected indelibly to my memories of Durga Puja because of an insignificant pair of shoes.

Baba was a stern figure—there was always a distance between him and his children that defied my efforts to gain proximity. And so I would wait impatiently for Durga Puja—on the first day of the festive fortnight, Mahalaya, my father would offer prayers to his forefathers in the morning and then go out with the entire family in the evening to buy us shoes.

Durga Puja was not a time for shoes alone. But the matter of new shirts and shorts or trousers had already been taken care of at readymade garments stores in Howrah. Tailors with measuring tapes around their necks had not infiltrated the world of children yet, nor had the made-in-Bombay outfits wrapped in shiny cellophane made their appearance in our lower-middle-class life on the outskirts of the big city. We were still shamelessly dependent on the makeshift

Tuesday markets in Howrah and on small-scale clothes-makers in Agarpara.

But it was different when it came to shoes. This was the one area where Baba took a personal interest. From our house in Chowdhurybagan in Howrah he would take us down Harrison Road to the vicinity of College Street in Calcutta. He was partial to one particular shop there, though we found it monotonous to get our shoes from the same place every year. But he would remind us that when he was young, the shoes for the children of the local jomidar's family were always supplied by this very same shop: Graduate Shoe Store. Perhaps this annual shoe-buying expedition was how that fatherless adolescent boy from the village fulfilled his childhood wishes.

He would hold long conversations with us in the shop when buying us our shoes, and help us choose as well.

We were a large group of brothers and sisters. The girls would get their shoes first, followed by the youngest of the boys. When it was finally my turn, my father would sometimes ask the salesman, 'What are the damages so far?'

Back then I didn't understand the reason for his anxiety, but the fact is that he was a lawyer in a small-town court with an average earning, and the father of many children—a massive financial responsibility, especially at this time of the year. And the court being closed for over a month during this festive time meant reduced earnings; lawyers in this land earned the least at the precise time their social expenditure peaked.

Reflected in the gigantic mirror in that shop on College Street, Baba's face suggested he was paying more attention to the price tags than to the shoes. He wouldn't say it in as many words, but he seemed to be hinting that I pick a cheap pair of shoes. His expression made me pick the least expensive pair available, even though I was not old enough to properly understand the deep mysteries of earnings and expenditure.

Back home my siblings said I had chosen the worst shoes, that I had no taste. This annual humiliation would exhaust me, but I couldn't tell anyone that selecting these cheap, poor shoes had made Baba happy.

That year too Baba had taken us to College Street. After snacks and sweets at Dwarik's sweetshop, we arrived at the shoe store. But this time I wasn't willing to lose out. However, my father's financial condition seemed even more precarious than usual, for he began checking the total costs even before it was the turn of the brother born just after me.

Examining the price tags, Baba extended a cheap pair of shoes towards me. At once I demanded the most expensive option. My father tried to convince me to take the cheaper shoes. 'Looks like a very good pair,' he said.

I was upset with him. I had never asked him for anything expensive, but he was trying to dissuade me now. Taking advantage of my silence, he asked for the cheap shoes to be packed. But now his son rebelled openly.

'Let me take the expensive shoes,' I said. 'When I grow up I'll buy you the best pair of shoes there is.'

My father gave in at that. It must have put a big financial burden on him, for he purchased nothing for himself. But my promise had brought a strange, wistful smile to his face that day.

That was the last time we bought shoes with our father. His untimely death soon afterwards cast our family into crisis. The clouds finally lifted after many trials and tribulations, but through all that I never forgot that mysterious smile.

Meanwhile I entered the world of literature. I had a pleasant dream on the night before Mahalaya in which Baba was still with us. I had taken him to the shoe shop, and was telling the salesman to bring out the most expensive and modern pair of shoes. Once again my father's face broke into that unforgettable, wistful smile. And I woke up. I was miserable afterwards.

The writer Saradindu Bandyopadhyay was visiting Calcutta for a few days from his home in Poona. He was one of the very few people whose affection had breathed life into my barren existence. Even today I treasure the wonderful memories of this large-hearted man.

Having been brought up outside Bengal, Saradindu did not have much experience of the Durga Puja celebrations in Calcutta. He had seldom been in the city when his novels were published in the annual Durga Puja editions of magazines—something we had often laughed and joked about in his Poona home. 'Let's rent a room somewhere remote beyond Bardhaman,' he told me, 'and run away there. We'll return only if the reports about the novel are favourable, or else I'll escape to Bombay directly via Allahabad.'

I hadn't forgotten the dream I had had of my father. I could afford to buy gifts now, but the person I wanted to give them to was gone. I wondered why Baba had come back in my dream now, considering how long ago he had left. Finally I made up my mind. To lighten my burden on this holy day, I would buy a pair of expensive shoes for a father figure whom I cared for deeply. It was with this intention that I arrived at Saradindu Bandyopadhyay's house in south Calcutta one morning directly from Howrah.

He laughed loudly at my proposition, and then called out to his wife. 'Sankar has decided to boot me out this year.'

I begged his pardon piteously. 'I know I've made an arrogant proposition; no one presents shoes to those they respect. But please grant me this opportunity, it is essential that I buy you a pair of shoes.'

Suppressing a smile, Saradindu said, 'Making me happy with a pair of shoes is a very difficult task, Sankar.'

I had more than a hundred rupees in my pocket, money was no object. I said, 'The more expensive your choice, the happier I will be.'

He still had a disbelieving smile on his face. As if asking, *Why brag about something you cannot do?*

I was adamant. There were many shops nearby, I had enough money in my pocket—there was no cause for concern.

Finally he said, 'Very well, since you insist. But I've warned you already, don't blame me if you cannot satisfy me.'

His wife, who was present, was smiling secretively but she didn't say a word.

Our first stop was a massive Bata showroom. There was a crowd of Puja shoppers. 'Your most expensive shoes, please,' I told the salesman.

'Put your foot here.' Extracting his foot from his shoe, Saradindu planted it on the measuring stool, whereupon the salesman seemed to panic: They didn't have shoes in his size.

I stormed out in a bad mood. Saradindu was still laughing. Instead of giving up, I took him to several other shoe shops, but the salesmen in all of them ran away on seeing the size of his feet. My obstinacy mounted. We took a taxi to the old shop on College Street where I made Saradindu sit on a bench. I looked at him in the mirror, as I had my father all those years ago. Here too no shoes that would fit him were available.

Out on the pavement, Saradindu said, 'Don't blame me, I did warn you. But I came with you so that you wouldn't misunderstand me. I don't get readymade shoes for these spade-sized feet anywhere except Russia.'

I was wondering what to do when he said, 'Let me give you a suggestion, my boy. Why not buy me an umbrella or dhuti instead?' And so a fine dhuti it was, but it was a gilded gift, not real gold. No dhuti could substitute for shoes for my father on the occasion of Durga Puja.

In the taxi, on our way back to south Calcutta, I asked him from where he got his shoes.

'I place orders with a shoemaker in Poona,' he said. 'He has a wooden frame the size of my foot.'

I made up my mind to visit that shoemaker with Saradindu on my next trip to Poona and fulfil my dream. Wretched as my luck is, I never got the chance.

Even today, I am reminded of both my father and Saradindu when it's time for Durga Puja. Long ago, as a child, I did something wrong when getting new shoes; try as I might, I have not been able to undo it even after all these years. My father and Saradindu Bandyopadhyay continue to vex me every autumn.

Durga Puja

Whenever the Durga Puja festivities are imminent, I am reminded of my mother. Like the goddess, she too fought many battles to protect us from danger. Even amidst the grand puja celebrations many heartbreaking memories leave me forlorn.

Every year, well before the advent of Durga Puja, Ma would remind me, 'Start the shopping now.' The pressures of writing often delayed this activity, and I would be scolded for my tardiness. My mother was convinced that shopkeepers increased their prices the closer we got to Durga Puja.

Ma had memorized the shopping list for everyone, but she never cared to write it down herself. She was seldom satisfied until her eldest son put pen to paper and took on the role of her scribe. Two names were always missing from the list—her own and her eldest son's. Knowing full well that the aforementioned son was not one to buy anything for himself, she would slip out one afternoon and use the money she had stashed away to buy him a dhuti. Similarly, the son would also go shopping at least once for his mother despite her reluctance. It was an easy project for the colour of a widow's sari never changed, nor did its style. Only the price went up every year. I had no choice but to report a lower price than the actual one, or she would have worried about how her son would carry the burden of the growing expenses for an enormous family.

Some people will smile mockingly. I don't have anyone now who will worry and make a fuss about such matters, for whom I have to buy white saris. I recall an incident from childhood, when Ma was floundering with eight children after my father's death, and the insurance money was yet to come in. How could those who were barely surviving expect to celebrate Durga Puja with gifts? A little money came in from pawning a small inherited mango orchard in Gobardanga, and was used for the youngest children—Ma had decided that some of them would get shorts and some, shirts. She waited every day for the postman to deliver the money order, but there was no sign of him.

Finally the first day of Durga Puja, Shoshti, was here, and my youngest brothers cried themselves to sleep because they hadn't got new clothes. Early the next morning Ma handed me some money to buy clothes for the little ones; I was not particularly old myself. It felt embarrassing to go shopping on the second day of Durga Puja, Shoptomi. Everyone would know we hadn't been to the shop earlier because we weren't able to get the money, whereas we wanted to give the impression that we belonged to the set of people who claimed they did last-minute shopping because they never had any time. I bought the clothes, my youngest brothers stopped crying, and Ma too was thankful to see the smiles back on their faces. I asked her when the money from Gobardanga came, but she evaded my question instead of answering it.

I learnt the inside story later. Although still a minor, I had already begun earning. Once, I got some extra work that had to be done overnight and was paid Rs 30 for it. I was thrilled with this unexpected earning, and the feeling rubbed off on my mother. I was dying to buy her a new sari, which she desperately needed. But she said, 'Some other time. For now you'd better get back my gold bangle which I had pawned to so and so.'

I had no knowledge of this until then. The person who had lent her the money said, 'It was on Shoptomi morning. I told her it wasn't right to pawn your jewellery during the festival, but she wouldn't listen.'

Eventually those trying days did come to an end, and it was no longer difficult to give everyone new clothes for Durga Puja. But every year during Durga Puja, on Shoptomi morning, I can still see my mother secretly pawning her gold bangle for money to buy clothes for her youngest children.

Luchi or Khichuri?

My father was not a Hindu priest, but his father had been one. Moreover, there was a renowned Sanskrit school and priests' residence near the Howrah neighbourhood where I spent my childhood and youth. As children, many of those who went on to become priests were my playmates. Like everyone else, they too were interested in football and theatre and films when they were young. But poverty was one of their curses. Those who performed the rituals to gods and goddesses for the well-being of ordinary people never ate or dressed well themselves. I couldn't blame those among them who regretfully moved away from the family profession in search of a better life.

Our feasts during Durga Puja were of a certain kind before my father's untimely death in 1947, and those during the first festivities in independent India completely different. Earlier, we were deeply interested in getting the inside information from the family that conducted the Durga Puja rituals in their home. How much of the enormous quantity of fruits and sweets that was served to Ma Durga and her family did they consume themselves, and how much did they leave for devotees? I was astonished when enquiries revealed that Shiva, Durga, Kartik, Ganesh, Lakshmi, Saraswati & Co. were pleased that offerings were made, but they never actually ate any of them. I realized that it was precisely because they don't eat anything that these gods and goddesses are revered so much here on earth. I was also told that the day they started devouring the food offered to them, the very nature of devotion might change.

Despite being on their feet continuously for four days during their visit to earth, and not touching even a morsel of the variety of extremely edible offerings served to them, Ma Durga and family were still on the heavier side—the goddess herself, her husband, and her beloved son Ganesh were definitely overweight. The reason for this, I've been told, is that the daughter-in-law Ma Durga brought home to take care of the entire family's nutrition was a little partial to her own husband, Ganesh, who had developed a belly as a result. The snake he used as a belt gasped constantly to keep his stomach under control.

Elaborate Durga Puja rituals were conducted in one of the houses in our neighbourhood. The son of the owner informed his friends in private that a high mound of laddus was offered to Ganesh, whose wife had prepared no diet chart for him. There was no need to either for in heaven there were no heart attacks, no cholesterol, no heart failure—all of which made one's life as a god most pleasurable. No wonder Mahishashur had dethroned Indra at the first opportunity and usurped the seat of power in paradise.

One's curiosity is limitless at that age. I got inside information on Kartik too. Far from being the commander-in-chief of the gods—there is no account of his having fought Mahishashur—he actually married a woman named Devasena and became 'Devasenapati' or commander-in-chief of the army of the gods. The goddess was put in charge of bringing up children. If in doubt, read the *Devibhagavatam*.

I used to envy my priestly friends in the neighbourhood, for I had been told that the *Devibhagavatam* clearly states that the offerings to the goddess must subsequently be served to Brahmins. Offer honey on the first day of the rituals and pass it to Brahmins; on the second day offer jaggery and then give it to Brahmins to ward off unhappiness; on the third day, coconut; on the fourth, khoi or parched rice; and on the fifth, black sesame to dispel the possibility of death. The young children of priests confessed that all of this was symbolic, no one could live on such rubbish.

This led to more enquiries about the food served to the deities. Ma Durga's favourite items were payesh or rice pudding on Sunday, milk on Monday, bananas on Tuesday, fresh ghee on Wednesday, powdered sugar on Thursday, sugar lumps on Friday, and ghee made from cow's milk on Saturday. In our childhood we were also curious about what Mahishashur, built as he was like the bodybuilder Monotosh Roy, survived on during these days. The young priests told us pityingly, 'You fools, the bull is vegetarian and eats grass and weeds.'

What about Ma Durga's mount, the lion, then? Is the king of beasts also forced to eat all kinds of near-inedible substances under pressure from Durga and family as well as circumstances? I have been to the Alipore Zoo many times—no lion there will consider eating such things.

There was no scope for bringing these subjects up at home. Ma would fast on the first day of Durga Puja, but make sure we got her share of the luchi. On the second day the feast was vegetarian, but the menu was of a different kind. On the third day most people eat khichuri, but a generous ancestor in the Mukherjee family had done succeeding generations a tremendous favour by instituting the consumption of luchi on this day. On the fourth day, of course, it was a grand spread of mutton. Can anyone claim Ma Durga didn't decapitate Mahishashur to ensure we ate meat? But for these additional pleasures we had to starve, no, fast till the flower rituals were completed in the morning. There is a world of difference between starving and fasting. It took until Baba's death for me to realize that one is mandatory and the other voluntary.

We had Durga Puja celebrations in the forty-seventh year of the twentieth century too, the first in independent India. The absence of my father had brought us perilously close to penury. It wasn't obvious on the first two days, but the danger signs were clear when I saw no arrangements on the third day to knead the dough for the luchi. My young mind refused to consider the expenses involved in getting all the ingredients.

And so I asked unreasonably, 'They're making luchi in everyone's house, why not ours?' Ma had managed to procure some khichuri for us, but that wasn't good enough. As far as I was concerned, she was at fault! My great-uncle had said long ago that we would eat luchi, not khichuri, and the leftover luchi would be had for dinner too.

Furious, I said to my mother, 'What if I don't have the khichuri?'

'Don't even think such a thought on an auspicious day, it's a sin.'

'So what if I commit a sin?'

'Your mother will die.'

But not even this warning made me back down; I was certain it was her fault that we weren't going to have luchi.

Suddenly we heard there was a grand feast of luchi for children at Chowdhurybagan. Angry with my mother, I went there directly. Mounds of luchi were being brought in, disappearing in a flash. I was to eat with the next batch.

My mother didn't say a word when I went home much later, perhaps because it was an auspicious day. She only asked, 'What did they give you with the luchi?' I didn't answer. She probably read the truth in my face; like the Goddess Durga, all mothers in this land are mind readers. I couldn't bring myself to eat for someone had said, 'This is for poor people, it's just being called a feast for children so that they don't feel slighted.' I wasn't poor.

Ma had not eaten yet. Now she pushed her plate of khichuri towards me. During that Durga Puja my mother fasted without even a sip of water on Shoshti, and then again on the third day, Ashtomi, because of her eldest son's whimsical behaviour. Apparently the more you fasted at this time, the better your life would be.

Many years have passed since then. Life has changed greatly with the passage of time. Thousands of restaurants—from Chinese to Thai, Italian to Greek, Continental to American, Punjabi to South Indian—compete to feed people during Durga Puja, from Bengal's own lobster to bekti, koi, and other fish, from the first course to the last. For gourmets, being in Calcutta is mandatory during Durga Puja. Five stars, seven stars … many more stars than can be in the sky get busy serving up banquets to celebrate the visit of the goddess.

Thanks to her generosity, I have both the opportunity and the status to be invited to many such feasts. But I still feel the pain of having tormented my mother on that long-ago Durga Puja afternoon, so much so that even luchi turns to ashes in my mouth.

The Meaning of the Word 'God'

Writing about Ma, writing about Bibhuti Da, writing the untold stories of Mr Barwell's life—all of these will need both space and time. It isn't reasonable to trust memory always; once you've crossed sixty, it's best to write things down. So many memories vanish while waiting to be written about.

But why write these things in the first place? Certainly not for self-satisfaction, there is no greater sin in society than self-promotion. What we need is acknowledgement. Some unbelievable but true examples to ensure that the wretched of the earth in the generations to come do not lose faith in the world entirely. To them I have only this to say: This world has not yet become devoid of love. I have found succour repeatedly amidst strangers on the tortuous road of life. Basking in their generous love and affection has enabled me to survive in this largely heartless, loveless world. I bow my head again and again to the human gods who live within many. Like evergreen trees they stand in the endless desert in order to restore our faith in society, to kindle the humane within us. Some might say this is apotheosis, but I don't care. I have no objection to worshipping anyone, dear reader, for instead of wasting my time pursuing gods in heaven, I have gathered the resources for my arduous pilgrimage on earth from humans worthy of being revered and remembered.

The rented home in Bongram in which I was born was known as Noni Babu's house. A wealthy Noni Babu somewhere must have been its owner. Even by small-town standards it was an ugly structure. Only those who have lived all their lives in rented houses know the misery and distress of this form of existence. Middle-class snobs refer to those who never acquire a permanent address with the derogatory Bangla term *bashare,* whose English equivalent might be 'renters'. When it came to arranged marriages, renters were usually low in the pecking order. Still, after the untimely death of his first wife, Nibha, my father had no difficulty in finding another bride in the form of my mother.

My father bought some land in Bongram in December 1933, shortly after my birth. A few years after this, there was a minor quarrel with the landlord. Connoisseurs of art, literature and theatre used to gather beneath a lychee tree every evening, which finds reference in Bibhutibhushan Bandyopadhyay's writings. The pillars of the local community were present as well. One particular evening the discussion veered round to rented houses, and there was unanimity that it did not suit the eminent lawyer Haripada Mukhopadhyay to live as a tenant. My father's post office savings book had no more than two hundred rupees in it. One of the participants in the evening gatherings was an established businessman named Jahan Ali Biswas. He said, 'I will supply bricks, cement, and everything else you need, pay me later.' Someone fetched a religious almanac, glanced at his watch, and said, 'The most auspicious hour is right now.' To think was to act. A lantern was lit, and one of those present, Manmatha Chatterjee, offered two bricks. Everyone set off in the darkness to lay the foundation for Haripada Mukhopadhyay's new house.

It was the things my father had to do to complete this building that made him leave Bongram. He ran up huge debts and his earnings as a small-town lawyer were not sufficient to repay them. Unfortunately a redrawing of the jurisdiction map had reduced the number of cases in Bongram. This was when my father ran into a judge, who used to respect him greatly when he was posted in Bongram.

Learning of the upheavals in my father's life, the judge said, 'You're so talented, you should leave the subdivision and go to a large town.' My father said, 'Even if I move it will take me three or four years to get a legal practice going. This profession is impossible when you have mouths to feed at home.'

The judge said, 'I'm a judge for the Howrah district now. I can help you get an income of two hundred or two hundred and fifty rupees. I have a case which needs a receiver. Register with the Howrah court as soon as you can and inform me immediately.'

And so by a twist of fate I had to abandon paradise and move to Howrah via Sealdah Station. At that time anyone who got off the train at Sealdah Station was considered a 'Bangaal' from East Bengal.

We found shelter in a building at the end of an alley leading out of Chowdhurybagan Lane in Howrah that would put even the lanes of Kashi to shame. It was very easy for strangers to lose their way. Our house was numbered 18/L, and the one opposite ours, 18/K. This was where, on my first day in Howrah, I met Badal Chandra Basu—whom I addressed as Badal Kaku.

He was a most unusual man, one of the two persons who left a deep impression on my life, whose images live on in my heart and mind even after their passing. I wrote a couple of stories about him long ago, in which Badal Kaku was transformed into Asru Mama.

I realize that one does not meet someone like Badal Kaku without enormous luck. The sheer number of incredible characters to be found in Bengali households is a matter of real wonder, it's just that we don't get to know of them.

Badal Kaku's story runs thus: After passing his matriculation examination from Mugkalyan School, he drifted to Howrah in search of a living and, unable to make any headway, learnt Pitman shorthand. Such neat and efficient stenographers were rare even in the British era in India. Having mastered shorthand, he joined the English company Kalamazoo, where he grew to be a devotee of its head, Mr Livingstone.

Although this Mr Livingstone took his leave from India after Independence, he kept in touch with 'Bose', and they wrote to each other regularly. Livingstone wrote twice a month, and so did Badal Kaku. The final letter came from Livingstone's daughter, who wrote, 'Dear Mr Bose, your letter arrived yesterday. I am sorry to inform you my father, your friend, passed away last week with all his faculties intact. Your regular correspondence kept him connected with India; even on his deathbed, he was awaiting your letter.'

Even though he was blindly devoted to Livingstone, Badal Kaku was a staunch swadeshi. He would say, 'The British as businessmen are not the same as the British as rulers. Britain made a big mistake in ignoring the role of the businessman and occupying the one of the ruler.' That Badal Kaku was right was proven later, for the genuinely efficient British firms enjoyed unbelievable business success after 1947.

A portrait of Mr Livingstone hung on Badal Kaku's wall. Along with those of Mahatma Gandhi, Netaji Subhas Chandra Bose and Napoleon Bonaparte. Abbott's *Life of Napoleon* was part of his personal collection, and he would often read to me from it, though none of it made any sense at that age. But I listened carefully to his explanations; if anyone had succeeded in giving the English sleepless nights, it was apparently the Frenchman Napoleon.

Badal Kaku was an idealist. Intent on ensuring his younger brother received the best education, he chose not to marry. You could call him a strict moralist too—he neither smoked nor drank; not even tea was served at his home. Only once did he buy a cup and saucer for an emergency, in case Mr Livingstone visited. He was an eternal enemy of cheap songs and cheap culture. He walked to and from his home in Howrah to his office on Clive Row, and was never late in nearly half a century of work life. He never took casual leave, except on two days. That those two days were dramatic ones should be evident to the experienced reader.

Badal Kaku's greatest regret and failure was his younger brother. He had dreamt of helping his brother achieve what he had not been able to himself. Spartan discipline to me was just another term for the 'Badal Basu regimen'. But his younger brother felt so oppressed under this extra pressure that he revolted one day. Shattering his elder brother's hopes and defying all his mother's pleas, he left home. That was the first time Badal Kaku took the day off from work, as he did the next day. It was a historic event. Worried by the fact that Bose was not in office, and had not given any advance information either, Mr Livingstone himself appeared at Badal Kaku's Howrah residence. That was my first glimpse of him.

Being one of eight siblings was a most troublesome affair. My mother was so busy having a succession of children and carrying the burden of the enormous family that I was deprived of her attention till the age of thirteen, when my father died. As for my father, he was usually distant. When he came from the court, he met his clients, read law books, and occasionally reprimanded his junior colleague Girindranath Basu and his clerk Jogen Manna. But I did get his company once for several months at a stretch, when the word 'evacuation' was spreading across Calcutta, along with 'blackout' and 'baffle wall'. Subsequent generations learnt of load shedding, but had no idea of the significance of blackouts. Two more words have disappeared during our lifetime—'famine' and 'cholera'. There can never be a famine again in any circumstances, since its name has been changed to 'drought'. Cholera too has been renamed 'enteric fever' or something like that.

Back to those days. With everyone at home engaged in the battle for survival, no one had the time to satiate the endless curiosity of a growing boy. That was when two individuals took on important roles in my life—my father's clerk Jogen Manna, whom I referred to as 'Mastermoshai', and Badal Kaku. The latter had unlimited time for me. He took me seriously, and gave thoughtful answers to all my questions. He used to keep the *Chambers Dictionary* handy when reading *The Statesman* every morning, and when he came from work, he would sit down with the newspaper again after a snack, underlining many of the words with a sharpened, fine-pointed pencil. As he read, he expressed his anxiety about the ups and downs of the Second World War. He wanted the British to be walloped by Hitler's forces, but he didn't want them to lose for that would harm Livingstone. There was a dearth of petrol in Calcutta at the time, forcing Livingstone to resort to a horse-drawn coach, which even I had the opportunity to ride in.

After poring over the newspaper, Badal Kaku would put it away it so carefully that every copy seemed fresh and untouched. For my part, I would wait impatiently for these newspapers to be sold by the kilo. This business of selling the newspapers was something of an event. There would be a series of negotiations with a succession of scrap buyers and a deal would eventually be struck with the highest bidder. Then came the checks on the weights being used—Badal Kaku had caught numerous buyers cheating on weights. Next he meticulously counted the money he had received. After the buyer had hoisted his sack on his shoulder and started to leave, he was suddenly called back urgently. Am I in trouble, he'd wonder. But no, the reason was different. The proceeds from the newspaper sales had been divided into three portions. One would go to Badal Kaku's mother, one would be used to buy lozenges for me, and one would be given back to the scrap buyer as a gesture of goodwill. Most scrap buyers were astonished by such behaviour—they had never encountered such a strange customer.

From Badal Kaku I learnt the value of dedication to work. 'There are hundreds of people seeking my money,' he would say, 'the landlord, the newspaper vendor, the milkman, the coal seller, the grocer, the maid, the servant, the cook, the shopkeeper, the doctor, even the pickpocket. But there's only one person willing to give it, that's Mr Livingstone of Kalamazoo. So the entire world must be placed on one pan of the scales and Livingstone on the other.' I didn't realize the significance of what he had said then, but I do now. The pen-pushing Bengali has earned countrywide infamy for their neglect of work and responsibilities. Our decline began the day the social Bengali converted the workplace into the drawing room, and refused to accept work duties in their heart.

I am astonished every time I think about Badal Kaku's discipline, punctuality and work ethic, which were matched by how neatly and well he organized his things—everything was always in its place. From the moment he awoke till he went to bed, his timetable was absolutely rigid—the schedule could not be changed even slightly. And then there was his self-reliance. He washed and ironed his own clothes, and cleaned his shoes with the air of an artist; I cannot believe I saddled him with the responsibility of looking after my shoes too.

Badal Kaku would tell me about events happening around the world, and listen to my opinion earnestly. The daily goings-on at the Kalamazoo office, Mr Livingstone's observations, or the future of the Calcutta Football Club established by the British were all at my fingertips. Badal Kaku reported his conversations with Mr Livingstone in English, which helped me overcome my stiffness with the language at an early age. This unofficial tutoring in English proved a blessing when my search for a job brought me to barrister Barwell's door on Old Post Office Street later in life. Without my knowledge of the language I would have lost many an opportunity—and perhaps *Kato Ajanare* would never have been written.

We used to address Badal Kaku's younger brother as Pochu Kaku. He too loved me greatly and was instrumental in my admission to Howrah District School in December 1939, where I started directly in class three since the school didn't have classes lower than that. I benefited from skipping those classes, for when my father died in 1947 I was already in class ten. Had I been in class seven in keeping with my age, I would never have been able to take and pass my matriculation examinations. Even in those days, anyone without a bachelor's degree had no social standing in our country, and someone who had not even passed their school-leaving examination was practically an outcast.

Life in the district school did not prove particularly happy. Calcutta was engulfed by the fear of Japanese bombing. The evacuation began, and we went to Bongram, but then my father and I came back, for he had to earn a living, and I had to go to school.

But what school? The military were stationed in our school building. Classes had been shifted to the morning section of the girls' school, but that too was closed. One of my father's clients said, 'Ask him to try at Vivekananda School, Haripada Babu.'

My father was engrossed in his work, so I appeared by myself at Vivekananda School on Khurut Road in the middle of the term, seeking admission. That was my first glimpse of Sudhangshushekhar

Bhattacharya. Swarthy and a little on the heavy side, he was dressed in a milk-white khadi panjaabi and dhuti. Makhanlal Chakraborty, the headmaster at my old school, was always seen in a suit.

It was love at first sight. Sudhangshu Babu was astonished to discover I was there by myself. Fortunately there was a shortage of paper, so the admission test was conducted orally. He asked me to speak on a topic of my choice. This was no problem for me—I knew all the conversations between Badal Kaku and Mr Livingstone by heart. I said a few words on Mohun Bagan versus Calcutta Club. I don't know what the headmaster saw in me that day, but he was convinced I would grow up to be famous. Jugal Babu came in to ask if I should be tested in arithmetic, but Sudhangshu Babu said, 'No need, brilliant student.'

Unfortunately, thanks to mathematics, I was never brilliant when it came to examinations, for which Sudhangshushekhar and his brother Himangshushekhar were perpetually regretful.

Both brothers were dedicated to Vivekananda's ideals. And yet they were fiercely independent. They lived like monks, having passed all the tests of a life of renunciation, and yet they were householders—only in name, for neither had married. Devoted to their students, they seemed wedded to their school.

It needs many lifetimes of piety to get such extraordinary teachers. What Sudhangshu Babu taught us did not need to be looked up in textbooks afterwards. His firm adherence to discipline and punctuality, alongside his modesty, percolated into the behaviour of hundreds of students over the years.

Sudhangshu Babu was at the root of the events that led to my becoming a writer. At the weekly literary meets, he would encourage us to write on various subjects. I had no ambitions of becoming a writer, but during class one day Sudhangshu Babu asked who among us were entering the essay and speech contest.

I sat quietly, but for some reason he assumed I was participating. Thus began my life as a writer—with the blessings of my guru. I was like a puppet in his hands.

Sudhangshushekhar was equally adept in Bangla and English. He believed it is hardest to write simply. Just as an uncomplicated person is everyone's favourite, so too does uncomplicated writing win everyone's hearts. But someone who has not succeeded in digesting complex subjects cannot write simply. He also emphasized brevity. 'You must know where to stop,' he would say. 'You've seen the train at Ramrajatala Station, haven't you? Unless the train stops precisely where it should, the carriages overshoot the platform, and getting on and off becomes difficult.' Next came wit, which, he insisted, was like the salty and sour flavours without which the entire meal becomes bland. 'Look at how Thakur Ramakrishna does it, he uses wit and humour to make all these indigestible things easy to take in, people derive both pleasure and reassurance from reading him even today.'

The 'Sudhangshu school of writing' was my first and primary resource when I began my journey. Sudhangshu Babu followed the same principles in his own writing too, never using five words where one would do. I did not realize then how valuable this style was when it came to writing in Bangla. Other writers spend years searching and experimenting to learn this, but Sudhangshushekhar gave it to us as a gift.

He would go out for a five-mile walk every evening, starting on Khurut Road and going to Ramrajatala via Kashundia. In his pocket would be an old newspaper, which he would read on the railway platform if there was time, watching the BNR Bombay Mail go by. He was usually accompanied by a favourite student on these jaunts.

I thank the god of good fortune for the wealth of rare knowledge I gleaned as Sudhangshushekhar's walking companion for several years. This form of education through conversation began among the ancient Greeks—the legendary Socratic dialogues—and Sudhangshushekhar was an incomparable exponent.

A believer in strict discipline, he didn't tolerate any deviance. The students had to assemble on the grounds every morning and sing devotional hymns. One day, I allowed a friend to persuade me to stay on in the classroom. After the prayers when the headmaster asked which of us hadn't joined, I confessed. There was no mercy, I was kept standing for three hours. I haven't received too many such blows in my life. Many were delighted to see the plight of one of the headmaster's favourite students, while others were surprised. I was so hurt I assumed this was the end of the relationship.

But the unexpected took place that day. Since I did not go to Sudhangshushekhar's house for the evening walk, he came to our house himself. I had to go on the walk with him, during which he behaved as though nothing had happened that morning. It seemed we might get late returning from Ramrajatala that day, but he was unmatched when it came to punctuality. In these situations he ushered his student companion into a bus, paid for the ticket, and made sure everyone got home in time before he went back to his own.

The two brothers led frugal, thrifty lives. Their only indulgence was treating guests to tea. Anyone who turned up at the appointed hour would get a cup of tea made personally by one of the brothers on a kerosene stove. They drew meagre salaries, but were devoted to the school. It was their dream and their endeavour to ensure that the ideals of Swami Vivekananda were inculcated in the new generation.

Sudhangshushekhar had the rare ability to convert even a solid stone into a juicy sweet, an ability that he was eager to pass on to his students. Hundreds of books have been, and will be, written about Ramakrishna and Vivekananda. The number of articles is beyond count. But all of them are rehashed—how many of the writers say anything novel, or throw new light on the complex lives of their subjects? This was where Sudhangshu Babu stood out. He would tell me, 'Read for yourself, don't eat pre-digested food. Immerse yourself directly in Ramakrishna's and Vivekananda's writings, see if you can find things that appeal to you. Always remember that Ramakrishna was the infinite tranquil sky, and Vivekananda the turbulent Atlantic Ocean. Somewhere in the distance, beyond the range of our vision, the sky and the ocean meet.'

On the basis of whatever little writing prowess I had demonstrated, the headmaster had expected me to make him and the school proud. Why did you have to get me into extra trouble with such expectations, Hadu Da? I will not be able to fulfil any of them, and sooner or later you will feel all your efforts have gone to waste.

Fate dealt me another blow. My father fell ill around the middle of 1946, when he was diagnosed with high blood sugar. His condition worsened during the horrifying riots that year, and then, late one night in April 1947, he left for the other world. I had gone to bed a short while earlier to snatch some rest; I woke up to the sound of my mother sobbing. The city was under curfew, and one seemed to have been imposed on my future too.

I didn't exactly know then what grief means. I will not demean myself by denying that the survival of the family appeared more important to me at that point than mourning my father's death. Genuine grief came much later; I was somewhat settled in life then. It was the day in 1955 when my first book, *Kato Ajanare*, was published. I took the first bound copy home and handed it to Ma. She took it but didn't open it. A few moments' silence, and then both of us began to weep. Relief overwhelmed us: The danger had passed, we wouldn't starve to death now. Suddenly my mother said, 'Your father used to write. He'd have been very happy to see this book.' I too would have been delighted to see him in a new role. You wouldn't have had to bear the responsibility for running the household alone, Baba, I would have taken care of it. All we would have wanted from you was for you to stay with us, just stay. Look, your son Sankar is a writer now. That night I was truly grief-stricken. Grief that involves self-interest is not real grief, it is only regret for loss.

I had lost faith in myself after my father's death. Sudhangshushekhar had observed our suffering from a distance. He waived my school fees even before I asked. Himangshushekhar used to take coaching classes for students; he invited me to join without even mentioning fees. Those who claim kindness has vanished from the world are unfair to such human beings.

After passing my matriculation examinations, I went out every day in search of work, walking all the way to Howrah Station, then across Howrah Bridge, along Strand Road, to Esplanade. I grew familiar with every tiny room in every building in the area, but not one of them had a job to offer.

Again, Sudhangshu Babu assumed the role of a saviour. I needed a job desperately, but couldn't bring myself to ask him. He realized the situation and dispelled all my embarrassment and hesitation. 'We need someone at the school,' he said. 'Why don't you do it?' He had no need at all to give me a job, the offer was made only out of consideration for me. I was terribly embarrassed all over again, knowing he would expect me to make a success of myself.

Do not put me in such a position, O Lord, allow me to be lost in the human jungle, free me of my shame.

I got the chance to observe Sudhangshu Babu even more closely during my time as a teacher at Vivekananda School. His happiness lay in sacrificing all pleasures and dedicating himself to the task of shaping the new generation. One Naren Dutta had said some things long ago, and here Sudhangshushekhar was, calmly applying himself to ensure that every word was reflected in the lives of his students. They meant everything to him, in them lay his salvation. Ramakrishna had said little boys are pure milk, just warm it a little and serve to the gods. Sudhangshushekhar possessed the unlimited patience needed to warm this milk little by little, day by day, month by month, year by year. Without any doubt or hesitation. Why should there have been any, after all? His faith in what Ramakrishna and Vivekananda had said was boundless, there was no question of their having made a mistake.

Meanwhile, I managed to get a job with the Birla Company. Sudhangshu Babu said, 'What I pay you barely covers your family expenses. Take the new job, but don't tell anyone. I'll make sure your post remains available, you can come back if something goes wrong there.'

I didn't have to go back. Instead, there was a new opportunity. I had mastered shorthand and typing at M.N. Dutta's typing school. There I met Bibhuti Roy, fondly known as Gana Da. His brother Anil, who was my schoolmate, had introduced me to him. Bibhuti Da was the clerk to Noel Barwell, the British barrister of Calcutta High Court. His employer was getting old and fearing that he would soon have to look for a job, Bibhuti Da was revising his shorthand skills.

Bibhuti Da had found another job, and suggested I replace him in Mr Barwell's office. I had some doubts initially. What if the old man died suddenly? But Bibhuti Da had blind faith in his conviction that anyone who came into Mr Barwell's circle would be blessed with good fortune.

'Do you want to remain a typist all your life,' he asked me, 'or do you want to see what life is?'

I had by then abandoned all my dreams at the Bamboonagar Burning Ghat; all I wanted was to survive somehow. But what if I could grow into a bigger role? That wouldn't be bad at all!

Sudhangshushekhar heard me out, and then said, 'Go ahead. Remember what Vivekananda said: "The effort to fulfil your potential in the face of constant adversity is what life is."'

A new story unfolded after this. I was reborn in Mr Barwell's chambers, where I learnt to see the world from a new perspective. And how I became a writer after his unexpected death is a story known to many.

I have already mentioned what I did with the first bound copy of *Kato Ajanare*. I gave the second one to Bibhuti Da. Wrapping his arms around me, he wept quietly. Noel Barwell had been to him what Vivekananda and Ramakrishna meant to Sudhangshushekhar. As for the third copy, I gave it to my former headmaster in his home in Kashundia. Sudhangshu Babu wasn't someone whose expression revealed his feelings.

'I did it, sir, what you had wanted. I am coming out of the darkness of the well, sir, I can see the light.' I had tears in my eyes. Sudhangshushekhar considered his students' success his own. Not being one given to offering blessings, he embraced me. 'Who am I to bless you,' he said, 'god resides within you, glory to god.'

Sudhangshu Babu was like a friend and companion during this phase of my life. He was kindness incarnate—people like him have left the world poorer by not having families of their own. But then they had greater responsibilities, which included nurturing the next generation, and setting the foundations of a new era. Families get you far too involved, and unless you neglect them every step of the way, your vision for the world cannot come true. All those who strove to fulfil their larger dreams for society were known to have been unfair to their own near and dear ones—from Buddha to Vivekananda, from Gandhi to Subhas Bose, it's the same story.

'I didn't go to the trouble of marriage,' Sudhangshushekhar would say, 'since that would come in the way of running the school properly.'

I had never expected the headmaster of my school to discuss these things with me like a friend.

Many years have passed since then. I had not imagined Sudhangshushekhar's life taking the turn it did. A darkness had descended all over Bengal in the 1970s—much like the period of chaos that the *Matsya Nyaya* talks about. From Vidyasagar to Ashutosh, the dagger of hatred spared no one. I was told Sudhangshushekhar was no longer going to his school. Next thing I knew, he was in hospital. When I went to see him there, I sensed his disillusionment and disgust in every word he said. The discipline and punctuality that had been the foundation of his work had disappeared from Bengal. Another person visiting him at the hospital said he would send a young boy to meet Sudhangshushekhar. The latter promptly replied, 'No, don't. Teenaged boys make me uncomfortable.'

But were these boys not supposed to be pure milk? Had the milk begun to sour? Sudhangshushekhar was too ill to be asked such questions.

He retired from his job subsequently in what was a tumultuous decade. Hurt beyond belief, he chose to exile himself from the institution that had been his life, where he had spent fourteen, sixteen, eighteen hours every day.

Sometime later he sent for me and said, 'Help me make a will. I have some paltry savings and this house I have inherited.' I assumed he was going to bequeath everything to the school, but to my astonishment, he didn't even mention Vivekananda Institution. Instead, he told me, 'My father used to teach in a Sanskrit school. Start one in this house if you can. Take the help of the Sanskrit teacher, Nityananda. This is best. Maybe Bharatvarsha can be excavated from the earth again.'

I did not have the courage or impudence to offer advice. Nor could I bring up the matter of the school. It was as though his lifelong dream had been shattered right in front of my eyes. After paying his premiums every month, a man is told the insurance company has gone bankrupt.

We sat there face to face. It was essential to talk, absolutely essential. But I couldn't summon words to my lips. Finally I recalled Vivekananda. 'The effort to fulfil your potential in the face of constant adversity is what life is,' I said.

Sudhangshushekhar stared at me blankly. I gazed at the frail old man for a long time. It seemed to me that a tree had been cruelly uprooted.

There was a particular joy in becoming a teacher in the very school where I had studied. I savoured this pleasure to the utmost. A principal reason for this was that Kanai Da was still teaching there, and who could be joyless in his presence? Few know him, he is not famous, either by his own name or a pseudonym. Yet I consider myself honoured to have been in his company. It makes me wonder why these 'insignificant' people do not find a place in the history of mankind.

Much later, I was on my way home after work one evening when I heard that Kanai Da had passed away. Early that morning, while everyone was still asleep, giving the slip to Vivekananda School,

Kashundia, and the monastery, the water insect had surreptitiously returned to the water.

I got off the bus and went directly to the school, where I saw a scene that was unprecedented. All the doors and windows were closed. On any other day the lights would be on in the school office overlooking Netaji Subhas Road, as well as in several rooms on the first floor. But now everything was dark—as though the mains had been switched off, allowing the building to sink into a giant vat of liquid darkness.

Still I couldn't turn my back on this sight. I gazed in silence for a while at the building that was awash with memories of Kanai Da. Then I began walking towards Hadu Da's house in Kashundia. Many of the students who were unhappy with him for obvious reasons often called it the tiger's den. The cognoscenti referred to it as a modern Sanskrit school, where locals converged every morning and evening for adda. One day I must write a great deal more about this shabby, neglected building on Kashundia Street in Howrah. This was where a cup of tea was earmarked for Kanai Da twice a day. He used to spend so many hours here, and was seen in the drawing room so often—no matter the time—that many mistook him for a resident.

Today the place was shrouded in silence, like an abandoned building, as though everyone here had vanished together a long time ago, and no one had dared go anywhere near it since.

But no, I was wrong. Peeping through the all but closed window shutters, I found someone sitting inside. Even with the feel of winter in the air, he was waving a handheld fan slowly. This was the spot where Kanai Da had sat every day, chatting with us, getting into arguments at the top of his voice, shouting, 'You think you know everything. What I'm saying will be accepted even by the Supreme Court, you will have no option but for a mercy petition.'

Hadu Da was sitting next to Kanai Da's customary spot like a stone, some ghostly power moving his arm with the fan.

One look at him made it clear he had no awareness of the surroundings. At least a dozen plump mosquitoes were peacefully sucking blood from his bare torso, not hesitating to perch on his back and even his ears. Hadu Da was frozen, without the slightest desire to get rid of them. Some empty tea cups were scattered on a small table. A full cup of tea sat in front of him, cold now, a thick film of cream on top.

Entering, I realized it wasn't an abandoned building after all; there were others. 'That's Kanai's cup,' whispered Patterson Da, a lifetime member of Hadu Da's daily adda sessions. Hadu Da had asked for tea for Kanai Da too by mistake—old habits die hard, after all. But Kanai would not be coming to claim it and raise a tempest in a tea cup.

I said nothing, leaving in silence. Patterson Da—Rabindranath Patra—followed me out. I waited for him to catch up with me. Together we walked towards the Ramakrishna–Vivekananda Monastery on Naskarpara Lane, in silence, like students at a school for the profoundly deaf.

People called it the Ramakrishna–Vivekananda Monastery, but we had done away with the first two words and referred to it as just 'the monastery' or 'the ashram'. It was a group of committed bachelors from this ashram who set up Vivekananda Institution, inspired by the great men the monastery was named after. The environment at the ashram was not very different from the image conjured up by the word. There was no unnecessary excitement, the place became quiet and tranquil after the evening prayers.

Tonight it was even more silent than usual. The lights were not on. In the beam thrown by a distant lamp post, I could indistinctly see some of the residents staring into the pond, lost in their own worlds. This would never have happened had Kanai Da been present. He would have rushed in as he normally did and shout, 'What's wrong with all of you? Have you fixed silencers to your mouths? I don't understand you lot, frankly. I have no idea how you can just dress up and sit quietly on those benches. Nothing doing.' He would grab their arms, drag them to the edge of the pond, and flop down on the steps leading down to the water. Then the adda would begin.

But who was going to start an adda tonight? Kanai Da's gilded ship had left us behind and sailed for some unknown destination.

I couldn't stay there; I walked away. Patterson Da didn't try to stop me either. On any other day, everyone would have objected loudly, 'This won't do! How can you leave so soon?' Tonight we were all immersed in our own grief.

I went back home, reflecting on my loss. Let this one evening, this Saturday, be Kanai Da's evening. Tonight there was no literature, no politics, no economics on my mind, only Kanai Babu, Kanai Da, Kanailal Bag.

The writing pad lay on the desk. Perhaps Hadu Da would request Shankari Da or me to write about Kanai Da's death in the insignificant magazine of our insignificant school. Or perhaps he would pick up the pen himself. I could predict what he would write in his flawless Bangla:

> The late Kanailal Bag had an association of dedicated service and support with our school and the Ramakrishna–Vivekananda Monastery from childhood till the day of his demise. His relationship with both of these institutions was so close and intimate that the question of whether his loss can be compensated for is not even relevant. We are inconsolable with

grief after Kanailal's death, we have no choice but to bear it helplessly.

He has left us at a mere forty-eight years of age. He passed the entrance examination from our school and joined us in the capacity of teacher in 1932. After his entrance examination he underwent training in automobile engineering and acquired the necessary skills, but when it came to selecting a vocation, he elected to teach at Vivekananda School. Perhaps he did not really have a choice in the matter, for he began as an infant member of the community of young men inspired by Ramakrishna and Vivekananda to found the Ramakrishna–Vivekananda Monastery and, in natural course, became one with this brotherhood. A formal disciple of Swami Virajananda, Kanailal continued to discharge his debt to his country and his mentor till the very last day of his life.

Kanailal was a simple and uncomplicated man. He was not partial to succumbing to emotion and was given to performing his tasks with close attention. An unostentatious, humble man, he ensured the dignity of the establishment he belonged to. His wit and eloquence made his company especially pleasurable for his friends and elders, while his students came to be closely acquainted with his kind but firm disposition.

I pray to Sri Ramakrishna to grant eternal peace to his soul.

But there were other ways to know our Kanai Da too. A philosopher has said a man can be king at least twice in his life—as the groom on his wedding day, and as the sleeping monarch who departs to eternal life on the day of his death. Kanai Da, however, was crowned only once, having voluntarily abjured the first opportunity with a vow of eternal celibacy. Today he was king, but only for a day; the kingdom was his, but only for this brief period.

Who would remember him when the earth returned to its position after a year of revolving around the sun in its orbit?

Those who want their names written permanently in the ledger of the world have to pass stiff examinations. This money-minded world hunches over its red accounts book like a wizened moneylender. Provide all the details, down to the last paisa, of your joys, your sorrows, your sins, your piety, your acceptances, your sacrifices, your good deeds, your misdeeds. Then the old man will add subtract multiply divide, and only if there's a sizeable surplus at the end will your name go into the ledger.

But had Kanai Da provided his accounts, or even wanted to? The geriatric usurer will roll with laughter if I try to intercede on Kanai Da's behalf. To tell the truth, I don't have the courage to dismiss his derision. And yet, there was nothing I wouldn't have done for Kanai Da once I had met him.

I remember those days very well. I had just enrolled in school, and a teacher who always humiliated students who hadn't done five pages of handwriting was about to take class. Some of us were waiting glumly for him. Even giving up games of hide-and-seek during the tiffin break and writing in large script at the speed of the Bombay Mail hadn't helped fill more than two pages. Necessity is the mother of invention—with a crisis looming, it occurred to me how wonderful a writing machine would be. Who would fear handwriting assignments after that? All the bad-tempered teachers at school would be taught a lesson.

I was about to applaud my brainwave when a friend sneered, 'The British invented a machine like that long ago. In fact there's no need to go to their offices to see it. Keep your eye on the school office, you'll see one.'

I didn't trust him at first. But the very next day I saw a man in the school office loading a sheet of paper into a peculiar machine and using it to write it without even following the movement of his own fingers. I couldn't believe my eyes. A man writing on a machine without even looking? Who was he—a human being or a cursed angel?

My friend was astonished. 'You don't know him? Haven't you seen him in the other building?'

How was I to know him? I had not had the chance to study in the other building, having leapfrogged the primary section horse to nibble the high school grass on Khurut Road.

'That's Kanai Babu,' my friend whispered in my ear.

It was my turn to be astonished. I had never met him in person, but even in this inflationary market his slaps were supposed to be cheaply available. He was generous with his pinches too, charging next to nothing for them. I had been harbouring the mental image of a stocky, terrifying person by that name. Now I savoured the joy of gazing at a tiger from a safe space. Suddenly I heard a voice: 'You, come inside.' That's when I realized I had stepped inside the tiger's lair instead of watching from a distance. My friend dashed away. Entering with a tearful face, I said, 'I didn't want to come see it, sir, they made me.'

Solemnly unloading the sheet of paper from the machine, Kanai Babu said, 'It wasn't you who wanted to see it, it was your brain.'

Taking a sip from the cup of tea next to him, he loaded another sheet of paper in the machine. Meanwhile I was cursing the side of the bed I had got out on that morning.

'What's your name?' I managed to answer this question and was about to protest my innocence again when a clacking sound began. I shut my eyes in fear—he must be practising his slaps—but when I felt no blows being rained on me I opened them again. I was surprised to see my name shining brightly on the sheet of paper inserted into the machine. Before I could overcome my astonishment, I discovered a flowery border set around my name.

I still remember the triumphant delight with which I returned to my friends with this valuable object. And that I started thinking of all the other stern teachers as harmless creatures. Only one star shone brightly in my sky—Kanai Babu. Could Jugal Babu or Himangshu Babu or even the headmaster himself use this machine to write or create floral borders?

I had been hoping to meet Kanai Babu once more when I ran into him on the street one day. I said, 'Will you write my name again with a border of flowers, sir?' I asked deferentially. 'I'll paste it in my handwriting exercise book.' Paying no attention to my palms joined in supplication, he said, 'That's not difficult.'

Not difficult?

I stood on the road in surprise as Kanai Babu, dressed in his trademark crisply laundered white shirt and white dhuti, vanished at his customary pace.

Had I already been a writer on that May evening, and someone had asked me write about Kanai Babu, I can state with conviction that I would have created a character who would have made Buddha, Ramanujam, Shankaracharya, Alexander, Akbar, Napoleon, all of them insignificant and redundant. Could any of them operate a machine without even looking at it? And even if they could, would they have brushed aside a hesitant young boy's request with 'that's not difficult'?

I didn't know then that I would meet him repeatedly on the streets, at the school, in trams and buses, or that the dreamlike illusions at the dawn of my life would be shattered under the weight of the pragmatic world in the afternoon, and a day would come when I would learn to operate the machine myself. Learn too that typists are not counted among the successful people of the world, that only those who succeed at nothing end up mastering how to type and tap away at the box. Nor did I imagine that I would be elevated to Kanai Da's level as a teacher in Vivekananda School, that he would say in the same school office, 'We're amateur typists, not very good at our job. You type this, Sankar, it will turn out much better and be done much quicker.'

But what use was it thinking about these things tonight? Surely the soul of someone who had made us laugh all his life and given us a rip-roaring time would not be pleased at our shedding tears over him. Kanai Da couldn't stand cry-babies. 'Tears won't do,' he would say. 'Be loud, get into trouble, accept punishment quietly from your elders and teachers, then go off to play—that's what boys are supposed to do. I don't get these fellows who moan and whine all the time.'

Seizing the opportunity, I'd ask, 'Is it true your slaps can be had as cheaply as in historic times?'

'Don't you understand it's because of the slaps that you have a sharp brain?'

Kanai Da wasn't one for long-drawn-out discussions. 'You think chatting with you will put food on my table?'

A few moments later he was playing cricket with the class four boys, using a wicket made of bricks. Monastery workers of his age kept calling out to him, 'Come on, Kanai, we have work to do.'

Kanai Da couldn't be bothered; he could be heard telling the boys after scoring a boundary, 'It's all in the wrist. You won't get me out even if you bowl at me all day.'

By the time I was in a higher class and had grown a little sharper, I discovered along with my classmates that Kanai Babu was actually Kanailal Bag. He taught in the junior classes and collected the school fee from senior students. Our dealings with him were limited to that one day when the monthly fee was due. He would sit behind a window and we would slip the fee book through the grille and place it under his nose. Scanning it through his glasses, he would make a mark with a red pencil, stamp it and tear off the counterfoil before returning the fee book.

Sometimes he would flare up. 'This one's learnt nothing yet. A donkey in class four, a donkey now. Magazine fee instead of examination fee, fan fee instead of magazine fee. Have to report him to his guardians.'

As the poor fellow at the receiving end of this criticism left with the fee book, his face bleak, Kanai Da would laugh. 'Don't curse me, it'll make me choke on my tea. I'm not really going to report you.'

It didn't escape his attention when I chuckled in the queue at this. 'What's so funny? Have you seen your own handwriting?'

On hearing this story many years later, one of Kanai Da's childhood friends said, 'That's Kanai. He sounds angry, but it doesn't come from his heart. And he can't sleep nights unless he's had a joke at your expense. You know how he glares at little boys when they can't do their sums? That's all for show. You can joke about him too, he won't mind. In fact, he'll be very pleased. You can pass off all the made-up stories and lies and scandals as his. You have no idea how many funny rumours there have been about him in school.'

The same friend told me another story. 'This one time we were told to translate something to the effect of great men usually come from great families. But someone responded from the back without a moment's hesitation, great men come from a reliable source. Everyone burst into laughter, but no one knew who had spoken. The teacher asked who this reliable nephew of Mr Chambers was.

No one would own up, but there was always Kanai, so we named him the reliable source.'

After a pause, he continued, 'Kanai would never get upset. Take sports. You couldn't have a team without him no matter what the game. But he was unanimously blamed for every goal conceded, every defeat. One particular mistake in volleyball even came to be known as the Kenaian smash!'

I don't know which bench Kanai Da occupied as a student, but during his working life he never sought to be prominent. And yet, when it came to work at the school and the monastery, he was happiest doing the most complicated tasks, the ones that needed the most effort.

Some people in the world are like salt—seldom visible, but everything turns bland without them. At community feasts they knead the dough and fry the luchi but are the last to eat. They do the back-breaking work but earn no praise. For meetings and celebrations they're the ones who arrange the chairs, decorate the stage, distribute the invitations, but not the ones to dress up and welcome the guests. Away from the spotlight, they prompt the actors but don't don the armour to play the role of the king. No one gives them awards; their names are not published in newspapers. And yet no feast, no meeting, no play, no celebration can be held without them—life itself comes to a standstill if they're not there.

Not that the world cares. Anyone who seeks entry to the sanctum sanctorum of the collective memory of the human race must pay a fee. And that is what I'm afraid of being asked: Who was this person on whom you're lavishing your eloquence?

Who was he? He did not have a PhD, he did not have an MA, in fact he barely passed his matriculation examination. He could type, he could drive, but he was a primary school teacher. The world might ask, what did he give humanity? I will have to lower my eyes in silence. Perhaps I will be asked pityingly, did he at least teach the works of Subhas Chandra Bose, Rabindranath Tagore or Saratchandra Chattopadhyay to his young students? Again I will have to lower my eyes.

But the embarrassment caused by these questions is not for Kanai Da to bear, it is reserved for his students. For those who knew him, who saw him up close—who understood the magnitude of their loss early that morning. For the echoes of this loss would not fade in a day. Every time there was a celebration at school, as the teachers rushed about and the students shouted in gay abandon, they would be reminded of this bereavement.

During Durga Puja I would see Kanai Da in a different avatar. Someone who has not been part of the puja festivities at the monastery will not know how big a space it occupied in our lives. The festival took on a unique form. For four days a contingent of joyous young people spent all their hours here, nothing else mattered. Large groups of people, some familiar and some strangers, came and went. And Kanai Da took care of everyone—from ensuring they had managed to view the idol and received their share of proshad, the food offered to the deities and then passed around for devotees, to finding them a place to sit and rest that was not being monopolized by young boys.

There was another tradition here—though no monetary contributions were sought, many people wanted to contribute nevertheless.

Kanai Da would man the cashbox round the clock with a smile on his face. He was there even at midnight. 'You never know, what if someone turns up.'

And it did not end there. Badal Babu, another teacher, might say angrily, 'We've been here nearly two hours, Kanai, not even a cup of tea. Is this how the management works?' Making the tea or distributing it was not Kanai Da's responsibility, but it was he who went off to enquire, muttering in rage.

Sometime in October, when Naskarpara Lane echoes with the beat of drums on a golden morning, when the residents of Kashundia stroll down the dark red path within the monastery to the veranda with the tiled roof in expectation of holy proshad, when Patterson Da hands out sweets and tea, all of us will feel someone else should also be here, among us, that someone or something is missing.

The Greatest Gift

It is time I tell the entire story. It goes back all the way to my childhood. Much of it is already lost forever and what little remains will disappear with me. No records or marble plaque or memento will tell the world that in a dark, narrow blind lane in this gigantic metropolis a young man befriended a lonely teenage boy. Theirs was a friendship whose memories linger all these years later, defying the ravages of time, and wish to remain alive longer still.

It is now four in the morning. Most of the exhausted people on earth are still sunk in sleep, their bodies resting in preparation for the battles awaiting them. I have switched on the table lamp and am sitting with paper and pen and the desire to write. There are many incidents in this world that I do not approve of, that are worthy of my criticism. I'm considering attacking one of them, asking why they occur, of protesting against them, and then putting down a prescription of what should be and why. There is no dearth of subjects and allegations; a great advantage of having lived so long is that I know many people who have caused considerable injustice. Not even unending censure will do justice to the task.

I reflect on how peculiar humans are. On the one hand, they cannot live except in each other's company, but on the other, they continue to heap oppression and unfairness on the weak and the poor who are conveniently at hand. Society is a maze of contradictions—its members have fed me, clothed me, educated me, treated me when sick, given me shelter, and kept me alive, yet there's no end to their wrongdoings. It is they who have shackled fellow humans in chains, it is they who have sung songs of freedom; it is they who have terrorized people with naked weapons, it is they who have whispered in our ears that we must not fear, for we will win, for the doors will open. An entire lifetime can be spent in fury against this society, in unmasking the evil, in protesting, in stating how things should be. But the time available to us is limited, none of us will be here forever.

I should gather these disparate thoughts and sweeten them with grace from my heart like syrup over ice, but my mind will not settle on such weighty matters.

Instead, it seeks to fly off like a sparrow on small, feeble wings to my childhood in Howrah, to Biharilal Chakraborty Lane, which allows entry but no exit. That's how it is with blind lanes. Look at me: I entered the lane nearly seven decades ago with my parents, after which there was the Second World War, the Atom Bomb, the partition of my country, the unfurling of the flag of independence, and, with great effort, even my physical body taking wing—but I, Sankar to my mother and Shankushaheb to Badal Kaku, have remained there, stuck simply because there is no way out. Here in the early hours of the morning I have realized the harsh truth, that even after so many changes in my life, after travelling to various cities and ports, my heart has not changed its address—I continue to live in the decrepit building standing at 18L Biharilal Chakraborty Lane, for a blind lane implies you cannot exit.

Perhaps this inability to exit has harmed me, perhaps it has caused incalculable damage. Then what about Badal Kaku? Could there have been a greater gain than having him in my life?

It so happens in some people's lives that despite all the wretchedness they win lotteries and become millionaires. Add my name to this list, for without expectations and without any effort this luckless boy from Biharilal Chakraborty Lane met Badal Chandra Basu, without whom all other gains in my life would have become meaningless. Not just that, I might have been a failure myself, and I certainly wouldn't have had anything to tell the world in the early hours of the morning.

Recently a cement company advertised in the French style with a slogan to the effect that one's house should be one's identity. It has created some discomfort in the upper echelons of society who complain that this consumerist culture has reduced humans to a level where a house is a person's identity. I can understand the rationale behind the protest, but may I humbly remind readers that this business of a house being a person's identity was the unpleasant truth even in the third decade of the twentieth century. Cement companies of the time knew this only too well, but they remained silent because cement had vanished from the open markets thanks to the World War. Many in our generation spent their entire lives waiting for a time when cement would be available again without having to seek a favour from the government or bribing someone.

Let protesters say what they will about the French-style advertisement, but when I got off the Eastern Bengal Railway train at Sealdah Station with my parents and rode a horse-drawn carriage for the first time to set foot in that dank, dark lane in Howrah, that house was our identity. The serpentine lane grew progressively narrower; 18L was located at the point where it could squeeze the breath out of a human. Directly opposite was 18K, where Badal Kaku lived. A habitation of tin- and tile-roofed structures stood all around us, known collectively as a slum. Around these stood a few one-storeyed or two-storeyed buildings, each of which had a number of residents who were called 'renters'.

In those impossible times the first thing everyone wanted to know on being introduced was whether we were tenants in the slum or in one of the buildings. I remember Badal Kaku asking my father, the lawyer, what the difference between tenants and renters was. The reason for his enquiry was that the landlord had surreptitiously reduced all the tenants to renters on the receipts he gave for collecting rent.

There is another odd piece of business that is yet to be wiped from my memory despite the intervening years. Wherever I'd go in the neighbourhood, the first question was: Where do you live? When it became clear that my address wasn't in the slum, they would follow up with: Whose renter are you? That I couldn't be anything but a renter seemed obvious; the only question was, whose? Almost every renter in the neighbourhood was Biharilal Chakraborty's, after whom the lane once known as Chowdhurybagan was named. While other streets are renamed on the basis of wealth, accomplishments, or sacrifices, here the change of name was inevitable, though I wasn't old enough to bother about it.

The first grand entrance into my limited world was made by Badal Chandra Bose. It is still a matter of infinite wonder and some mystery about how he became Badal Kaku, and I Shankushaheb that very first day. His mother was my great-aunt, he was a bachelor.

As a child I was quite precocious, and that irked my mother often. I had the bad habit of asking people close to me the kind of questions that created serious problems, even if temporarily. Let me offer some examples. Once, I asked my widowed maternal grandmother in Shyampukur, 'Why did you pick an aged husband for my mother?' Near and dear ones knew she was my father's second wife, with a vast difference in age between them. Tears filled

Didima's eyes. Instead of answering, she made feeble enquiries about who had put me up to asking this question, was it my mother or a neighbour? (It was neither.) Although my tearful grandmother couldn't answer the question, I learnt, and evaluated, the circumstances much later—my maternal grandfather's unexpected financial crisis, the sudden death of my father's first wife, and so on—but by then it was too late.

On to another instance of my foolishness. Badal Kaku and his family lived in two rooms on the ground floor. His mother occupied one of them with her deities, and he the other. Framed pictures of two unusual individuals hung on the wall. One was a formidable man on horseback, on his way to valiantly conquer remote mountain ranges perhaps. The other was of a frail, toothless old man, his dhuti hitched up to his knees. I couldn't fathom how he had mustered the audacity to laugh at the hero on horseback. Nor could I understand why Badal Kaku had given them space together in his room. Eventually I found out the man on horseback was Napoleon, who had at one point threatened the might of the English. But why was the toothless man laughing? Despite my young age, Badal Kaku never talked down to me during our discussions. He told me the toothless man had managed to rout the English without using a single firearm. I was greatly reassured to know he was still alive, but was saddened to learn the horse rider had died long ago in captivity after losing to the English in war.

There was a room, there were pictures, there was Kaku, but no Kakima. It was enough to pique a precocious child's curiosity. In the evening I would often switch off the light and lie down beside Badal Kaku on the floor. Much of our weighty discussions happened then. As I grew older I learnt that those who wish to win the hearts of the young reject the gulf in their ages and treat even their youngest acquaintances as contemporaries. This is best, though I have personally never succeeded at this. It is my own fault that I have been deprived of the precious chance of being a favourite of youngsters.

Thus I had the temerity to ask Badal Kaku, 'When will your wife come, Kaku?'

He was taken aback at first, but soon had the situation under control. He even gave me an answer, explaining that the kakimas of this world torment the thakumas. And since his mother wouldn't be able to bear it, he hadn't married. This made sense to me. I agreed with him that anyone who might torment the person I called Thakuma should not be brought home.

The trouble began the next day. Badal Kaku's mother drew me aside and said, 'What have you said to Badal? What am I supposed to have told you?' I realized then that she must have been blamed for my inquisitiveness. Badal Kaku was under the impression someone had put me up to asking the question. 'Never ask him about marrying,' Thakuma told me. I never did. Afterwards I came to know that Badal Kaku had opted for eternal bachelorhood lest his widowed mother and fatherless younger brother suffer financially, not budging from his stance despite his mother's pleas. This made his younger brother's rebellion against him and subsequent decision to move out deeply hurtful and humiliating.

Badal Kaku led a very disciplined life, whose value or significance I did not grasp then. He used to wake up early every morning, open the door and wait for me. I was his closest friend, despite the three decades between our ages. I would meet him when he had almost finished cleaning his teeth with a neem twig. He didn't believe in toothbrushes, choosing instead to dip a twig in a bucket of water overnight and using it the next morning. I knew he had once quietly presented an Englishman with a bundle of neem twigs. I also knew why it had failed. The Englishman had told him, 'Thanks so much, Bose. Both my wife and I tried these, but they're far too bitter, and we don't want to start our day with this kind of a taste in our mouths.'

I was of the same opinion. However, Badal Kaku had advised the Englishman to be patient for a month. 'The bitter taste will go away.' The Englishman couldn't do it. Badal Kaku believed the Britishers of that era were too self-indulgent. They had lost to Napoleon because they lacked persistence. Who knew what their fate would be under Hitler's aggression.

Irrelevant as it might be, let me state something here. One day Badal Kaku proudly announced that pins had disappeared from the market, but he had hit upon the perfect solution—he had assiduously collected acacia thorns for his office. Let researchers be informed that acacia thorns had played the role of pins for several years in the offices of wartime British India, just as Badal Kaku's English employer had used a horse-drawn carriage instead of his car for five years to deal with the shortage of petrol and tyres. We had not yet graduated to toothbrushes at home. My mother would take the ash leftover from using cow dung cakes in the clay oven, pound it to a fine dust and store it in an earthen pot. Why not in a tin? Allow me to inform researchers once more that all tins were on their way to the war.

Badal Kaku had hoped his English employer would be forced to give up on toothbrushes and toothpaste because of their unavailability, since the thin aluminium with which toothpaste tubes were made in those days had also been commandeered for the war. But, alas, the Englishman managed to get hold of toothpaste from the Bengal Club store somehow. He was delighted to discover he could keep his teeth clean with half the normal amount of toothpaste and double the life of each tube.

Because my father went to the Howrah District Court to practise as a lawyer, I had assumed that everyone in the world had their breakfast and went to some court or other to practise as lawyers. The first time I heard the words 'office' and 'job' were from Badal Kaku. Once he was done cleaning his teeth, he would slice the neem twig down its length and use it to clean his tongue, explaining to me why morning dental care wasn't complete without this. Then it was off to the river, some two miles away, at top speed. Returning like a machine, Badal Kaku would bolt his food and then rush to office in a colourful shirt and white dhuti. On foot, obviously, which meant three miles more, past Howrah Station, over Howrah Bridge, and on to one road named after Robert Clive, followed by another, Clive Row. Badal Kaku had whispered to me the secret of how to make this journey on foot painless, which can inspire the bigwigs of advertising even today. 'Flex shoes,' he told me, 'when you have them on even a hundred miles feel like going next door.'

Badal Kaku had more information to add. 'You won't get this quality if you buy them at any old shop, you must buy them only from Cuthbertson Harper opposite the Governor General's residence.' Apparently Cuthbertson Harper had been secretly appointed to supply shoes to the Governor General. One more thing—Badal Kaku wouldn't slip on the Flex shoes immediately after buying them, he would first summon a cobbler to fix additional half soles. There was sufficient economic justification for this strange behaviour—doing so would ensure the soles never wore out.

Once, Badal Kaku gave me a gift of a pair of shoes from the British store. Needless to add, I too got half soles added before even trying them on. Because the modified shoes made me totter, which came to the notice of my schoolmates, I had to face a fair number of taunts. But despite the mockery, as a worthy disciple of Badal

Kaku's, I firmly believe there's nothing funny about his scientific innovation that extends the longevity of Flex shoes.

Both 'job' and 'office' were mysterious words to me at one time. Badal Kaku found himself in some difficulty over this. He said, 'Everyone has to serve, but because that sounds like a servant's work, they use the word "service" so that their self-esteem is not hurt. What does your servant Kalindi do?'

'He obeys Ma's and Baba's orders,' I said.

Badal Kaku explained that in an office everyone had to obey the top officers and the head clerk. Doing this for thirty days meant you were paid a salary, and handing over the salary to one's mother at home meant she could use it for expenses for the next thirty days. Those who could save some money after expenses opened an account at the post office or put it in a little pot at home.

'And those who cannot?' My precocious self was full of questions.

'They borrow money.'

It was from Badal Kaku that I first uncovered the mystery of debt. After coming to Calcutta from Bagnan, Badal Kaku had tried to ward off poverty by pawning his mother's jewellery. Because he couldn't pay the money back in time, the jewellery was forfeited, a matter he regretted all his life. Badal Kaku always thought twice before incurring any expense, and advised me not to spend money I hadn't earned already. 'Never take a loan,' he warned me, 'because loans have babies called interest, and this interest multiplies like tadpoles, hopping about everywhere without caring for anyone.'

Even in these final years of my life, I think often about Badal Kaku's lessons on loans, although I am aware that people borrow money not out of choice but necessity, just as my mother did, several times, because there was no food at home. My father had died by then. Ma had a gold necklace which she had to forgo; we could redeem it from the lender. Much later I got a gold necklace made for her with the takings from my first book. But it was a bauble compared to the one that disappeared after being sentenced to life at the pawnbroker's.

That service comes from the servant is a vital truth which Badal Kaku instilled in me early on. Everyone in the world is intent on extracting money from you, but there is only one source of income. So you must learn to put the entire world on one pan of the scale and your work on the other in order to balance them. That was what he did himself; no matter what the weather, he always went to work. His favourite saying: repairs for buildings, taxes for landowners, attendance for employees.

Thanks to his profession as a lawyer, my father was the receiver of the Basu estate in Khariap, which was how I mastered the ins and outs of the landowning business at a young age. As a resident of Biharilal Chakraborty Lane, the importance of repairing decrepit buildings where renters live was not unknown to me. What I learnt from listening to and observing Badal Kaku regularly was the importance of attendance when in a job. And not just the daily attendance, but the everyday battles to ensure this attendance. Thakuma would wake up at the crack of dawn to light the unoon and start cooking while Badal Kaku rushed to the Ganges to bathe, and then present himself at the Kalamazoo Company in Dalhousie like clockwork. He taught me how to race against time and arrive everywhere a little early.

On his way back from work too he travelled on foot. Upon arriving home his first task was to remove his clothes, wrap a gamchha around himself and clean his Flex shoes for the next day. 'Those who say shoes should remain just that, shoes, and not expect any attention are mistaken. Our shoes are our mount, the English judge people on the basis of their shoes.'

Long before I met Badal Kaku's employer, Mr Livingstone, in person, I knew intimately what his daily routine at work was like, what colour shirt he wore on a particular day, what he had told others and when, what he had eaten for lunch, and how restless he became and at what time on the days the Calcutta Football Club had a match to play. Mr Livingstone's words were like gospel for Badal Kaku—the accounts that I was given over days and months and years, and what I still remember in defiance of the oppression of time, are enough to write a Mahabharata on Britain's foreign trade in the mid-twentieth century.

My proximity to Badal Kaku had taught me to live with conflicting ideas without letting their inherent contrariness trouble me. Neither he nor I had the slightest doubt that the British were the best at business and that Kalamazoo's loose-leaf binder was the finest in the world. Both of us agreed that this notebook, which although bound also allowed its pages to be separated as required, was a revolutionary innovation. May the company prosper, and may Mr Livingstone live to be a hundred—such was our ardent desire.

Why, then, the pictures of Napoleon and Gandhi? Because both had made it their mission to get rid of the British.

Back then I did not understand the significance of the strange analysis of British history that Badal Kaku had woven for me. Even during those dire times he was confident that Mahatma Gandhi and Mr Livingstone would cohabit in India. I was worried that the first thing Mahatma Gandhi would do on becoming the king was throw the British out. Mr Livingstone would no longer be able to live here, which was probably why he kept his house in England spick and span.

Badal Kaku and I had separated from the mainstream. We wanted both Mr Livingstone and Gandhi maharaj to be victorious, to live together in harmony. God alone knew how this might be achieved. Badal Kaku had chosen me as the only listener for his analysis of world history, and I used to pay close attention to his words, confident that he couldn't possibly be wrong.

I did worry about what might happen if Mahatma Gandhi threw Mr Livingstone out of the country. After his evening bath Badal Kaku would sit on the floor and assure me that the British had done business in India to their heart's content before they started ruling us. We would simply have to learn the business of business from them. The British had made a huge error in giving up shopkeeping to sit on the throne, the two were not the same and couldn't be managed simultaneously, which was why they had ended up neglecting their businesses. I couldn't imagine Mr Livingstone had not discussed this vital question in private with his stenotypist Badal Kaku.

Then one evening Badal Kaku suddenly changed his tune. 'Gandhi himself is a bania, he's from the trader class,' he said. 'So the only cause for concern is that one bania is trying to come to power at the expense of another, but it isn't the job of banias to be kings.' He pondered deeply on this, poring over every line of *The Statesman*, and consulting the *Chambers English Dictionary* whenever in doubt about a word. Eventually Badal Kaku calmed down and did not withdraw his support to Gandhi maharaj.

Today, after all these years, in the final phase of my life, I still remember what Badal Kaku said: It isn't the trader's job to be king. Whenever the scales have been replaced with the sceptre there has been trouble in the world, a crisis has erupted every time a businessman has turned his attention to something else.

If Badal Kaku were alive, I could have asked him another relevant question. When the sceptre is again converted by choice into a pair of scales, when the king wants to become a shopkeeper again, is the outcome a good one? I'm referring to the role of the state in commerce and industry. It has taken us more than half a century to realize in our bones that when the king starts selling things while still on the throne, not only does it not solve all the nation's problems, but it also exacerbates many of them.

From the tales of his office that Badal Kaku narrated to me in my childhood after he came back from work, it was clear that managing a business was very difficult, no less complicated than running a kingdom. His close association with Mr Livingstone and the innumerable official letters that he typed up every day gave Badal Kaku the impression that no one could measure up to the British when it came to trade and commerce.

If you ask people my age, you'll hear about the ARP, Air Raid Precaution, instituted in Calcutta to combat the spectre of aerial attacks from bomber planes. The arrogant behaviour of its local members, all dressed in a particular kind of uniform, did not always elicit public support. One day I told a nervous Badal Kaku that the neighbourhood young men had expanded ARP to mean A Royal Pummelling. Although he knew this would cause Mr Livingstone both disappointment and concern, Badal Kaku felt morally obliged to convey the information to him.

Though called a World War, for us it was the English versus the Germans, and although both combatants had their supporters, most of us didn't understand why we were paying the price. I didn't either, despite my precociousness, but I had no choice other than to listen to the discussions of the adults from afar. Badal Kaku was worried about the future of Indians as well as that of the British. It was true that a dark tomorrow awaited the world if England didn't win the war, but why would a country yet to gain its independence fret about a change of guard? Why should its people shed their blood on a distant battlefield to protect its lords and masters? Badal

Kaku rued the foolishness of the English, he felt they should grant India her independence and rope in Gandhi. He had no doubt that in mistrusting Gandhi, the English were only demonstrating their own stupidity.

There was plenty of reason for ordinary people to be fed up with the ARP forces. The same unemployed people who used to loiter around the neighbourhood were now turning up at parades at odd hours of the day in uniforms and gleaming shoes, eating whatever they wanted at snack shops and taking new buckets of different sizes, free of cost, for their homes. With buckets disappearing from the market, ordinary people could no longer buy them to store water. The ARP forces were even supplied food grains and other kitchen essentials at low prices. They behaved as though they would be the ones to lay down their lives when the enemy invaded through the aerial route, and the English should therefore allow them a few days of pleasure in their brief lives.

The locals, however, had a different viewpoint. No matter how much they paraded up and down in military style in their shiny uniforms—left, right, left—once face to face with the enemy, the ARP would get 'a royal pummelling'. It was about them that this rhyme was composed furtively: 'Get ready, soldiers, eat your daal and rice / Vomit on the battlefield, won't that be nice / The stink will repel the enemy, they'll vanish in a trice.'

Badal Kaku knew this rhyme would mortify Mr Livingstone, which caused him some pain too.

It was a very strange time, with everyday essentials unavailable. No grains, no daal, no kerosene. With no paper to write on, we practised our handwriting on slates all over again. As far as we knew, war meant guns—why, then, was paper in short supply? Badal Kaku would explain to me what *The Statesman* was saying, but he probably didn't understand it entirely himself.

People want to wipe out memories of bad times as quickly as possible. Is there any other explanation for all of us having forgotten the depths of despair the lives of ordinary people touched during the war?

Let the new generation know that the rice-loving Bengali of that era was forced to consume rutis for the first time. After being thwarted for several centuries, wheat finally infiltrated the Bengali kitchen successfully. But the amount was rationed—even buying bread meant that the quantity of wheat allotted to you would be reduced proportionately. It wasn't just food grains and oil, clothes were difficult to get as well; you had to submit the coupons that came with the ration card and queue up to collect new garments. Which meant you couldn't buy an unlimited number of shirts or trousers or dhutis or saris. Many were forced to remain half-naked at home, wrapped in nothing but a gamchha. No one could throw any light on the situation because lights were switched off in the evening. It wasn't load shedding because of inadequate power supply; it was the age of blackouts in the city of the black hole. Street lamps were turned off, blinkers were put on the lights at home, and the windows were hidden behind veils and burkhas. Amidst all this were the threats from the ARP troops. If even a sliver of light escaped outside, you'd be reported to the police.

But, my dear boy, the moon in the sky is not going to obey your orders. What will you do on moonlit nights, ARP? Badal Kaku would explain to me that full moon nights were particularly worrisome, for that was when Japanese bomber planes could attack Calcutta.

The keeper of records in Badal Kaku's office, Atul Kaku, used to live nearby. He, however, used to say, 'Don't worry, neither Hitler nor Tojo will be able to withstand the bites of Calcutta's mosquitoes. Even if they occupy the city they won't know where to run when the mosquitoes attack them.' But there were objections to this. 'How did Clive manage to survive the mosquitoes of Murshidabad and build a house in Dalhousie?' This was where Badal Kaku would jump in. 'What you don't realize is that Clive didn't come here to rule, he came here as a businessman.'

Even as a householder, Badal Kaku believed in a monk's way of living. No tea, no paan, no smoking, no going anywhere near a cinema hall, love songs from films to be considered poisonous, and only plays about Chaitanya allowed by way of theatre.

He'd been to the cinema just once, and I had had to accompany him. The order had come from Mr Livingstone himself. So Badal Kaku bought tickets for New Empire in Esplanade and we entered together. Before the main feature, we were shown a documentary with detailed descriptions of what patrons should do to protect themselves in case of an air attack, where to take shelter, how to cooperate with the ARP, and so on. As soon as it ended, Badal Kaku, to my surprise, left the hall without watching the main film. My heart's desire remained unfulfilled.

Badal Kaku was probably a little lonely. Many people didn't want to listen to what he had to say or disagreed with his views, which was why he treated me as an equal and told me everything on his mind, some of which I haven't forgotten even now. Perhaps many of these thoughts originated with Mr Livingstone. Badal Kaku would say we always get what we want, and are kept away from what we don't want. So we must be very careful about our desires, and remember that we can never get what we didn't want in the first place. 'Even a thousand friends may not be enough,' he would tell me, 'but one enemy is all it needs. You will see this foe on land, in the water, in the sky, everywhere.'

He never skipped work, except the one time when he didn't go to the office on two successive days. It was a heart-rending sight, for his younger brother, for whose education and betterment Badal Kaku had chosen to stay single all his life, had rebelled and left home. He couldn't be blamed either, for Badal Kaku's regime was impossibly strict. No tea, no cigarettes, no character-destroying film songs, no roadside food that ruined one's health. Anything you wrote had to be revised twice, you must have the dictionary by your side when reading the newspaper, staying up too late affected concentration, studying early in the morning was the best ... who could possibly live with so many rules all the time?

As I've said, there were no arrangements for tea in Badal Kaku's house. Yet this same man took me to buy cups and saucers the day after his brother left because Mr Livingstone, worried at the absence of his favourite B.C. Bose, had sent word through Atul Chakraborty of his intention to visit Badal Kaku at home. Badal Kaku had decided to offer doi-chire—flattened rice in yogurt—to his guest, but then he changed his mind. We shared our views on this: There was no harm if the English drank tea or smoked or ate beef stew, that was their habit.

Many years later I wrote a story about how Badal Chandra Bose relaxed his rigid principles temporarily to give Mr Livingstone an aromatic cup of tea in newly purchased crockery. In the story Badal Kaku appeared as Asru Mama, who was considered by some to be an imaginary comic character. I did not respond to this allegation for a long time, since Badal Kaku was anything but comic to me. He clung with all his might to the values he believed in and, flouting everyone's suggestions, chose to accept an immature boy as an equal, a friend, and opened his heart to him.

My life would have remained incomplete without Badal Kaku in it. I was lonely despite being part of a large family. Burdened with a thousand household responsibilities and the task of giving birth to and raising eight children in a row, my mother became more caregiver than companion. My father too was perpetually busy with the battles of life, and had neither the time nor the opportunity or even the mentality to face a barrage of questions from a curious child. And then came that horrifying night when he left us for a land where no messages reach. I don't know where my loneliness in this bewildering desolate world would have taken me, but Badal Kaku's affection and indulgence revived me. With no effort on my part I was given the answers to many tough questions this world poses—much of my incomplete understanding of things was compensated for.

Badal Kaku took my hand the morning after my father died. I was thirteen, and hemmed in by unknown fears. Badal Kaku understood the severity of the situation, but what he said was, 'You will have to struggle a bit, Shankushaheb, but I can see clearly that eventually everything will be all right because of your own efforts.'

As luck would have it, all the crises did indeed come to an end. Badal Kaku's quiet lessons came to my aid every single step of the way. I do not know what he had foreseen during my darkest days, but I do not hesitate to admit that without his companionship, love, learning and inspiration, my life would have remained half-formed.

Our Hadu Da

My lineage is one of teachers. My grandfather, who died young, taught in a Sanskrit school, just like seven generations that preceded him. In those days there was no money in teaching so, as a secondary profession, he presided over religious rituals.

My father was a talented student of science and had also acquired a degree in law. But the work he was proudest of was reflected in a framed citation that the students of Calcutta's Hindu School had given to him, their mathematics teacher, when he left. It was written in verse, and even in his last days my father used to derive great joy from reciting it.

Once, I remember a completely unknown gentleman had turned up at our home in Howrah where he was treated in a manner befitting a son-in-law. The mystery was unveiled in due course—my father had taught him mathematics in school. Since that episode was over, I didn't understand why our adult guest was still drawn to my father. But later in my life I experienced the reversal that converts a student's attraction for their teacher into a teacher's attraction for their student.

Since we're talking of lineage, I might as well point out that my father had picked a schoolteacher as a groom for his eldest—and favourite—daughter. His son-in-law Nakulchandra Roy's family was steeped in teaching too. My father did not object when my elder stepbrother Gaurisankar wanted to teach after passing his MA examination, although there were several other options he could have pursued. His fame as a teacher enhanced our family's reputation. Although his daily hardships never ended, he would proudly assert till the last day of his life, 'My students mean everything to me.'

Bordada, as I called him, loved literature fiercely. 'It was because he was a schoolteacher that Bibhutibhushan became such a great writer,' he would say. I was in the habit of flinging barbs at the time. 'No one besides teachers become writers in Bengal,' I'd retort. Bordada would smile. 'Look at Rabindranath. He was punished and humiliated in school as a child, but he did not lose faith in teaching. He was a jomidar's son but he set up a school in Santiniketan.' He wouldn't stop there. 'All the revered people in the world are teachers. Buddha, Jesus, Muhammad, Sankar, Ramakrishna, Sister Nivedita and Mother Teresa—what were they if not teachers? They seemed to have been born only to enlighten us.'

Bordada was an extremely popular teacher himself. When he taught Bangla in school even a stone could absorb the fragrance of literature. He often forgot that his students had to study more than just Bengali literature, and going beyond the syllabus was a luxury they could ill afford. Still, he believed students never made a mistake in evaluating their teachers; they had the natural ability to tell the good ones from the bad.

Bordada was delighted to hear that in some countries students also give marks to teachers the way teachers give them. I was no match for him as a student. Once, when he was in a difficult financial situation, I took him to an Englishman for employment. He was about to start the new job when he suddenly hesitated.

'No,' he said to me, 'at least one person in the family must be a teacher. You had better switch to a line of work that will support the family.'

I didn't care for this blind faith in students. I told Bordada when I got the chance, 'The scandal that the students of the Bowbazar branch of the Metropolitan School on Creek Row created in the last century has never been remedied. The same school where you teach had appointed Narendranath Datta as the headmaster. Two months later the students of classes nine and ten sent in a written petition saying this teacher is useless, he doesn't know how to teach. The petition went to Vidyasagar, who was the owner of the school, and simply on its basis he said, "Tell Naren not to come to the school any more." Can you imagine—someone who was born to teach could not fulfil the expectations of the students of Metropolitan School Bowbazar?'

Bordada was a little embarrassed, and then he said, 'I believe there was a conspiracy. One of Vidyasagar's close relatives did not want Naren to be installed as the headmaster.'

To put him at ease, I said, 'Just as well, or Narendranath might have lived and died as a well-known headmaster, and we wouldn't have Swami Vivekananda.'

Without the creation of Vivekananda I would have been in trouble too, for then I would never have been a student and then a teacher in Howrah's Vivekananda Institution. Nor would I have become a writer. But that's a long story, for another time.

Before continuing with my own journey, let me emphasize again that Bordada was an unparalleled teacher. Whatever he taught—English, mathematics, history, geography or grammar—was easy to understand. I have repeatedly found evidence that good teachers can make even stones easily digested.

Bordada would also say that every educated person should compulsorily teach for at least one year, just like mandatory military service in many countries. One's eyes aren't really opened properly unless one has been a teacher. Bordada believed Vidyasagar could not have become 'doyaar sagar', kindness incarnate, had he not been a teacher.

Towards the end Bordada would say that it was because Vidyasagar wrote books and made some money by publishing them that we benefited from his kindness and generosity. Ishanchandra Ghosh, the headmaster of Hare School, had come into a little wealth by investing in the share market, and instituted the Ishan Scholarship. Mahendranath Gupta, who wrote *Sri Sri Ramakrishna Kathamrita*, used to be the headmaster of three schools at the same time, and later became the publisher of extraordinarily successful books, which allowed him to provide financial support to others. The legendary governor of West Bengal Harendrakumar Mukherjee was a fount of charity because of his stock market gains. Acharya Prafulla Chandra Roy could devote his life to his students because he did not marry and have a family.

No, I've not picked up my pen here to write paeans to those who taught other people. Just as every person's mother is the greatest heroine of their life, so too do a couple of teachers remain in memory as larger-than-life heroes and heroines. I have not yet met a single person who isn't eager to talk about their teacher. And if I were to meet such a person, I wouldn't waste my time talking to them, for there is reason to believe that someone who has not discovered a hero in a teacher has something lacking about them.

Is there anyone more unlucky in the world than those who cannot weave a golden web of memories about their mother and their teacher? Fortunately, I am not one of them. I had the ten-armed Goddess Durga incarnate as my mother, and teachers who gave meaning to my life as a human being, shone a light to dispel the darkness, inspired me on my journey over long, difficult roads. They cautioned me, reprimanded me, corrected me, and were also overcome with happiness when I succeeded because they considered my successes their own. There is a charming section on wish fulfilment in the final episodes of the Mahabharata, where the heroes killed during the battle of Kurukshetra returned to their loved ones briefly. Were such reunions possible in my life, I could have spent a long time talking to my favourite teachers.

From time immemorial teachers have been split into two groups: those who predict simian futures for their students, and those who envision greatness. If I were to find myself within reach of both, I would tell the first, 'I didn't turn out as badly as you'd feared,' and the second, 'Forgive me, for I could not fulfil your expectations.'

The word 'master', often used in Bangla for teacher, has various meanings in English. Someone who owns slaves or has servants. A master is also an expert, highly skilled at something. 'Like master, like man' is the English proverb—it suggests that there is a great possibility of a student's developing in the same mould as their teacher. Perhaps this is what is known as a gharana here—the guru–shishya parampara, the teacher–student tradition.

My father has not been in my life for a very long time. I was thirteen when he died, and yet I was luckier than him, for he was just five when his father passed away. Baba didn't speak much with his children, but he was garrulous in the company of friends. There was both pleasure and learning in eavesdropping on those conversations.

I remember my father telling Satish Babu, who taught at the Howrah District School, 'Teachers have the greatest role in ensuring that humans remain human. Why are humans so far ahead of other creatures? It's because what we learn in our lives is not lost with our deaths, the next generation inherits it. The baton that gets passed on in this relay race is what is called education. Every twenty-five years or so, a new generation has to learn old ideas afresh. And it is teachers who perform the crucial task of ensuring this. Despite being short-lived, human beings have mastered the art of perpetuating knowledge for eternity, which no other species has succeeded in yet.'

Listening closely, Satish Chandra Tafadar said, 'You've made the whole thing quite romantic, Hari Babu.'

This same Satish Babu used to teach us arithmetic and craft in primary school. Much to my shame I was good at neither, which filled me with such fear that I would run away whenever I saw him. My very first teacher in school could not become one of my favourites, although he had a huge contribution in ensuring I was admitted to the school.

I must now mention the first person I called 'Mastermoshai'—my father's legal clerk Jogendranath Manna. From Monday to Friday, he would spend the nights at our house, and then leave for the village of Raghunathpur near Uttarpara-Bali on Saturday, returning on Monday morning with a gunny bag stuffed with fresh vegetables. Besides being my father's clerk, Jogen Babu was also the accountant of the Khariap estate, where my father had been appointed the receiver. Since there weren't enough rooms in our Chowdhurybagan house, Jogendranath Manna and I would sleep in the front room. And because he was the one who taught me to read and write and gave me my initial lessons, I used to address him as 'Mastermoshai'.

I haven't seen a greater embodiment of patience and kindness in a teacher. Busy with his own work, he would sometimes struggle to answer the thousands of precocious questions I had about life and the world, often saying helplessly, 'I don't know.' But it was impossible for a young boy to believe there were things in the world his teacher didn't know. I assumed he was evading my queries, which put him under added pressure and made him feel even more helpless. I realize now that he had no means to expand his own knowledge. But he was never irritated with me, nor did he ever reprimand me.

My real lessons with him began at night, when we lay down next to each other after dinner. Exhausted after a long day, he wanted to go to sleep at once, but I had already slept a bit and was fresh for stories. It was through Mastermoshai that I became familiar with the world of stories, from him that I learnt how to tell them. The sheer number of stories he told me over the days and months and years was beyond count. When he claimed to have run out of stories, I would threaten him, 'You're going home, you'd better bring back new ones.' Once or twice I even scolded him, 'What do you do at home anyway?' It didn't occur to me that he had a family that waited for him all week. As far as I remember, Mastermoshai's salary was Rs 30 a month, besides board and lodging, and he made some extra money from clerking. Still, I never saw him fretting about his finances.

Just before I was to join the Howrah District School, my father became deeply perturbed on testing my arithmetic skills. Sending for Jogen Manna, he gave him a piece of his mind. 'As his teacher are you supposed to tell him stories or make him do his sums?'

Mastermoshai listened in silence. Then began a monumental effort to teach me arithmetic. Stories were banned, and as everyone knows, when something is banned we are drawn to it even more. That was my first experience of a desperate craving. Mastermoshai had been told that too many stories would not leave enough room for arithmetic. Many years later the masterly writer Bimal Mitra told me just the opposite—someone who cannot hold a complicated mathematical problem in their head will never be a brilliant writer.

My father used to say in annoyance, 'Mathematics isn't like your stories. You can say anything you like in a story, but that's not the case with mathematics. Here, there can be only one answer. A story can end in various ways, depending on who's telling or writing it.'

Baba wrote books in his youth, tasting some success as a young playwright for Kohinoor Theatre on the general stage. Now, in the process of taking me to task, he ended up making me think: Why doesn't god love mathematics? If a story can have three different outcomes, why can't a sum?

At that time an unbelievable experience came my way. God looked on me favourably—addition, subtraction, multiplication or division, whatever the sum, each time I tried it a different answer emerged! Jogen Manna was so worried he didn't dare report it to my father. He would tell me, you can have many answers to a sum, but only one of them is right, all the others are wrong and will fetch no marks. Which one is right? Who has taken this decision? Why isn't one of the wrong answers correct? Why isn't the correct answer wrong? My favourite teacher would be bombarded by a barrage of such tough questions from his precocious student.

All these years later, when I look back, it seems that the questions I asked were not mathematical but philosophical. It is in search of the answers to these very questions that I have been conducting an enquiry through literature. You might wonder whether I've succeeded. I have sometimes asked ageing monks who have dedicated their entire lives to their chosen task whether they have arrived at the place they set out for, abjuring lucre and worldly comforts. Their answer was strange: 'I won't lie, I haven't arrived there yet. But the journey is the joy, it makes up for all the suffering.'

There were many renowned teachers in Howrah District School, but I didn't have the chance to be close to any of them when I joined. I only remember the headmaster, Makhanlal Chakraborty, who used to dress in a hat and boots. He had a degree from England

and, as far as I remember, one of his sons studied with me in class three. The headmaster would sometimes walk past our classroom in his suit—the lord alone knew what he was inspecting—but his very presence gave us palpitations: What if something were to happen?

I made many friends in this school, and some of us are still in touch. But Howrah District School could only provide satisfaction, not delight. The delight came from Howrah's Vivekananda Institution. With the district school closing down in 1941 because of the Second World War, and its reopening uncertain, I went to Vivekananda School in 1942, just after I had turned eight, to seek admission.

I came to like the teachers' room immensely. The headmaster was seated in a room adjoining it—dressed not in a suit, but in a khadi panjaabi and dhuti. It was love at first sight. Spotting a tiny boy peeping into an area marked 'No entry for students', the solemn headmaster asked, 'What do you want?' Time for self-defence. Recklessly the boy said, 'I want to be admitted to this school.' It wasn't a particularly memorable reply, but Sudhangshushekhar Bhattacharya loved it. 'You're here by yourself?' More astonishment.

I had my first taste of romance in real life. Taking me into the teachers' room, the headmaster made me stand on a chair and said, 'Explain to everyone why you're here.' With the goddess of learning seated on the tip of my tongue, I spoke without fear. The outcome was as desired, everyone was impressed. Then one of the teachers said, 'Should we test his arithmetic?' A cold current ran down my spine.

The headmaster rescued me. 'No need,' he said, 'admit him.' I still shudder to imagine the turn my life would have taken had my arithmetic skills been tested that day.

But another teacher cast some doubt over my age. 'Is he a dwarf, sir? Considering he's going into class five ...' This was an aspersion

I had to suffer for several years because I was smaller than my classmates, being younger than them.

Vivekananda School was not at all glamorous. The rooms were small, even the former kitchen had been converted into a classroom. There was no playground, and barely any space to move about. The students used to call it a chicken coop. But the headmaster, and other teachers and employees inspired by his ideals, had made arrangements for broadening our minds—even the school bearer shared the same dream. Some people can grow up in large spaces and still be small-minded, and others can spend their lives in a cage and still be generous of thought. It is because nature has kept the door open to this possibility that we can be certain of progress and mental development.

In the first phase of our lives, Sudhangshushekhar was our headmaster, but once we had passed our matriculation and left school, he became Hadu Da to everyone. His brother Himangshushekhar, our Guiram Da, was a remarkable teacher too, a lifelong bachelor. The brothers were extraordinarily close, though they argued bitterly sometimes; Guiram Da was the headmaster's greatest critic.

They led truly spartan lives. A schoolmate of mine named Sachin, who was in touch with them till their passing, knew a great many details. For instance, that Sudhangshushekhar owned only three khadi dhutis, three thick khadi panjaabis, and two inner vests. When there was a tear he used a handkerchief to mend it. Sachin said Hadu Da never owned a personal cupboard or a trunk to keep anything valuable, he never even kept track of money.

As Sachin put it: 'Hadu Da would sign on the receipt on payday, Himangshu Babu would collect the salary. As long as their eldest brother Shashankashekhar was alive, Himangshu Babu would put his own and his brother's salary beneath Shashankashekhar's bed.

He never counted the money. Shashanka Babu knew their salaries, and on one occasion he asked, "Why is there ten rupees extra?" Himangshu Babu said, "I have no idea." When Gobardhan Babu from the cash department was asked the next day, it turned out they had mistakenly been paid ten rupees more.'

At one time the school was in dire financial straits. I taught there for some time in this period. When things were very bad, the first people to be paid after the students had deposited their fees were the teachers who were married. 'They have families,' Sudhangshushekhar would say, 'their needs come first. I have Guiram, we'll manage somehow.'

Our Shankariprasad Basu was a favourite student of theirs. He often had the audacity to ask mischievous questions. Once, he brought up the matter of Sudhangshushekhar and Himangshushekhar's spartan lifestyle, and commented on the headmaster's inner vest, which was quite perforated by then. Hadu Da smiled and gave a historic answer, 'Vests last longer when they have holes.'

The Bhattacharya brothers were frugal with their meals too. Another teacher went to their house one evening to find the headmaster at dinner. A very simple meal of boiled papaya and unripe plantain, along with a little rice and some rutis. The guest assumed they were trying to save money by cutting back on rice. 'It's just the two of you, sir,' he blurted out, 'why eat ruti? Why not just buy rice at the market?' Selling rice in shops was forbidden at the time, but money could get you anything you wanted. The headmaster replied, 'I cannot speak up against the black economy if I buy rice in the black market.'

A former student who owned a rice mill offered some of the high-quality rice he produced. 'How will you reconcile your stocks?' Hadu Da asked with a smile. 'You know birds peck away at the grain when it's put out to dry, sir,' answered the student. The reply came at once, 'Are we birds? We are fine as we are.'

Sudhangshushekhar was a careful spender, but his heart was with his students, and he gave away any money he had left over. Himangshu Babu had given him a wallet, into which Hadu Da kept aside some money every day for lunch. That was all the relationship he had with money. When he retired from his job at the school he returned the wallet to his brother, since he had no need for it any more.

With no clothes to speak of besides those for everyday wear in their possession, the brothers did not even own a suitcase. Once, when travelling to north India, they had to borrow both suitcases and warm shawls from a student. They indulged in only one luxury—on Vivekananda's birthday, Sudhangshu insisted on wearing freshly laundered clothes.

To tell the truth, having a teacher like Hadu Da was a matter of rare fortune. He was unmatched when it came to simplifying complicated subjects. It is from him that I have acquired a penchant for clarity in my writings. He taught us not to pick up the pen unless we were certain of being able to write simply, no matter how abstruse the theme. 'If you know how to boil it properly even a pebble can become as soft as a potato,' he would say. And he had proved to us many times that this was not untrue.

This mission to be understood easily had marked Sudhangshushekhar's entire life. I had once asked him what Ramakrishna's most useful advice for ordinary people was. Without a moment's hesitation he answered, 'To unite your mind and your tongue. To hold on to the truth.' Not an easy undertaking, but Hadu Da did it in the face of all obstacles.

Once, a particularly favourite student of his brought a boy to be admitted to the school. 'If the boy doesn't get good marks it means we're depriving someone else,' Hadu Da told him candidly. The embarrassed former student never recommended anyone else for admission.

Despite being soft-hearted, Hadu Da did not baulk at sternness when it came to following rules. 'Only by following the minor rules do you develop the ability to follow the major ones,' he would say. He would become frantic in his efforts to inculcate discipline in his students. But then the very same person said later, 'I was a rascal myself in school, which is why I know when these boys are being rascals.'

He used to write a diary, excerpts from which were published alongside reminiscences by students. I discovered a most unusual man in this diary. There was an entry on the writer of the *Kathamrita*, the formidable headmaster Mahendranath Gupta, which is worth reading.

> The chair that Sri M used in school had no armrests. He chose not to have such a chair. He could not touch his own mother's feet out of embarrassment. I am delighted to discover that at least in these two matters I have something in common with a great man. I have never touched my mother's feet either, I was too embarrassed. There's no end to my regret about this. After my mother died, I did it in a way no one could see.

For all of us who came into contact with him, Sudhangshushekhar was the great headmaster of a very small school. In the course of teaching, observing and reading, he created his own philosophy, at whose core lay an integrated flowering of head, hand and heart.

There was another aspect to him, all but invisible to most. He had realized that just as teachers influence students, they too are unknowingly influenced by students. He had once admitted that students sometimes have a moral impact on their teachers—their honesty, for instance, inspires those who teach them in classrooms. Qualities like loving one's school, not lying, not trying to fool anyone, also have an effect on teachers.

I am yet to find out why his students were devoted to him despite all the punishments they received at his hands. Shankari Da and I agreed that Hadu Da was not a social reformer in that sense, he did not create any institutions besides the school. He avoided meetings and gatherings, his behaviour with strangers was incoherent, he lacked the ability to move people with his words, and yet anyone who knew him would say, 'There won't be another like him.' Shankari Da had a valuable observation, 'He had made duty his creed, and later I realized, he had made his creed his duty too.'

It wasn't only in school that Hadu Da drew me close with his affection but also afterwards, during my extreme financial crisis. I would have been devastated without the job he gave me. And just as being a teacher in his school saved me from economic humiliation, it also gave me the chance to know the headmaster from a different perspective. Being in the company of such a person leaves little to ask of life thereafter. I want to say proudly, 'We're students of Vivekananda School. Sudhangshushekhar Bhattacharya nurtured us personally. We might make mistakes, but we will never do anything wrong.'

My Mother's Friend

THERE'S NO COUNTING THE NUMBER OF TIMES I HAVE SEEN, since adolescence, married women in Bengal beating their heads on the ground in front of the silent idol of Lakshmi, the goddess of wealth, and acquiring bruised foreheads for their efforts. My long-suffering mother used to say that the goddess may not speak much, but her eyes are everywhere, and even the slightest sign of bad behaviour will make her instruct her mount, the owl, to fly off quietly into the night. Not even her permanent representative in the household, the one we call grihalakshmi, will come to know.

No one knows better than Bengali women that this capricious goddess is always on the verge of leaving. As my mother would say, 'Who can tell from her calm demeanour that her heart is constantly seeking opportunities to go off somewhere else?' A lady who lived in the neighbourhood used to tell Ma, 'That's all for show, Didi. She's the eternal resident of rich people's houses, she doesn't feel restless even when they do bad things. All her animosity is reserved for poor people.' My mother would become fearful. 'You mustn't say that, Lakshmi. You must live up to your name.'

Lakshmi Mashi's response to this was, 'Forget it, Didi, her exploits only make the rich richer, and the poor poorer.'

Ma would tell her to speak softly; what if the deity heard? 'The goddess didn't have it easy either,' she would say. 'After springing from Brahma's body her beauty and her qualities made her such an object of envy that her very life was in peril. The other gods and goddesses had decided to murder her and share her beauty and abilities amongst themselves. It was just that because women must not be slain, on Brahma's advice they only shared her beauty and abilities amongst themselves without actually killing her.' Lakshmi Mashi was something of a rebel. She said, 'It's all very well to say women must not be slain, but what they do is to keep us alive by a thread and inflict all their torture on us.'

Lakshmi Mashi owned several slim volumes about the goddess Lakshmi. These contained inflammatory material too, and whenever she was upset or angry, Lakshmi Mashi would come over and rant at my mother. 'Listen to what she's been up to, Didi. Someone said to her face, the learned and the wise do not get your bounty, all of it is enjoyed by the vile, the indolent, and the gluttons. You do not value justice.'

My mother's household was spilling over at the time. With eight children at home, Ma was desperate for the goddess Lakshmi's generosity. She would pay no attention to what Lakshmi Mashi would say. 'It must be some sin I committed in childhood,' was her refrain. 'Once I used tulsi leaves as a bell for the goddess, my mother ran up and said I had ruined everything, Lakshmi couldn't stand such practices and was bound to punish us.'

Even after the goddess left our Howrah home without notice upon my father's death, my mother continued to pray at her feet. Lakshmi Mashi drew me aside to inform me the goddess wasn't trustworthy at all—on a mere whim she could render an entire family bankrupt in a moment. She felt not the slightest shame in occupying the laps of heartless, unprincipled debauchees. Who could possibly have named her Lakshmi!

Lakshmi Mashi had reason to be angry. Abandoned by her husband, she was financially dependent now, living next door to us as part of a distant cousin's household, where she slaved all day and heaped copious abuse on her divine namesake. 'Lakshmi is far too biased,' she would say. 'She doesn't even understand the suffering of her own kind, she heaps misfortunes on women. I don't see men performing rituals for her, but they are her chosen ones, I never see a woman in her good books.'

Lakshmi Mashi chose her own path later, running away with a man. Ma was unhappy. 'There's no knowing how the goddess Lakshmi will punish rebels,' she said.

I was on Lakshmi Mashi's side at the time, reposing no faith in the goddess's goodness of heart. What was the reasoning behind her brutal oppression of those who had not rebelled against her but merely used the wrong kind of leaves by mistake during the rituals?

Following my mother's orders to track Lakshmi Mashi down after she had left home, I came face to face with an entirely different world. I was told she was characterless, but my experiences showed me humans appear the same with or without character.

If anything, our former neighbour was blooming, realizing the potential of her beauty now that she was well looked after. The truth was that men who had pocketed the goddess Lakshmi now rolled at Lakshmi Mashi's feet. I did not have the maturity at the time to know what form this thing called character takes, and what a family gains or loses in its absence.

Lakshmi Mashi served me a meal with great care in her new home, gave me some money, and said, 'Don't tell Didi. You'll need it to get about.' Then she added, 'Tell her I'm well.' Not being employed herself, she found it difficult to imagine how she could help me find a job, but still she said, 'Let me see what I can do for you. He doesn't visit me every day, only three days a week. Come and see me any day besides Wednesdays, Fridays and Saturdays—I have no work on those days.'

I didn't understand then what influence Lakshmi Mashi had on the person she referred to as 'him', but I did afterwards, upon reading Ramakrishna. In some parts of his books he had referred to Golap or Golapi, the mistress of someone referred to as Borobabu. An applicant for a job with Borobabu was making no progress when someone suggested, 'Go tell Golapi, that will work.' The applicant went to her with a request to put in a word. 'With whom?' asked Golapi. 'Borobabu,' said the jobseeker. 'I'll tell him tonight,' she said. The next morning someone turned up at the applicant's house, telling him to start work immediately.

I met Lakshmi Mashi's 'special person' in his office. But times had changed greatly from Ramakrishna's days, rules had been tightened, and the job market had deteriorated. 'Meshomoshai' tried his best, but nothing was easy in a Bengal that the goddess Lakshmi had already begun to put on the losses side of the ledger.

One day I arrived at Lakshmi Mashi's house to find it in turmoil. Thanks to her 'special person' her house was being raided for black money. It seemed his legally wedded wife had tipped off the police.

I went home disappointed, but did not say anything to my mother lest she be upset. I did ask her why the goddess Lakshmi was so hesitant to pass on wealth to women who prayed to her so ardently. Ma told me something I didn't know: Lakshmi may be the goddess of wealth, but she had foolishly handed over the cash to Kuber to manage—and Kuber worked according to his own fancies. There was even a bank by his name at that time, but for some unknown reason Kuber himself collapsed in this wretched Bengal.

Who is Kuber? Ma told me the very rich people say he's the goddess Lakshmi's husband. But how can that be, for she is Vishnupriya, the one whom the god Vishnu loved.

There was one more question I didn't get an answer to: Why are all the wealthy people of the world men? Why do Lakshmi's fortunate sons rule everywhere, why not her fortunate daughters? Lakshmi Mashi had said this injustice would not last forever. But until then the goddess Lakshmi had decided not to give wealth to anyone but men, and women would have to work twice as hard to control it for themselves.

The downturn in Lakshmi Mashi's fortunes did not worsen my mother's, for I had by then found a job with the barrister Noel Barwell that paid enough for our family's survival. In Calcutta Mr Barwell used to live in the now defunct Spence's Hotel, and his office was in Temple Chambers. I noticed rich men coming and going regularly in both these places, but very few rich women. One of them was a fortune hunter who, after trying her luck at various ports, eventually became Queen Mira Adityanarayan towards the end of her life. She appears early on in my book *Kato Ajanare*. Many of the women who came to the lawyers had been cheated by men; a few had even become bankrupt. Pawning their bodies to the goddess Lakshmi's inner circle, some of them asked for nothing more than financial stability. Others were trying to protect their reckless husbands from their latest infatuations, most of whom were foreigners or Anglo-Indians. The goddess did not offer a circle of protection to Hindu women, for there was no religious objection to polygamy at the time.

Not that every woman who came was a client. Consider Mrs Pakrashi, the centre of attraction for high society at that time, who was my employer's social acquaintance, and knew me as a result. I got to know her better subsequently at *Chowringhee*'s

Shahjahan Hotel. Exquisitely beautiful women from poor families sometimes earned the friendship of rich men because of a quirk on the part of the goddess Lakshmi. When I saw Mrs Pakrashi with Mr Barwell she could charm the world with her looks. Had I been familiar with the scriptures, I could have quoted from them directly instead of attempting to choose words of my own—'radiant in her own spirit, resplendent in her beauty, endlessly captivating, her complexion like beaten gold, dishevelled under her jewels, clad in yellow garments, a gentle smile on her face, eternally youthful'.

Mr Barwell's chambers near the High Court and Spence's Hotel in Dalhousie Square were like important places of pilgrimage. How many among all the women I met within a short period at these two places could I depict in *Kato Ajanare* or in *Chowringhee* anyway? Some of them were royal consorts, some flashing-eyed wives of shameless capitalists, some hostesses in hotels, some dancers, some air hostesses, some lovers who had risen from history books only to disappear in them again. None of them were blessed by the goddess Lakshmi before entering the arena; they were forced to pursue both riches and ruination.

The greater the wealth, the larger the problem. The goddess's male favourites whom I encountered on the road of my life were uniformly vile, tormenting the learned and refusing to value justice. But I also met a number of joyful men who were not in her good books, such as Satyasundar Bose, aka Sata Da. Not everyone is born to judge and weep, many lucky men can establish normal, easy relationships even with unlucky women.

I have not yet recounted the aftermath to my Lakshmi Mashi's life. Although the man who led her out of the blind lane in Howrah had abandoned her, she did not surrender to fate. Eventually she became a sought-after entertainer who often flew off to Delhi or

Bombay, where I ran into her a few times. Her affluent guests would book luxury hotel rooms in those cities in advance.

Lakshmi Mashi read my *Chowringhee* with great attention. 'It's a very busy time now,' she told me, 'when I have some time on my hands I'll tell you my entire story. Tell everyone I don't pretend to be someone I'm not. I have no discomfort, I've bought a flat and a car, I have a driver, I go to the Dakshineshwar Temple every month, I give money to the poor. Mine isn't a profession where you cheat people, I give them some pleasure and accept compensation. Those who receive pleasure can give more if they wish.'

The human jungle that I went ever deeper into in search of characters offered me no evidence of the goddess Lakshmi's just ways, which is why my novels filled up with the bad battles being waged by good girls.

My novel *Jana Aranya* was published in English translation as *The Middleman*. No novel should need additional explanations, but I did write an afterword about some of Bengal's luckless women. For instance, I knew a sex worker named Rosie. Once, I had failed despite all my efforts to sell some bailing hooks to a jute mill. But a competitor won the purchase manager over by offering him a night with Rosie, and bagged the order. Annoyed by my foolishness, Rosie told me, 'You are a bloody fool! Why didn't you tell me earlier?' In the afterword I wrote, 'In this world the mother serves up the daughter for cash, a brother offers his sister, a husband presents his wife.'

In this greed-tainted world, a mother can unhesitatingly peep through a crack in the door to check how much longer her daughter is going to spend in the arms of a client, and return to the next guest and announce calmly, 'Not much longer, I knocked on the door, just a few minutes more. That's the problem with my daughter, can't get a customer off quickly and send him on his way; she wastes too much time.'

The passing of time simplifies many complicated things. Countless young women are sinking into darkness as we middle-class people refuse to acknowledge the games that the goddess Lakshmi plays. But on this full moon night when the goddess is meant to be worshipped, we can wipe off our resentment and annoyance and ask her clearly, 'Why are you so miserly when it comes to handing over money to women? Why is your cash stuck with Kuber? Those who say he doesn't consider women worthy … are they wrong?'

Those who are afraid whisper that somewhere in some Purana it says Lakshmi did get married to Kuber, but there is no report of a divorce.

Still, when it comes to the embodiment of the goddess Lakshmi, I can only think of my mother. In beauty and qualities, in affection and behaviour, she was as reassuring as the deity, a giver of largesse. But the parsimonious goddess deprived her of the power of money. Today I feel that had our mothers been empowered to earn, there would have been no difference whatsoever between them and the goddess.

Several years into my literary journey, I did notice Bengali women adopting simple solutions to difficult problems, ignoring all manner of opposition and joining the workforce without allowing their grace and glory to be impaired. Both husband and wife have begun to earn together with joy—a sight that delights me no end. Yet it was just the other day that there were heated debates on the streets over whether women would be able to retain their honour if they started working in offices and factories. It wasn't too long ago that the sight of a woman working in a government or private organization would lead to great excitement and curiosity.

Sociologist Benoy Sarkar, a true thought leader, congratulated these bold new steps taken by Bengali women. Today it seems strange that we Bengalis regarded this entirely natural and essential step with suspicion. The goddess Lakshmi must have chuckled.

Working couples in foreign countries are called two-paycheque families. Those who imagined that the placid hearts and minds of Bengali women would be radically transformed once they tasted blood in the form of money have been proven hopelessly wrong. Those young ladies who have set out to worship the goddess Lakshmi before getting married have brought new glory to Bengal's women.

I was delighted to be able to place just such a woman, Paramita, at the heart of my novel *Nagar Nandini*. Like many other Bengali women, Paramita Mukhopadhyay is cheated by her classmate. Later, the same man is in trouble at his workplace, and the person who goes to conduct the enquiry from the distant head office is none other than Paramita. She is perhaps the first woman executive in Bengali literature.

The currents of time have brought many more changes to Bengal on the goddess Lakshmi's wishes. There are now women who earn lakhs every month, not that you will know it by looking at them. It is being said that an annual salary of a crore for a woman may soon materialize too. When the goddess Lakshmi finally evades Kuber's plot and decides to accord equal importance to women and to men, the rituals performed for her every Thursday will become even more meaningful.

My Mentor

PLACE: NO. 107 KHURUT ROAD. TIME: EARLY 1942. Character: Your humble servant, whom his fellow students in class five kept annoying with the label of being a Bangaal from Jessore. The other character is the now-deceased protagonist of this piece, the apple of our teachers' eyes, Shankari Da of class nine. He was also the star of the students' literary society. I had assumed he had no disappointments in his life—he was good at studies, good at sports, good at public speaking, and was a literary star in the making.

The pride of our school was its self-governance, or what the students jokingly turned into 'shallow governance'. The students themselves were in charge of law and order—and those among them who became senior functionaries in this self-government wielded considerable influence and commanded attention. When everyone gathered for prayers before studies began, the students of the senior classes would make the necessary announcements. Our greatest hero was Bota Da, whose full name was Batakrishna Mitra. It was these announcements that led to my first glimpse of Shankari Da. He began his announcement with 'Look, my friends'. The time to know him well hadn't come yet. I got a closer look at him at our literary meetings where he would read out his work regularly.

I have to admit Shankariprasad's essays were rather ponderous and studded with a number of perplexing words. His Bangla a la Vidyasagar would frequently rob me of my self-confidence. At home I would run the words he had used through my mind and feel quite miserable. Why couldn't they have popped up in my thick head first? The opening line of Shankari Da's speech to a packed auditorium on the occasion of Vivekananda's birth anniversary remains alive in my memory more than fifty years later—'boundless time with no beginning or end have I made finite by the inception of my life.'

My head spun. I remained overwhelmed by this opening line for quite a few days. When I sat down to eat I could see boundless time with no beginning or end in front of my eyes, on the way back from school I had the temerity to make it finite. For a few days I attempted to construct a similarly profound line, but failed miserably. Despair overwhelmed me; my dreams of becoming a writer seemed on the verge of being wiped out.

I was down in the dumps when I got an invitation to read my own work at the school literary meeting. I confessed my plight directly to the headmaster, Sudhangshushekhar Bhattacharya. We would go out with him on evening walks sometimes, strolling along Circular Road from Kashundia to Ramrajatala Railway Station. The headmaster chuckled on hearing my predicament, refusing to take it seriously. 'Not everyone can be Shankari,' he said. 'Switch from boundless time with no beginning or end to something else. Use completely domestic language, the way Ramakrishna did.' I realized that he was gently hinting that I should steer clear of Vivekananda. And yet it was Vivekananda who was our hero then, we didn't concern ourselves with the priest from Dakshineshwar. In fact we found it difficult to understand why a bright and bold young man like Vivekananda paid so much attention to him.

Still, Shankari Da had reached the stratosphere with a single sentence; I bowed my head to him from a distance, for he never appeared to be within reach. But a chance visit to the playing field of the Ramakrishna–Vivekananda Ashram changed things for me, when I found Shankariprasad had paused his efforts to sandwich eternity and was playing football with great gusto. As a footballer he could by no means be called lacklustre.

It was this ever-popular Shankari Da who later offered me a long-lasting sanctuary of affection. 'Don't call me Shankari,' he said, 'that's feminine gender. My name is Shankariprasad.' It proved impossible to go by the intricacies of grammar, and he remained Shankari Da, our natural guardian. I was thin as a reed at the time, with a bulbous head—to reduce the circulation of the epithet 'Bangaal from Jessore', Shankari Da himself named me 'potato-on-a-toothpick'. Later, he said, 'How was I to know you would by a quirk of the Maker become a "coconut-on-an-urn"?'

Shankari Da's first love in this period was Rabindranath Tagore, many of whose poems and aphorisms he had memorized. A number of Bangla words evoked wonder in me, but there was no dictionary at home so I could not tell their meaning. Our beloved headmaster Hadu Da had instructed us not to use words whose meanings we were unaware of. Later in life Shankari Da would tell me, 'This valuable advice from your guru saved you. I still believe that they who can turn pebbles into seedless dates for readers will triumph.'

'Read these,' Hadu Da would order us, handing over mysterious texts written by Vivekananda. Shankari Da was the only one we could turn to. He would explain the essence of karma yoga and bhakti yoga in brief. But when this didn't seem to appeal to my taste, he would say, 'Why don't you try reading Swamiji's travel writings and letters?' When even this did not elicit a suitable response, he gave up in disappointment and handed me over to the gourmet

Gayaram Kirtan Da, who surreptitiously informed me that when it came to cooking, eating, and hosting meals for others, Swami Vivekananda was second to none. Shankari Da was relieved to see this had appealed to me. 'To be a writer,' he would say, 'you have to be aware of both the positive and negative sides. It isn't enough to know the details of how he cooked polao, you must also know why he was vehemently opposed to guavas.'

That was when I made Shankari Da my guru in literature. No education, no memory, no command over English—the lord alone knows why I felt the desire to be a writer, but Shankari Da gave me refuge. Although he was fully versed in the all-rounder Rabi Thakur by then and had turned his mind to medieval poets and their poetry, his body was still involved with playing sports and watching them. Beyond school, he flourished in the wider arena of college, winning a string of gold medals. Our teacher Himangshushekhar Bhattacharya used to say boys are of two kinds—peacocks and dogs. Dogs are gorgeous as puppies but become uglier as they grow older; peacocks are not attractive at first, but when they display their full plumage they are wondrously beautiful. Our Shankari Da had only passed his matriculation in the second class, but in his MA examination he stood first class first. One of our classmates was a simple thinker; he asked Himangshu Babu, 'And what about those who are beautiful neither before nor after?' Our teacher was not in a good mood, he said, 'They are monkeys. Like you. No change.'

Until Shankariprasad left school, I remained familiar with his exploits at every literary gathering, accepting his leadership wholeheartedly and never considering rebellion. He used to live in a house right next to our monastery. He might have been a resident of the monastery had there not been a bamboo slip fence in between. The monastery had a library, and here too Shankari Da appeared as the principal player. We would leaf through books and magazines in the reading room, but the same question would keep haunting me—how had this person demonstrated the audacity to contain boundless time with no beginning or end? And the accompanying question: Had he thought it up himself, or borrowed it from someone? When I eventually asked him one day, he said, real writers absorb, they don't purloin. It is possible to acquire other people's ideas without stealing them, this is how one can widen their learning.

After completing his MA Shankari Da became a schoolmaster at about the same time as me. Around then Sarat Da—Sarat Kumar Ghosh—from the school was a close friend. On Sunday mornings he would appear at Khurut Road to complete pending work from the school. I would be there too. We referred to him as the Saratchandra Charitable Outdoor Trust, for it was he who, via Gajen, treated us to tea and snacks. Occasionally Robin Da—Robin Mitra—insisted on taking over the task, and renamed the institution Rotary—for the responsibility would be rotated. Shankari Da would be present at some of these so-called Rotary gatherings, where different aspects of his pleasant personality would reveal themselves.

I discovered Shankari Da had altered his thinking radically. He now said there was no use being stern or harsh; the greatest challenge in the world was to win hearts gently. Since suffering is endless in this world, create bliss wherever you can, make people happy—joy is the essence of creation, after all.

Shankari Da used to allow me some extra indulgence during this phase. Perhaps it was out of pity, for my education had been abruptly curtailed, and I had no identity other than that of the youngest teacher in the primary section. So his affection for me went a long way. We used to entertain ourselves by attacking him, doing our best to catch his mistakes or to annoy him. Pleased by this, he would smile and egg us on. From afar anyone would think a minor war was under way, but it was nothing like that; our love and respect for him were intact, none of that was open to question. Still, it was a game. Our discussions ranged over the entire world—from football to the Maker of the universe, from cricket to poetry, nothing was out of bounds. When the debate threatened to peter out, Robin Da would use his sense of humour to instigate a renewal of the argument. Feigning self-defence, Shankari Da would make all kinds of jokes that, if noted down systematically, could have been made into a book.

I should point out that his thoughts always flowed in more than one direction. Sometimes towards cricket, sometimes towards Bharatchandra, sometimes towards Chandidas. We used to joke that cricket was not a sport, only a barbaric expression of colonial culture, leading two men with sticks to make eleven other innocent men slave all day. At other times we questioned how Vivekananda and Bharatchandra could be served up in the same bowl. They had only one thing in common, one was born in Howrah, and the other passed away there. Shankari Da would hear us out, indulge our questions, and then defend himself. We would battle it out, smiling all the while, and Sarat Da, sizing up the situation, would send for a second round of tea. It would not be unfair to say some of Shankari Da's best writings about cricket came from the fake Rotary addas.

The crisis in my life had begun when Shankari Da's fame was spreading through the neighbourhoods of Howrah. After my father's untimely death, I had no desire for the company of those close to me. Scraping through the matriculation exams, I had enrolled for the Intermediate course, all my dreams having already gone up in flames on Baba's funeral pyre. I was haunted by just the one question: How would someone with no connections get a job? The only persons I could turn to were my mother and my headmaster Hadu Da. He would send for me, ask after me, and tell me Vivekananda had been plunged into a similar crisis, which he had overcome. Eventually, out of kindness, Hadu Da ignored all protocol and gave me a temporary job at the school.

Shankari Da didn't give up on me either. When we ran into each other he didn't ask how I was surviving. Instead he would say, 'You mustn't stop writing.' Strangely, he was convinced that I would be a writer one day, and adoring readers would queue up for my autograph. It felt like a cruel joke, but for some reason Shankari Da was unwilling to shed his conviction. 'A new age is upon us,' he would say, 'bringing triumph for those who have learnt to convert pebbles into seedless dates.' His conversations with us suggested Neville Cardus was most certainly a greater writer than Shakespeare, and it was Bengal's misfortune not to have a Neville Cardus of our own.

Later, when I was working as the barrister Noel Barwell's clerk, I used to recount my daily experiences at the Sunday addas. It was here that the inception of my book *Kato Ajanare* took place. This was followed by more changes in my life, but I remained addicted to the Sunday adda. One day, I took some of the chapters I had written to show them to Shankari Da.

My luck had changed earlier when Bibhuti Da led me by the hand from Vivekananda School to the precincts of the High Court, where I gained a new identity, that of clerk to a barrister, the Englishman Noel Frederick Barwell—it was a most unusual experience. Shankari Da would sometimes make me ride pillion on his cycle and take me back to our Chowdhurybagan house from the adda, and there he would listen to accounts of the happenings in my life with great interest. At the time, I was walled in by hopelessness with no power or water supply at home, and our lives dependent on just two lanterns. Shankari Da didn't care for any of this though. He had surmised that I was in touch with a new world, the kind that the world's greatest writers are willing to sacrifice everything for. I had no faith, but he had taken it for granted that something exceptional was about to take place. Not that my happy days at Temple Chambers lasted long, for my employer had a heart attack during a court appearance in Madras and died in a nursing home there.

Soon afterwards I began to surreptitiously write about my recent experiences, which had tickled Shankari Da's curiosity greatly. Sometime later, when the opportunity arose for the piece to be serialized in *Desh* magazine, he said, 'If at all I understand anything of literature, the time has come for one twenty-year-old young man to give autographs.' As the instalments kept appearing, a renowned author advised me, 'Don't empty out your bag of experiences, spend it carefully.' Shankari Da didn't agree. 'Give it everything, you can think later about what comes afterwards.'

He wrote a long review of my first book in the *City College* magazine. 'Ramakrishna didn't care for the practice of law. And although he came from a family of lawyers, Vivekananda wasn't well disposed towards it either, he even argued with his brothers about it. But he made no adverse comments on clerks, you found the right gap in the field to hit your boundary.'

Shankari Da would say, 'Cowards can achieve nothing. A writer's mind is like a perpetually full wine glass, the more you empty it, the more it fills up.' This dictum proved useful to me. As for Shankari Da, after tasting the flavours of different kinds of writing, he was intent on going deeper into literature about the Ramakrishna–Vivekananda movement. Bengalis wanted to see him as the bard of sports writing, but he was keen on embarking on another pilgrimage, and had even decided what it would be. India needed its own Marie Louise Burke, he felt, for it was necessary to re-establish Vivekananda against a contemporary backdrop. This path of dedication may not lead to encounters with hundreds of thousands of devotees, but then a genuine believer does not pawn his work to ensure a traffic jam on the literary highway. Still, our own Marie Louise Burke, Shankariprasad Basu, achieved the impossible. I don't recall there ever having been such a large number of mesmerized readers for a serious book in Bangla, as there were for *Vivekananda and Contemporary India*. 'Many people leave their homes to establish the Ramakrishna–Vivekananda movement globally,' I told him, 'and here you are, giving up your original calling to switch from literature to history.'

Perhaps there were no other paths, but this one also earned him unimaginable popularity. From the chief of the monastery to the chief justice, from other judges and barristers to film stars and even ordinary people, everyone was an enthusiastic reader of the book, swearing by the information presented in it. Apparently this was exactly what had happened in the West, where there was a rush everywhere from libraries to kitchens to read *The Decline and Fall of the Roman Empire*.

Shankari Da's back-breaking labour to excavate Vivekananda had to be seen to be believed. Visiting various cities of India year after year, almost penniless, rummaging through unhealthy dust-caked documents without a care in the world, taking down everything by hand in a technology-less world, and spending the night absolutely anywhere.

Still Shankari Da did not lack for a sense of humour. After he received an award from the Sahitya Akademi, he told me when I went to meet him, 'I cannot protest against what Ramen said.' Ramen, who was at hand, repeated his observation. 'When you copy in exams they rusticate you, but here Shankari copies shamelessly under the guise of research and gets a national award.'

Whether it was the retrieval of hidden gems, or poring over collections and anthologies, his effort evoked nothing but wonder in the rest of us. Thousands of pages of handwriting, half of it comprising sharp analysis—some of which made it to the press, while the rest remained in his house in Olabibitala Lane. I worry about the fate of all his unpublished work, especially the working papers. Scrap paper has played a vital role in today's research into the Ramakrishna–Vivekananda movement.

Scholars and experts will evaluate Shankariprasad Basu's mind-bogglingly extensive work on Ramakrishna, Vivekananda, Sree Ma, Nivedita and Subhas Chandra Bose. All I will say is that it was he who instigated my senile audacity in my old age to write about the unknown Vivekananda. 'Wasn't it Syed Mujtaba Ali who told you,' he said, 'that a crow happily slakes its thirst in the slush where an elephant dares not tread?'

Nothing has been written yet about Shankari Da's dedication to erudition. I am sure his admirers will do it soon. I would like to talk about a few personal things. He was not greedy for either fame or acknowledgement. Whom should I dedicate my first book to? 'Not to me,' he declared. 'The next one, if you like.' This book was *Chowringhee*, which I dedicated to him with the words, 'To the producer, director and music composer of my literary life, Shankariprasad Basu'. This too became an object of his jokes—after several pirated editions of the book came out, he said, 'I can't criticize them, because they haven't left out the dedication page.'

For the benefit of those who consider my account something of an exaggeration, let me mention that even this does not say everything that should be said. Shankari Da could tell whether a raw piece of work had possibilities, and alongside this, he kept an eagle eye on the laboratory. Simply put, like the elixir advertised widely in almanacs, Shankari Da knew how to revive the dead.

And he bestowed his benedictions on me unstintingly. Even fifty years later I cannot forget the ways in which he helped me rebuild myself during various phases of my life.

He could organize information from thousands of pages in his head in an orderly fashion, but he was lackadaisical about his own affairs. I wrote out and then typed up his long application for a university job according to his instructions. A few days later he said, 'It didn't work out this time, I lost the papers on the bus.' Not one to quit, I stayed up all night and rewrote the application, typing it out the next day.

He expressed no annoyance when it came to attending literary events. On one occasion he said, 'They gave me a first-class train ticket. I told them, why didn't you tell me earlier you were going to buy first class, I would have got you a far worthier chairperson.'

I was involved in the selection of his bride too. It was a short list of candidates. He liked one of them, with three still to be met. Shankari Da said, 'Since I like someone, it won't be right to meet the others.' And he didn't.

A true writer, teacher and devotee, Shankariprasad didn't care for wealth or fame; he believed in respect and reverence. Although always courteous, he used his pen like a sharp sword to slice up his opponent without hesitation. This led those whose views diverged from his to slap the label of a blind devotee on him and belittle his huge project. But their effort did not succeed.

The accomplishments for which we know Shankariprasad would have earned him a knighthood and, subsequently, a peerage in the US. The pressure of work prevented him from seeking a PhD, though he did earn an honorary doctorate late in his life.

In sum, in these eight decades of my life I have not seen another writer so devoid of arrogance, so full of joy, so curious about myriad things, or so eager for the well-being of others. After Mahendranath

Gupta and Swami Saradananda, we haven't had anyone as good as him at bringing us the words of Ramakrishna and Vivekananda.

Shankariprasad proved that the beginning and end of creation is joy. Despite being in robust health all his life, this lively, energetic man had to suffer greatly in his last days. 'I suffer from knee pain because I'm not inclined to kneel,' he would say. When he fainted outside his house one day, he said afterwards, 'I was trying to understand what being in a trance is like.'

An admirer asked him on his sickbed, 'How are you?' He replied with a smile, 'It'll take half an hour to give you details about the ECG and X-ray and blood report. After which you will ask me why I'm not consulting Dr So-and-So. That will take another fifteen minutes. Thereafter I will be obliged to reciprocate and ask how you are. The conversation will go on for forty-five minutes more. I'd rather you told me what brings you to Olabibitala.'

Had I not been increasingly weighed down by age, I would have announced a new book at the end of this piece, 'The Ever-Smiling Shankariprasad Basu and Bengali Society of His Time'. But I dare not.

Sometimes I feel we got the best of Shankari Da the writer in his juicy pieces on cricket. As for his collected research on Vivekananda, it was like a fasting student offering flowers to the goddess of knowledge. It demonstrated enormous patience and painstaking enquiry, as well as an unmatched sense of duty and respect—but to experience the elation of creation, we have to go back to the cricket literature of his early days. I also wonder, what if Shankariprasad had entered the field of storytelling instead of surrendering himself to Ramakrishna and Vivekananda? Maybe Bengali literature would have got a writer the likes of whom have never been seen.

Vivekananda had once said about Ramakrishna that he could easily have created a thousand other Vivekanandas. From my own experience in the workshop of literature I can say that while my life would have been a failure without Shankariprasad as my guru, he could easily have created several dozen other writers.

Even in the life beyond literature that we have learnt to revere, Shankariprasad reigns as an emperor. The intention of extracting the essence from the hardest of rocks, a perpetual air of levity while trying to fathom life's deepest mysteries, uncompromising dedication, sacrificing small pleasures for great ideals, the conviction that the deed matters and not the outcome—these are the qualities Shankariprasad Basu demonstrated to us, in a way that has ensured future generations will never believe such a man lived among us in Howrah–Kashundia. Those who got his company are fortunate. Now in my twilight years, I feel he was not just the producer, director and music composer of my literary journey, but also the hero of the film of my life. I bow my head once more to him.

The Red Building

Ever since I arrived from Howrah I had wanted to learn more about this structure, but I have not till date laid my hands on anything worth reading on Calcutta's Writers' Building. It seems even British journalists visiting India would ask why a palace ruled by clerks was called 'Writers". Much later one of them told me, 'Your race has a tremendous sense of humour, that's how you've managed to give the name "Paradise" to the income tax office headquarters in Bentinck Street.' A self-flagellating Bengali explained, however, that all that happens in Writers' Building is writing in files, hence the name. If ever some other work is done there, the name will have to be changed.

When I was searching for a job to bring the smile back to my mother's face after my father's untimely death, I used to steal away to Dalhousie Square from Howrah and wander for hours near the red building. I had even tried to enter it, but the rules were very strict then—as soon as I walked up to the counter they would ask whom I wanted to meet. Since I knew no one's name but the chief minister's, I wasn't allowed in.

I did learn the secret of the word 'Writers" in the canteen, though. The young Englishmen freshly imported by John Company were called writers instead of clerks, and their first and principal address in Calcutta was this red building. They were still bachelors, with monthly emoluments of some twenty rupees. The cruel English didn't just plunder Bengal, they also oppressed their own youth with embarrassing salaries. But then meagre wages did not mean meagre exploits—after all, Robert Clive was one of these clerks.

I had no money in those days, but it was possible to hear many of the juicy stories told by seniors without having to occupy a chair in the canteen. Many of the experienced clerks at Writers' knew very well that John Company was an affectionate nickname for the East India Company. A number of those who became senior clerks at that time could have become IAS officers today, but of course these posts were reserved for the English before Independence. I used to envy them at first, but later I learnt their earnings were not particularly lucrative—at least those who believed in keeping on the straight and narrow.

The stories that circulated about John Company's young British clerks did not exactly cover Writers' Building with glory. Where were the lowly paid Britishers to go? They worked at Writers', which was also where they got board and lodging. I was glad to hear it was they who lent a fresh glow to Bengal's muri. Whenever they were peckish, the favourite snack for these thrifty Englishmen was this puffed rice, which they renamed 'Bengal Biscuit'.

I had applied several times for the post of bearer at Writers' Building and even given an interview on the second floor of the red building, but to no avail for I was not eighteen yet. The advice that came from the canteen circle was, don't write your date of birth on the application, and, instead of drawing attention to your matriculation certificate, call yourself a non-matriculate.

This time lady luck smiled on me; there was a temporary job as a bearer at the Bankura Agricultural Sales Market at the royal salary of Rs 52. But the organizers had an 'advance demand' of Rs 312. To this had to be added the train fare for Bankura, where I would have to collect the appointment letter, and arrangements for board and lodging for over a month. Calculations showed that I would be able to contribute nothing to my family in Howrah over the next year and a half. So I couldn't take advantage of the opportunity.

Many years later a powerful ICS secretary summoned me to the red building for professional advice. An admirer, he told me, 'We cannot afford advisers like you.' Unable to hold back my sorrows, I told the large-hearted secretary of my efforts to find a job as a bearer. 'There are many exceptional people all around you in this very office, but the system here has not been able to put them to use.'

Let me go back to my days looking for employment in the vicinity of Writers' Building. There were dozens of foreign business houses around the red building then, including kings of jute, queens of tea, emperors of paper, banking, insurance and shipping. Still there was a world of difference between the clerks in these companies and those in Writers' Building. Ramakrishna knew the secret, and whenever anyone visited him, he would ask whether they had a pencil—pension—or not. Whether the job came with a 'pencil' was crucial.

Finally I found a temporary source of sustenance in the legal neighbourhood of the High Court. Noel Barwell, the English barrister I worked for, would sometimes visit the offices of the chief secretary or home secretary or finance secretary on behalf of his clients. As his clerk, I too frequented the corridors of power, laden with briefs. The long application that Mr Barwell would dictate before visiting Writers' was for some unknown reason known as an 'aide memoire'. There was a long tradition at Writers' of letting things in through one ear and out through the other—from Lord Clive to Warren Hastings, no one was renowned for their memory. So, experienced British lawyers would leave behind a lively, well-written, anti-forgetfulness application before exiting the chambers of the powerful.

Noel Frederick Barwell was a goldmine of stories from the age of Clive to the Calcutta of the time. He also had a wealth of information about the young Englishmen of John Company at his fingertips. For instance, despite earning a pittance, each of these white men would swiftly engage a personal assistant, a coveted post for middle-class Bengalis. The personal assistant did their employers' shopping, took care of their finances—and even went out in search of funds when necessary. Yes, white men borrowed money incessantly, and were not averse to earning through illegal means, including the running of enterprises without using their own names. Some of them saw their fortunes soar in quick time, while others disappeared in a state of bankruptcy.

It is said that it was thanks to Writers' Building that they were nicknamed the 'Rich—or Rob India Come Home—Boys'.

British officers and clerks posted at Writers' used to be in a perpetual hurry, for their average lifespan in Calcutta was rather short at the time. That they had to avoid stomach ailments, malaria, or typhoid to survive meant their lives were at constant risk. Only after getting on the ship back home with all the illicit earnings made in the red building could they breathe easy. Many of them had long lives of leisure back home in England, living off the riches they had robbed India of.

Over and above the jobs in the red building, there were unlimited opportunities for earnings. Still, the Queen of England had deprived her favourite sons of some pleasures—they were forbidden from buying houses in this city and from marrying local women. In America the same white men had attacked and thrown out those loyal to their own country, severely denting the happiness of nationalist Englishmen.

The Mutiny of 1857 led to a number of changes in India—instead of John Company, highly educated, competitive young men arrived from their homeland to take over the task of ruling the empire. Those who had grabbed shares of the East India Company's monopoly over business acquired the new sobriquet of 'boxwallahs'. Taking their place in the spacious headquarters of big businesses set up around Writers' Building, they lived in luxury for decades. Some of their portraits can still be seen in the Royal Exchange building next door.

For some reason the British businessmen of Dalhousie Square stopped sending their briefs to Mr Barwell towards the end of his working life. Nor was he keeping well. On a whim he took me on a tour of Calcutta one day to show me the memorabilia of his ancestors. One Richard Barwell had in his time become Warren Hastings' right-hand man and acquired enormous wealth.

Passing Lal Dighi or Tank Square, we stopped outside Writers' Building. Suddenly Mr Barwell said, 'We have no children, you are like my heir. I had wanted to leave something to you. This Writers' Building was once owned by Richard Barwell. If the inheritance had passed uninterrupted down the generations, neither you nor I would ever have faced financial difficulties. Can you imagine the rent you could earn at today's rates? But something happened because of which my ancestor sold Writers' Building dirt cheap to John Company. You and I narrowly missed out on being the owner of Calcutta's number one property.' This revelation brought me great excitement. Imagine the transition from living in a rented house in a blind lane in Howrah to becoming the potential owner of Writers' Building!

After a penniless Mr Barwell passed away some time later, my mood would be transformed whenever I happened to pass Writers'. Here, I once ran into a broker I was acquainted with. Whenever a foreigner's house was demolished, he used to buy out the Burma teak beams and rafters, the window and door frames, the Italian marble slabs, and then sell them at a profit. But with most such houses in the city having been demolished already, he was going through a lean period. I felt he was greedily estimating how much money he could make if this genuine relic once owned by foreigners were to be demolished. I didn't care for this. He should have known Writers' Building was our capital and our last royal palace—and it could easily have belonged to me.

We Bengalis have created so many encyclopaedias and histories and anthologies after the Battle of Plassey, but not a single readable book has been written about the building that has been the arena of our deeds and misdeeds and suffering, the place from which we were ruled over for years.

For some unknown reason even the British have not chronicled the inside stories of this building. All we know is that the white arbiters of our fate who occupied Writers' changed their minds and moods in keeping with the times. The boxwallahs of John Company were nothing like the freshly imported officers from England who competed to join the ICS or their head and assistant clerks.

It is said that red tape was born in this red building. Bengali babus trained to be subservient were desperate to entertain their stern English masters. The one person whose name was often mentioned as a deity to be worshipped round the clock was the great soul Wakefield. Revolutionary Bengalis of that era had even considered inviting oil companies to recover all the grease that had been used here. Still, every Englishman at Writers' performed his duties most diligently as 'your most obedient servant'. You won't find this combination of royal haughtiness and karmic humility anywhere else.

Every detail of when each of these officers went on leave or was on furlough was printed in the government gazette. We're told that they would immerse themselves in a gigantic enterprise in the month before their departure from India—all subordinate workers would beg for a written character certificate, and the officers would patiently scribble with their fountain pens: 'I have known Babu So-and-So as the second clerk in my office for the past year. I wish this humble, hardworking, wise and loyal employee continued success.' The certificate would become part of the clerk's valuable family assets.

There were other sensational fairy tales too. An appreciative superior officer had purchased a jomidari in Orissa at an auction for his favourite head clerk. And yet, the brown-skinned Chatterjee Babu couldn't imagine eating anything touched by the boss he was devoted to. British and Indian histories had come ever so close to each other, only to stop at the dinner table. Not even independence in 1947 could bridge this distance. That the brown ICS officer, or their successor, the brown IAS officer, could not dispel the great Wakefield and his grease from Writers' Building is evident in the countless files still gathered in the archives for curious onlookers.

So much time has passed since then. I've heard many stories about the superstars of Writers' from veteran journalists and bureaucrats. Some of them have even become historical figures, especially West Bengal's first chief minister Bidhan Chandra Roy and Deshbandhu Chittaranjan Das's grandson Manu Ray, a favourite of the High Court precincts. It is probably Bidhan Chandra Roy who is etched into the history of the red building, like a dinosaur, for his far-sightedness and management abilities—and, at the same time, for his original profession. Apparently he diagnosed the illness of a sweeper in Writers' Building simply from the sound of his cough. Siddhartha 'Manu' Ray was an insomniac—the lights would be on in the chief minister's office even at midnight, and he would be making a succession of phone calls. Another occupant of the same office, Jyoti Basu ran a marathon by any standards, proving that mutually contradictory qualities can reside quite comfortably within the same person.

As the 'inevitable' heir to the childless Noel Frederick Barwell, the last English barrister of the Calcutta High Court, I had long been particularly interested in the wealthy and powerful Barwells of eighteenth- and nineteenth-century Calcutta. And once I learnt about the original ownership of Writers' Building from the horse's mouth, Mr Barwell himself, there was no holding back. Had dame fortune not mocked us, Barrister Barwell and I, his all-but-adopted son, would in natural course have become the lords of Writers'—this thought gave me a decided thrill in the electricity-less, ramshackle building in a dead end in Howrah that I called home.

Mr Barwell's ancestor Richard Barwell, the original owner of Writers' Building, came to Calcutta as a writer for the East India Company. At some Rs 20 a month, his monthly salary was nothing to write home about. But using a combination of intelligence and opportunities, Richard Barwell amassed the kind of wealth that not even our Mr Barwell could gauge. He was eager to see a portrait of his forefather—there must have been a giant oil painting of this confidant of Warren Hastings gathering dust somewhere in a famous museum. Mr Barwell's health was declining, his earnings were dwindling, he had sold his car, and he no longer had the strength to wander around the city with me to assuage my curiosity about his ancestors. Still, he did show me a black-and-white image of Richard Barwell in an English book one day. Not having noted its name, I couldn't locate it afterwards. Many years later I did find Richard Barwell again in a Bengali book published by P.M. Bagchi, the famous almanac printers, and tried to spot the similarities between Richard in the eighteenth century and Noel in the twentieth.

Besides the owner of Writers' Building, there were other Barwells of Calcutta whom my employer had mentioned to me. They were among the English barristers who had lucrative incomes and amassed considerable wealth after the Supreme Court was established in Calcutta.

One of them was Daniel Barwell, who found a place in the attorney William Hickey's voluminous and readable memoir. William Hickey, who took his oath as an attorney in court from Sir Elijah Impey, wrote:

> The first really pleasant party I was at after my illness was given by Daniel Barwell, who, as I have before observed, kept house with Pott and others. The most highly dressed and splendid hookah was prepared for me. I tried, but did not like it. As after several trials I still found it disagreeable, I with much gravity requested to know whether it was indispensably necessary that I should become a smoker, which was answered with equal gravity, 'Undoubtedly it is, for you might as well be out of the world as out of the fashion. Here everybody uses a hookah, and it is impossible to get on without.' Mr Gosling, less volatile and fidgety than the rest of the party, immediately said, 'Don't mind these rattling young men, Mr Hickey, there is no sort of occasion for your doing what is unpleasant, and although hookahs are in pretty general use there are several gentlemen that never smoke them.' I directly dismissed the hookah, never after tasting one.

Hickey referred to a 'barbarous' practice at the host Daniel Barwell's dinner—that of rolling up the bread into little balls like pills and throwing them at one another, which was known as pelleting. Not just men, even 'the fair sex' were adept at it. Hickey wrote: 'Daniel Barwell was such a proficient that he could at the distance of three or four yards snuff a candle, and that several times successively.'

Noel Barwell did not tell me what happened to Daniel Barwell eventually, but Hickey made a reference to it.

> In the middle of February my friend Bob Pott took leave of me and embarked in the *Ceres*, and towards the end of the same month Mr Daniel Barwell also departed with Captain Bogeis. Their voyage turned out disastrous and proved fatal to Mr Barwell ... Miss Mary Barwell, a maiden sister of Daniel's, an eccentric, odd woman, took it into her head that her brother had been basely murdered by the Dutchmen in order to possess themselves of an immense property in money and jewels ... She became outrageously violent on the subject, addressing letters to the Court of Directors, also to the different Cabinet Ministers, in consequence of which the most rigid enquiry and examination took place. The result satisfied every unprejudiced person that there was not a shadow of foundation for the insinuations and charges made by Miss Barwell.

Hickey also wrote of the predicament faced by the Board of Trade president William Burton. The directors of John Company brought charges of fraud against him. Burton defended himself at first, but when a rumour of a decree of £150,000 against him began to circulate, he escaped to the protection of the Dutch in Srirampur. From there he sailed for Europe on a Dutch ship, and began to live in Copenhagen after buying an enormous estate there. That was where he died.

Stories about the successful English lawyers of that age circulated within legal circles for quite some time. Let me offer a sample. 'The barristers only clamour for money.' There was no lack of them in Calcutta. 'All the Englishmen who came here to practise law became inordinately wealthy.' A contemporary complaint ran thus: 'Barristers charge far too much. Even if you only ask a question you have to pay a gold doubloon. If he writes a three-line letter for you, you'll have to count out Rs 800 at once. Making a will needs a fee, depending on its length, of five golden doubloons or more. A marriage contract is just as expensive. And those who happen to fall into their clutches for litigation are bound for bankruptcy. A barrister who practises for seven years and does not lose himself in gambling can go back home to England a millionaire.'

Historians of this state have honoured the writers of John Company with the title 'the first civilians of Bengal'. But the writers' salaries were scandalously low. The agents were in charge of depots, under them the writers occupied the lowest rung. In between came the factors and the junior senior merchants. In the beginning (1682), the annual income of agents was between £100 and £200, that of factors between £20 and £40, and of writers £10.

According to C.R. Wilson, the morning working hours were from 9 or 10 a.m. to 12 noon, and then another two hours in the afternoon till 4 p.m. Everyone gathered for lunch in a large hall. The cooks were British, French, Portuguese, or Indian. Everyone drank with their meals, but because imported wines were expensive, most slaked their thirst with country liquor.

Noel Barwell had thrown some light on their social life. On holidays the writers of the red building would go hunting, after which they would get down to eating and drinking. There was a great deal of competitiveness, bickering and fighting. We also have Shaista Khan's description—'a company of quarrelsome fellows, whose business dealings were not straightforward either'. Writers of books have termed these Englishmen 'quarter nawabs', 'half nawabs' and 'full nawabs'.

In his book *Calcutta Then, Calcutta Now*, Harisadhan Mukhopadhyay has provided generous descriptions of writers engaged by the Company. They began by working in the Company's offices, and then, when they had gathered some experience, were appointed at various business centres or depots. We even have a sample of the kind of language they employed when applying for these jobs in England: 'Having been duly educated in writing, Arithmeticks Merchants Accomply, he is desirous of serving your Honours as a Writer in India & prays therefore to be admitted accordingly, being ready to give the Security Required.' As the last few words reveal, British applicants had to make a security deposit even for this poorly paying job, which the parents of profligate children were compelled to cough up.

According to the book, beyond the salary,

> the primary means of income for the Company's employees were personal business enterprises, and, what was even more lucrative, gifts and bribes. The word 'interloping' crops up in connection with personal enterprises, which was to wilfully disobey all rules thanks to John Company's business monopoly. The Company's factors and writers used this facility of interloping to make copious amounts of money, spending it on royal luxuries.

They could not spend the unending stream of money flowing in through the tunnel of illegal businesses.

It wasn't as though news of the writers' reckless lifestyles and earnings did not reach the Company's headquarters in London. It has been written about in different books. One author pointed out that writers spent more than their legitimate earnings and passed on the burden of payment to the Company. Another said that the authorities in England would occasionally write strongly worded letters to Calcutta to keep their employees thrifty and under control. A letter to the governor of Calcutta in 1754 forbade lowly paid writers from using palanquins or coaches, on pain of demotion. Sometime later this instruction was modified to allow writers to use palanquins only during the monsoon and in winter. The letters added that offices were being prepared in Calcutta, which would ensure additional expenses for palanquins and so on would not have to be incurred.

Notably, however, this did not bring about any particular change. Mr Barwell referred to the warnings issued by the authorities in England in 1767, stating that young employees lacking in foresight were growing increasingly undisciplined, and unless better sense prevailed and they remembered their duties, they would be considered unfit for employment. Later, a 'supervisory meeting' was called to teach them a lesson. The new rules and regulations stated:

First, two servants and one cook were sufficient for unmarried employees.

Two, no writer could use a horse without the permission of the governor. Nor could they, individually or collectively, grow gardens.

Three, they would not be allowed luxurious attire.

Echoes were heard in England too. During the debate over Pitt's India Bill in the British Parliament, Mr Scott said in his speech that 508 civil servants had been sent to Bengal over the previous twenty-two years, of whom only thirty-five had returned, while another 150 had suffered untimely deaths. Of the 321 employees remaining in Bengal, it was doubtful whether even thirty-five would return in the next ten years. Most of those who had come back already had done so with less than £20,000 in savings, and some without even a shilling to their name.

Our Mr Barwell's forefather Richard Barwell was a lower-rung writer in 1756; in 1773 he became a member of the council. Noel Barwell's former driver used to tell me that as Warren Hastings' right-hand man Richard Barwell had amassed Rs 80 lakh before going back home in 1785.

At one time Richard Barwell used to live in a mansion next to St Stephen's Church in Kidderpore, but the creation of his that has withstood the ravages of time to remain standing even in the twenty-first century is, of course, Writers' Building beside Laldighi. The interesting nugget I unearthed when searching for more information was that the red structure was not the Writers' Building of the time; the original Writers', meant as a residence for the Company's clerks, was situated somewhere on Strand Road. After this there was a Writers' 2 as well, and finally the present one. I read that the 1776 lease for the land on which it stands is still intact in the Calcutta Collectorate. In sum, therefore, this was not Writers' Building at the time the Battle of Plassey was fought.

Talking of large structures means describing their surroundings too. So Laldighi, standing to the south of the red building, comes into the picture. The power-wielding Englishmen survived on the water provided by this tank, whose water level never went down. Rumour has it that the presence of secret channels of water at the bottom of the lake ensured it never ran dry. The banks were paved in Warren Hastings' time. Shyam Roy's temple was located in the same area, where Dol, or Holi, festivities would turn the water red, leading to the name Laldighi. The building housing Lakshmikanta

Majumdar's office, subsequently purchased by Job Charnock, stood here too.

The road to the north of Writers' Building is still named Lyons Range—Lion's Range to most people. A group of lunatics who smear history with filth as they please and change the names of roads and buildings has lived in the city for long. I must inform those who want to nurture their knowledge of the historical aspects of Laldighi that the Company sanctioned Rs 24 in 1750 to plant an orange orchard for the beautification of the tank.

Before being named after Thomas Lyons, this street was home to the residences of three famous people—two of them were Omichand and Mr Coales of the British Army who lost his life in the Black Hole tragedy. The third was General John Knox, who proved when Fort William was handed over to Siraj ud-Daulah that he who runs away survives.

The person who constructed the original Writers' Building was the same Thomas Lyons. But although formally owned under a different name, there is no doubt that right from the beginning it belonged to the Collector of Calcutta, Richard Barwell. Several writers have pointed out that the British politician Sir Philip Francis did not get along at all with his arch foe Sir Warren Hastings' long-time friend Richard Barwell, whom he labelled cunning, cruel and tyrannical. According to my employer, Richard Barwell became a member of Parliament after returning to Britain.

Thomas Lyons had lived in Calcutta from the time of the Battle of Plassey. To make shooting at Siraj's advancing forces possible, Lyons built the first version of the building on the land where Writers' Building stands today. In 1780 it became clear that Lyons had been working on behalf of someone when the East India Company took the building on rent for their apprentices directly from Richard Barwell—the agreement made no mention of Lyons.

Another interesting development was the advent of Hindi in Calcutta, with the red building as the epicentre. The lease that Lyons was given referred to the structure as 'company kerani ka baari' (the house of Company clerks, in a mixture of words from Hindi and Bengali). Lyons constructed nineteen apartments, and subsequently handed over the ownership formally to the man behind the scenes, Richard Barwell. Although the details are shrouded in mystery, it is surmised that after Lyons' five-year lease on it expired, he sold the building to Richard Barwell, who in turn handed it over to his trustees to manage on behalf of his children. Sir Elijah Impey was one of these trustees. The original monthly rent was Rs 3,800, and it is believed to have cost Thomas Lyons Rs 40,000 to build it. But Writers' wasn't referred to as a building, it was termed 'a bunch of boutiques'.

It remained the residence of the Company's bachelor writers for a long time after this. Only under Sir Ashley Eden, Governor General of Bengal, was the 'palatial building' transformed.

There has probably been no enquiry into when young Indian men quietly entered Writers' Building to serve the English writers. But a little investigation reveals that there were three levels—the English on top, Europeans next and Bengalis at the bottom. The Bengalis were pleased when referred to as 'native writers'. They earned between Rs 4 and Rs 20 a month. To tell the truth, Bengali clerks in Writers' Building were never known to be well paid. They were divided into two grades, upper and lower. Those in the upper grade knew English, and their loyalty to their British superiors was beyond question. They earned between Rs 8 and Rs 20 a month, compared to the range of Rs 60 to Rs 100 earned by European clerks.

But the title that earned special significance in that era was that of 'sarkar babu'. Some of its recipients went a step further and became moneylenders, creating a sensation in society.

The best written account of their presence in Writers' Building was laid out in Elza Fay's letters written from Calcutta between 1780 and 1782. In a letter dated 29 August 1780, she wrote,

> Though the lawful interest of money is but 12 per cent—enough you will say—yet 24 is given by the shopkeepers, who will lend or borrow the smallest sums for a single day, and ascertain the precise interest to the greatest exactitude, having the advantage of Cowrees, 5,120 of which go to make one rupee. The foolish custom, which subsists here, of keeping banians, gives rise to a thousand deceptions as no one pays or receives money but through the medium of these people, who have their profit on everything that comes into the house.

The words 'banian' as well as 'sarkar' are used. She wrote,

> The facility of obtaining credit is beyond what I could have imagined. The European shopkeepers are always ready to send in goods, and the banians are so anxious to get into employment that they outbid each other. One says: 'Master had better take me: I will advance five thousand', another offers seven, and perhaps a third ten thousand rupees … It is not uncommon to see Writers' within a few months after their arrivals dashing away on the course four-in-hand. Allowing for the inconsiderateness of youth, is it surprising if many become deeply embarrassed.

On Mr Barwell's encouragement I read many of the English books in his library. Mrs Fay wrote:

> Several have been pointed out to me who in the course of two or three years have involved themselves almost beyond hope of redemption. The interest of money being twelve per cent, and the banian taking care to secure bonds for whatever he advances, making up the account yearly and adding the sum due for interest, his thoughtless master (as he calls him—but in fact his slave) soon finds his debt doubled.

Another travelogue came into my hands at that time. It was by Fanny Parkes, who was in Calcutta from 1822 to 1830. She wrote a captivating account of things in November 1822.

> A very useful but expensive person in an establishment is a sircar; the man attends every morning early to receive orders, he then proceeds to the bazaars, or to the Europe shops, and brings back for inspection and approval, furniture, books, dresses, or whatever may have been ordered: his profit is a heavy percentage on all he purchases for the family. One morning our sircar, in answer to my having observed that the articles purchased were highly priced, said, 'You are my father and my mother, and I am your poor little child: I have only taken two annas in the rupee, dustoorie.'

Fanny Parkes also explained this custom of 'dustoorie' in Calcutta splendidly.

> Dustoorie is an absolute tax. The durwan will turn from the gate the boxwallas, people who bring articles for sale in boxes, unless he gets dustoorie for admittance. If the sahib buys any article, his sirdar-bearer will demand dustoorie. If the mem sahiba purchases finery, the ayah must have her dustoorie—which, of

> course, is added by the boxwalla to the price the gentleman is compelled to pay. Dustoorie is from two to four pice in the rupee; one anna, or one sixteenth of the rupee is, I imagine, generally taken. But all these contending interests are abolished, if the sircar purchase the article: he takes the lion's share. The servants hold him in great respect, as he is generally the person who answers for their characters, and places them in service.

I have not set my eyes on any drawings of this 'sarkar' or 'sircar'. But Fanny Parkes has given a fine description.

> The sketch of 'the sircar' is an excellent representation of one in Calcutta: they dress themselves with the utmost care and most scrupulous neatness in white muslin, which is worn exactly as represented; and the turban often consists of twenty-one yards of fine Indian muslin, by fourteen inches in breadth, most carefully folded and arranged in small plaits; his reed pen is behind his ear, and the roll of paper in his hand is in readiness for the orders of the sahib. The shoes are of common leather; sometimes they wear them most elaborately embroidered in gold and silver thread and coloured beads. All men in India wear mustaches; they look on the bare faces of the English with amazement and contempt. The sircar is an Hindoo, as shown by the opening of the vest on the right side, and the white dot, the mark of his caste, between his eyes.

There was clear evidence that she was in contact with the residents of Writers' Building. On 17 July 1824, she wrote: 'On this day, having discovered a young friend ill in the Writers' Buildings, we brought him to our house.'

She also mentioned a British civilian caught in a debt trap:

> A friend, now high in the Civil Service, contracted, on his arrival here about eighteen years ago, a debt of 15,000 rupees, about 1500/ or 1800/. Interest was then at twelve per cent. To give security, he insured his life, which, with his agent's commission of one per cent, made the sum total of interest sixteen per cent. After paying the original debt five times, he hoped his agents upon the last payment would not suffer the interest to continue accumulating. He received for answer, 'that interest never slept, it was awake night and day'; and he is now employed in saving enough to settle the balance.

Calculating along the ribbon of time, Richard Barwell's Writers' has witnessed four centuries, occupying Calcutta through the eighteenth, nineteenth, twentieth, and, now, twenty-first century. The rise and fall of Bengalis has taken place over the same period. John Company has created a remarkable fount of history in this very city.

Salaam Calcutta

IS CALCUTTA EVEN A CITY? PACKING MILLIONS OF PEOPLE INTO a few square kilometres of space does not automatically make a city. Take a look at the major cities of the world and you'll understand what the word really means. A city is where wealth is created every moment, where the innate power of humans is transformed into energy to achieve the impossible. A city is the victory column of a society, which humans themselves create through discipline and combined initiative. God created nature, and man has created the city. Decide for yourself: Is this goddamned Calcutta even a city?

Here servants are keen to make off with the small change from the shopping money, their ambitions peak at the desire to be the head bearer, and they spend all their time bickering with other servants. The British packed their suitcases to leave, the servants remained servants, and taking advantage of this golden opportunity, the brokers and dealers of jute and gunny took over ownership of trade and commerce in the city.

Traitors have eaten away at the heart of the city like woodworms in a manner that made it impossible to know something was wrong until Calcutta began gasping for breath. You will see them everywhere—try reading the history of the 100 per cent swadeshi institution named Calcutta Corporation. From Subhas Bose to Kamal Bose, there's been a succession of mayors. It was probably because he knew the city inside out by virtue of this position that Subhas Chandra Bose did not give the call for 'Calcutta chalo' and opted for Dilli.

Back to the woodworms. Thanks to them phones don't work, the roads are prehistoric, electricity is missing, streets are obstructed. London, Paris, New York, Chicago, San Francisco, Los Angeles, Tokyo—the last of these was number one in population (30 million) to begin with, now it's number one in wealth and resources too. Long live the Japanese; at least they've been able to rub the West's face in it and maintain Asia's honour. With the Japanese setting an example, Seoul, Hong Kong, Kuala Lumpur, Singapore have all woken up. The last is the next example of how the efforts of a single generation can transform a city. Their collective efforts have created a new term—'Asian Tigers'—to give white people sleepless nights. Calcutta too had everything once upon a time; Royal Bengal Tigers used to live here. Now the city is full of rodents, from rats to bandicoots. That second term originated in this country, from the Telugu, to refer to rodents the size of pigs. Footnotes are unnecessary.

Now for some history. So much exuberance, so many celebrations, to mark 300 years of the city—but 300 is no age at all. Howrah is 500; Cuttack 1,000; Varanasi 2,500; and Delhi about the same. We know the ages of Rome, Athens, Paris or London too—300 years is not even a fraction of their lifetime. But Calcutta is already close to kicking the bucket at 300—it's afflicted with diabetes, high blood pressure and tuberculosis all at the same time. Doctors say the first two can never be cured, they can at best be kept under control. Tuberculosis can be cured, but who is going to provide Calcutta with the treatment, medicine and nourishing food this requires? There are 10 million people and their collective capacity for love, but who's going to lead them, who's going to show the way?

Since we're talking of history, we might as well clear our throats and bring up unpleasant truths. Calcutta has always been at its best for outsiders. It wasn't Bengalis who founded this city, it was Job Charnock. All Bengalis did was sell their assets—a profession they know only too well. Bengalis are number one now when it comes to selling ancestral property, an unpleasant truth that Acharya Prafulla Chandra Roy spoke about sixty years ago. Even today, enquiries at the registration office will show the initiatives Bengalis take to hand over the land of their forefathers to others.

It's not just the founding but also the laying of the foundations of Calcutta's prosperity that was done by foreigners. Sadly, the humid, decaying city didn't suit their health, which is why the British became desperate to plunder our country to make extra money and go back home to live long lives. And so Calcutta developed as a centre for earning a livelihood, not as a cradle for the child or as a Kashi for the ageing. A habitation without babies and old people can never attain completeness—further notes are redundant. No city in history has survived without the power of trade and commerce. Akbar couldn't turn Sikandra into a city; the wealthy Americans' Washington, DC remained a village compared to New York; Islamabad cannot even claim to be a town. Things have flourished where political power and economic power have coalesced—look at London, look at Paris, look at Tokyo. Of late Delhi has joined their ranks as one of the fastest growing cities. No wonder Subhas Chandra Bose's war cry was 'Dilli chalo', even though Calcutta would have been the first stop on the way from Burma.

Some say Aryans did not quite understand urban civilization, that they demolished an extraordinary city like Mohenjo-daro on a whim. The learned named them Purandar—destroyer of cities. Since no one else was willing to entertain them, these Purandars arrived in a new guise in Calcutta. Like all noble-minded cities, Calcutta too cannot say 'no' to anyone seeking shelter.

Students of history know the destroyers of cities mount direct attacks, like the Hun emperor Attila, or the Japanese, who flew over the city to bomb it and shut down life. Whatever signs of life there are now in Calcutta are on the playing fields and in grand musical programmes in stadia. The residents themselves have forgotten how to play, nor are their voices melodious any more—the gaps are being filled by outsiders and artists from Mumbai.

To cut a long story short, 10 million people live in this city which has everything but where nothing is available. Trains exist, but in front of them are woodworms with flags. Power plants exist, but there are press releases with excuses of wet coal and punctured tubes (or fate?). Hospitals exist, doctors exist, nurses exist, other staff exists, patients exist in thousands, but there's no treatment; instead there are blockades, there is theft, there is jaundice, there is tetanus in the operation theatre. There's a minister in charge of all this, whom you will see every other evening on TV, emerging on the verge of tears from five-star nursing homes to express concern about renowned but unwell leaders. You cannot say the minister has no jurisdiction here, for they will immediately constitute a medical board with the handful of specialists who work at government hospitals if a hotshot admitted to Belle Vue Nursing Home has wind. The TV and newspaperwallas have realized as much, that's where they wait with their video and still cameras. And as for the news—it's all to be found at seminars, also known as study circles. There used to be just one venue earlier but thanks to Calcutta 300, there's now a second one: Taj Bengal. At these gatherings the chairperson is almost always a Purandar, and so are the chief guest, the convenor and the keynote speaker.

And yet, according to the woodworms, Calcutta is an incomparable city, there isn't another in the world so lively. An absolute lie! Apparently there's no city in the world that's safer for women. Another lie! Thousands of vulnerable girls and women are being played football with in Sonagacchi, in Kidderpore, in Kalighat. All of Calcutta is turning into a bordello—if you don't believe me, go to Esplanade in the heart of the city in the evening, you'll realize nowhere in the world are women subjected to as much torment and abuse as they are here. Everywhere else a woman in prostitution collects her money from her clients, here some other man grabs it from her.

Let's turn to history. It's said that Calcutta played practically the most important role in the freedom movement. An outright lie. How many white men did your revolutionaries kill, the small town of Medinipur can ask Calcutta. But no one even goes to Medinipur to learn about its role. Calcutta had an armoury too, but the death-defying courage to rob one came from the young men of Chittagong. Nothing took place in Calcutta other than a handful of fiery meetings—no salt march, no fasts unto death, not even loud cries of 'Quit India'. Yes, a memorable fight was put up by a Bengali youth named Subhas Chandra Bose—who hailed from Cuttack. But Calcutta behaves as though it owns Subhas Bose.

The most recent example of how skilful the authorities of this city are at stealing others' credit is *City of Joy*. The French writer Dominique Lapierre stayed in Pilkhana in Howrah, and named it 'Anandanagari', or City of Joy. But the honourable mayor of Calcutta flexed his muscles and claimed the title for his city. No one protested; the extremely parochial nature of Calcutta's newspapers is discussed everywhere. Neither they nor Calcutta's distinguished writers remember that there are other cities in West Bengal. Those living outside Calcutta find it impossible to read Bengali stories because all these distinguished authors assume anyone who knows the language also knows the topography of West Bengal's capital like the back of their hand.

What has Calcutta done for the world? Almost nothing. Whatever medical discoveries were made about malaria and cholera were done by British scientists, albeit using Calcutta's furniture. I admit that Aurobindo was born in Calcutta—but he made off from the city at the first opportunity, or else he wouldn't have become Sri Aurobindo. Vidyasagar? Made in Medinipur. Ramakrishna? Made in Kamarpukur. Vivekananda? It must be admitted he was born in Calcutta and studied here, but he got no attention until he became famous in America, and even then, the first to acknowledge him were Madrasis. And when he did come back he was harassed greatly—he was humiliated in front of the Dakshineshwar temple, and disgraceful rumours were spread about the monk who had renounced everything. Who knows what unhappiness led him to establish his monastery outside Calcutta, in Belur.

What about Rabindranath Tagore, you ask. That's a slight problem—he was born in Jorasanko, which is in Calcutta. The building is shown with great ceremony on TV on his birth anniversary. And on his death anniversary images of Nimtala Ghat, where he was cremated, appear on the screen. But all of this is symbolic. Until he was published in England and won the Nobel Prize, Calcuttans used to refer to him as 'that son of Deben Thakur's' who 'makes women dance on stage'. Afterwards, though, the same Calcuttans rushed to Santiniketan with garlands sweets certificates etcetera to take credit for the award. The poet gave them a fitting reply. He had suffered great persecution at the hands of Calcutta's

Bengalis, leading him to say regretfully, 'I wrote the line, "Beautiful it was to be born in this land, mother mine". I will erase it before I go.'

A curse is upon us. Calcutta's name has been wiped out from the list of the most respected cities on earth. The city of dreams has become a city of nightmares. A city of revolutionary ideas has turned into a city of processions. With new make-up, toadies, middlemen and pimps have become important people. The goddess of wealth has flown off on her mount, the owl, to Mumbai in revulsion. Everyone knows that wherever in the world the goddess of learning might be, she's not in Calcutta. All that the city has now are road blockades and cheap speeches—not the kind that Suren Banerjee and Bipin Pal made, but a few mincing words spoken directly to the TV camera by so-called leaders with slick faces, followed by the garlanding, almost in slow motion, of a photograph or a statue of someone dead. The people of Calcutta have even forgotten what sculpture means. There used to be some good examples made by European artists, but those have been removed. The statues of Netaji and Nehru that have been installed could easily provoke the people of Cuttack and Allahabad to file defamation cases against Calcutta.

It must be remembered that excellence has never been appreciated in Calcutta; dirty politics and factionalism have always triumphed. It is why a writer like Saratchandra Chattopadhyay couldn't get a subeditor's job. Why a poet like Mohitlal Majumdar didn't have the right to enter the teachers' room at the university. Reformer Ramtanu Lahiri's employment was not extended for a second year. Poets like Michael Madhusudan Dutt and Sukanta Bhattacharya died in penury, without medical treatment. Unable to kill the spirit of Jibanananda Das, the poet who wrote *Banalata Sen*, Calcutta killed him under a train.

You might say: This was a long time ago, what is the use all these years later of excavating the reasons that made Jibanananda Das leave his City College job? What, for that matter, is the point of finding out why a women's college in Howrah gave him sanctuary and a few moments of peace late in life?

Very well, I shall accept this argument and shift to the present. Just a few years ago a shy scientist made a discovery, working day and night on his own initiative, regarding test-tube babies. No sooner did the mass media indulge him just a little than the so-called intellectual society of Calcutta pounced on him. There was no lack of bigwigs inciting them. Eventually, driven to depression, Dr Subhash Mukhopadhyay, an Abhimanyu trapped by a formation hostile forces, died by suicide. Who knows why he dreamt of being an inventor in Calcutta. Having thick skin might have saved him; he would not have had to suffer an untimely death.

But can a single, solitary incident prove anything? I bow my head to this challenge. A remarkable artist named Ramkinkar Baij was born here in Bengal, in a remote village in the district of Bankura. Besides Debi Prasad Roy Choudhury, India has not had another sculptor of such eminence in the twentieth century. To view his 'Santhal Woman' you will have to go to Santiniketan, and to see his enormous sculpture of Yaksha and Yakshi, you will have to buy a ticket to Delhi and ask for the location of the Reserve Bank. Baij was very keen on having a work of his in Calcutta. Setting aside all embarrassment, he even responded to government tenders and sent samples. The honourable PWD Minister of State in Writers' Building derived great pleasure from rejecting him every time. Can you imagine? After severing the roots of the plant, the same minister attempted to water it afterwards by going to meet a dying Ramkinkar Baij at P.G. Hospital in Calcutta.

Have you seen the imported statue of Netaji Subhas Chandra Bose that Calcutta's powerful people installed in Shyambazar after rejecting Ramkinkar Baij's offer? Do not, for it is the equivalent of pouring acid into your own eyes. A famous architect visiting Calcutta said, 'I want to feast my eyes on buildings from the British era. But I will remain blindfolded till I am in front of them, the city has been filled with so many ugly structures that my eyes will be wounded if I keep them open all the time.' There's an English word: 'eyesore'.

It's no use compounding our disrepute by denying that Calcutta is a horrifying city aesthetically. Only a few buildings erected by the British shine dimly. But even these will not survive, an evil eye is upon us. The number of monstrous buildings created in the past fifty years is beyond count. Only three of them are pleasing: Tata Centre, Rabindra Sadan, Nandan.

Everyone knows its scope for appreciation is one of the biggest strengths of a city. It is this that draws creative people to the great cities of the world. Calcuttans will be deeply disappointed to learn of their city's track record in this respect. However, once something clicks, there's no end to shouting about it from the rooftops. Example? The world has been proudly informed that the roshogolla is Calcutta's contribution. But listen to what its supposed creator Nabin Chandra Das said with great sadness: 'In those days it was not very easy to make profits from running a sweetshop in Calcutta. Most customers bought on credit, there were practically no cash transactions. So it was a shop only by name, in reality it was a gathering place for the unemployed people of the neighbourhood.' After tireless efforts, Nabin Chandra Das developed his version of the roshogolla in 1868. But his fortunes began to decline nevertheless, because Calcuttans of the day barely touched the sweet they claim as their own now. Nabin Chandra Das received no support from the Boses and Ghoshs and Mitras—panfuls of roshogollas would remain untouched. 'Those who gathered at the shop to chat would consume them at the end of the day.' This was when a businessman from Rajasthan stepped in. His name was Bhagabandas Bagla. Charmed by the taste of the roshogolla, he began to publicize it using his own money. Yet no one remembers his name now.

Sweets like the ledikeni (apparently named after Lady Canning) and the paantua were also created around the same time. Calcutta has muscled its way into claiming these too, but may I offer a humble reminder that these were created by a man from Howrah. Since he was not from the city, Calcutta knows nothing about him.

Calcutta was a city of trade—it was the hub of both national and international trade, and it could have stayed that way. Crates of tea sent from Calcutta to Boston fuelled some of the battles during the American War of Independence. A local Bengali businessman would communicate through letters with a counterpart in distant America. He wrote of his keenness to visit that country, but said that his neighbours would ostracize him for travelling across the 'black ocean'. Calcutta is no longer the headquarters of big business in India (most of them have quietly left), but if you check, you will find that many of the major financial scams in this country originated in this city. The Mundras, Shethias and Dalmias whose wrongdoings have come to the fore all belong to business clans based in Calcutta.

Never mind the big fish, what about the small fry? Are you guaranteed a fair deal in Calcutta's markets? Ask those who shop there every day. Weights claiming to be 1 kilogram but actually no more than 600 grams are to be found everywhere. And still we boast of honesty.

Let me tell you a story of Tiretti Bazar—from 150 years ago. This is from an 1835 edition of the weekly Bengali newspaper *Samachar Darpan*.

> Police Appeal. Monday, 21 December 1835. The wife of a British soldier from the fort has complained to the Chief Magistrate on the abovementioned date of a person named Ramakrishna Dey to this effect: 'This forenoon I purchased some salt from the defendant's shop in Tiretti Bazar. Suspecting that the quantity given to me was not as much as I had paid for, I had it weighed at the police headquarters in Lalbazar and found it short.' The lady submitted the weight used for the scale, and the accused admitted to its being his, but submitted that it had not been used to measure the salt sold to the plaintiff. At this the plaintiff insisted that it was. The accused was sentenced to a fine of Rs 10 or, failing which, 20 days of incarceration with hard labour.

Calcutta had nothing, still doesn't, yet the authorities and newspaper subeditors are incensed when the city isn't praised. Anyone who lands in the city from elsewhere will be grilled about how they like the city. They will be asked, 'You have read Tyagor, haven't you? Watched Syatajit Ray's films?' Those who haven't find themselves in a fix. 'Great city,' they say with a chuckle, 'no money, no jobs, no clean air to make it liveable, but plenty of life, apparently. Warm hearts.' This, of course, is lip service, it's not true. The principle that people believe in today is 'Save yourself'. No one jumps up in rage any more when a woman is humiliated. Politics has been handed over to professional politicians. Other countries too have realized it's not worth sending more Sister Niveditas and Mother Teresas.

There was a torrent of lies on the occasion of 300 years of Calcutta. Putting up a hundred electric lights all over Victoria Memorial, the woodworms told everyone, 'You won't find another city as wonderful as this one.' Barefaced lies. Calcutta will make no progress till Calcuttans realize their own condition.

Unforgettable

WHY THIS ENTHUSIASM ABOUT THE PAST? TO BEGIN WITH, there are many advantages to becoming an author at an early age. I was born on 7 December 1933. Mr Barwell died unexpectedly in Madras on 20 August 1953. I was nineteen at the time, and that was when the preparations for my first book began. It was serialized from 1954 onwards. I had just turned twenty-one when *Kato Ajanare* was published as a book.

It isn't usual for the writer of a book to be around when it has completed fifty years in print. I have been granted a rare honour. I thank the god of fortune for this, with additional gratitude for the fact that the book has remained alive for half a century, that readers have not consigned the misty memories of a luckless young man to the dustbin of forgetfulness, that I have survived for fifty long years in the precincts of the High Court, the legal arena, and at home and abroad.

Two incidents took place within days of each other in 2005. I had severed connections with Temple Chambers on No. 6 Old Post Office Street a long time ago. I still remember every step I took when I was led into this building that first day by Bibhuti Da, but I had never been there since. The other day I had to get in touch with a renowned non-Bengali lawyer on business. A busy man, he doesn't make himself available easily, but the unthinkable occurred on the telephone, and, to my astonishment, Mr Garg said, 'I'm in the same room at Temple Chambers where you worked with Mr Barwell. You have made this room memorable, its doors are always open for you, please come whenever you like. After Mr Barwell's death his junior lawyer Shailen Majumdar used this chambers, it was passed on to me when he went to England. We believe Mr Barwell's spirit is here still.'

It made me very happy to imagine that an old memory was quietly alive even now.

The second incident took place the very next day. An acquaintance had travelled to Ranikhet in the Kumaon hills, where he had spotted the road named for Mr Barwell, seen his portrait in the local club, and heard the brief history that explained how the club was saved from extinction due to Mr Barwell's efforts.

The obdurate heart brooks no obstacle in its race back to the past. I was a mere boy when the Ranikhet Club incident took place. Bibhuti Da was a silent spectator to it all. The episode was a marvellous example of how much Mr Barwell loved India and how idealistic he was, of how his patriotism made him love the truth. Although he knew he might have to pay for it eventually, he didn't hesitate to stand up against injustice.

I have touched on the incident before, but Bibhuti Da's memories provided a great deal of new information.

Mr Barwell often visited his favourite hill station Ranikhet when the High Court was on vacation. It was in his residence there that he wrote two thick books on law, taking several weeks for each: *Laws of Insurance* and *Laws of Service*. The first was published by the famous Butterworth & Co., and the second by Orient Longman.

On one occasion in Ranikhet, Mr Barwell and Bibhuti Da were both very busy with the book they were working on. Neither had a moment to spare. Suddenly Mr Barwell handed a sheet of paper to Bibhuti Da with a frown. It was a notice for a meeting at Ranikhet Club. The agenda: Winding up the club.

Mr Barwell explained to Bibhuti Da that Ranikhet was a cantonment town where soldiers were camped. Regiments came, were stationed there for some time, and then made way for a new set. Many years earlier, when Mr Barwell used to be a colonel in the army, he was posted in Ranikhet and fell in love with the place. He had decided on the spot that if he were to return to civilian life and succeed in staying on in India, this would be his favourite haunt. Britishers do not use the word 'home' lightly, but he had made up his mind long ago that Ranikhet would be his home in the hills.

Ranikhet Club was established for soldiers and local civilians to pass their time. Subsequently, as with all other institutions, rules were drafted for the running of the club, and a system of membership fees initiated to fund the expenses. The money contributed by various regiments was not always spent in full, and the club's coffers began to swell. Besides cash, Ranikhet Club owned the most desirable property and assets—its building, a library, arrangements for all manner of indoor games, a tennis court, a garden, and even an enormous golf course. Mr Barwell had become a member of the club as a colonel in the army and had paid the fees regularly for many years, because of which he was included among the permanent members.

In the period I'm referring to, this 'Europeans-only' club was down to eight or nine members, ten including Mr Barwell. All of them were foreigners. With British soldiers going home after India became independent, the club's membership had not swelled. In addition to the massive property, it also had Rs 1.5 lakh in the bank.

The club rules included one which said that were the club ever to be wound up, its assets would be distributed equally among those who were members at that time. To wind up the club, a proposal would have to be passed first, and then another one a week later accepting the first proposal.

Mr Barwell was irked by the behaviour of his greedy fellow Britishers. In his opinion it was nothing but daylight robbery. It could even be called a crime. 'I will try my utmost to stop this. There is no rationale in not opening the club to the residents of Ranikhet only because of the greed for money.'

Mr Barwell attended the meeting and returned with a grim expression. 'The proposal to wind up the club has been passed. I tried my best to explain to them why this is irresponsible, but did not succeed. I was the only one who voted against the proposal. There is no option now but to prepare for battle.'

We will hear the rest of the story in Bibhuti Da's words.

'All work on writing the book during the holidays came to a stop. A case would be filed to stop this injustice. Mr Barwell instructed me to summon a local lawyer and make all the arrangements for litigation. He began to dictate the plea to me. The first draft was made and revised extensively. I typed up a second draft, and this too was revised. Type it up again, he instructed. Mr Barwell was not satisfied with his own work. This was a battle against grave injustice, there could be no shortcoming in the preparations.'

At breakfast the next morning Mr Barwell asked his favourite assistant Bibhuti, 'You've been typing the plea, Bibhuti, but have you read it?'

'At first I had no idea what Mr Barwell meant.' There wasn't much time, he wanted to file the case in the Almora Court the very next day. He had asked for an interim injunction, so that the winding up of the club could be postponed immediately. He had invited the government lawyer to tea.

Mr Barwell wanted to discuss the whole thing with Bibhuti after lunch. Bibhuti Da was not one to panic. He sat down with the club rulebook and Mr Barwell's plea, and when asked, presented his viewpoint without fear: There was no logical reason to file a case just then. He was of the opinion that until the proposal was accepted at the second meeting, the unjust decision would not have been taken. An annoyed Mr Barwell retorted sharply, 'It's clear what will happen at the second meeting.' Bibhuti Babu said there was no proof that those who had voted for the proposal the first time would not change their mind. His question to Mr Barwell was, does the law allow a case to be filed on the assumption of future injustice? Mr Barwell was getting progressively agitated, but his loyal friend's opinion was that it would be premature to file a case before the second meeting and the case would be dismissed on these grounds.

'I realized Mr Barwell was not willing to accept my opinion. Eventually he flew into a rage and said, "I know what I'm doing." But I wasn't one to yield, I said, "I am not your equal, Mr Barwell, but you asked for my opinion and I performed your bidding. There is no need for you to be angry. I trust you will not ask me for my opinion again."' In a fit of anger they retired to their respective rooms.

In the afternoon Mr Barwell handed the brief to the government lawyer and said, 'Please read this carefully, this is the final draft, you must file it tomorrow.' The lawyer pored over the brief with great attention and then said, 'The draft is flawless.' Mr Barwell said, 'But have you thought the whole thing through? Someone has given a different opinion.' He conveyed Bibhuti Da's viewpoint to the lawyer, who changed his mind immediately. 'This opinion is worth considering from the perspective of playing it safe,' he said. Mr Barwell said, 'The opinion hasn't come from a lawyer, the barrister's clerk who came up with it is sitting in front of you.'

Eventually everyone abided by Bibhuti Da's opinion. At breakfast the next morning Mr Barwell put his hands on Bibhuti Da's shoulders and said, 'I must seek your forgiveness, Bibhuti. You gave me valuable advice, and I misbehaved with you in return.'

'I was astonished,' wrote Bibhuti Da. 'Mr Barwell himself was apologizing to me.' Bibhuti Da said to Mr Barwell, 'Pray do not embarrass me. There is no question of forgiveness, please do not forget I am your clerk.' Bibhuti Da's opinion was that this kind of generosity of thought was extremely rare in the world.

The proposal came up again at the next meeting of Ranikhet Club. Once again Mr Barwell opposed it, but it was ratified. A case was filed without further delay and an interim injunction was obtained, so that the conspirators could not make off with the money or transfer the property to themselves. They had not understood Mr Barwell, they had assumed he wouldn't be able to resist the temptation of gaining riches overnight. They had not imagined he would spend money from his own pocket to save the club.

The case was shifted to the Allahabad High Court sometime later on the grounds that it involved complex aspects of the law.

Bibhuti Da had expected Mr Barwell to appear personally in court, but the British barrister hired the advocate general of the Allahabad High Court instead, besides the legendary lawyer Tej Bahadur Sapru.

Mr Barwell won the case eventually, and even obtained an order to recover expenses from the defendants. Bibhuti Da's memoir revealed that Mr Barwell had spent nearly Rs 15,000 back then. When the verdict was issued, all but one of the defendants left the country. Mr Barwell could have extracted the money from the one Britisher who had stayed back, but the latter pleaded for mercy. The large-hearted Mr Barwell could not turn him down. Eventually the club added new members and office bearers, who passed a resolution thanking Mr Barwell and reimbursed his expenses from the club's funds.

The complicated legal analysis that went into the verdict of Ranikhet Club led, I believe, to all the clubs in the country being converted into limited companies. One of the three Allahabad High Court judges presiding over the case was English. Dissenting with the other two, he had been in favour of allowing the club to be wound up. Where the matter got stuck was in the fact that as the club was not an organization with limited liability, the proposal to close it had to be accepted unanimously. And since one member had voted against it, the proposal had no legal standing. After all, if this were to hold, a group of members of any club could pass a resolution for it to be wound down and usurp all its assets and money, plunging the institution into a crisis.

All this, of course, was a long time ago. There is no reason to remember and recount the court case over an ordinary club. But what made it important was the battle between a set of selfish foreigners and a single compatriot of theirs who loved India, and did not want an institution in this country to be destroyed by the greed of a handful of Englishmen.

This case was of great significance in Mr Barwell's life. The commercial English society here never forgave him for it. Briefs from the offices of British attorneys stopped altogether. No one knew better than the English business community how to kill someone professionally, if not personally. But what was strange was that Noel Barwell would not be dissuaded from standing up against injustice despite the financial implications. It is those who forsake the desire for riches in order to oppose the untrue and the unjust whom we remember best. I too have not been able to forget Mr Barwell despite all the years that have passed.

The First Golden Harvest

JUST AS THE MEMORIES OF MY ADOLESCENCE AND YOUTH WERE becoming hazy and faded under a flurry of present-day experiences, a letter from the editor of *Desh* on the magazine letterhead sparked something of a crisis. The editor had ordered me to write about the old days—why and how I became a writer, how my books were published, etcetera. In simple terms, he had asked me to write the secret story of the storyteller.

Strangely, no sooner have I picked up my pen to perform the editor's bidding than the skies of Calcutta have suddenly turned dark.

Perhaps I should begin my story by talking about literature. Like many other girls and boys in Bengal, my first piece was published in the school magazine. I was a student of class eight then. When I went back home with it, far from encouraging me, my father scolded me resoundingly. Instead of being smart, he advised me, concentrate on arithmetic.

I was quite upset then, and a little hurt too. But later I realized why my father was annoyed. He didn't want his young children to make the same mistake he had made and lose their way in the forest in pursuit of the golden stag of literature.

Who knows what influence his viewpoint could have had on me eventually. But one day he launched his large family from two marriages on a sea of uncertainty and sailed away to the other side of the ocean of life. And my trials by fire began.

I was only thirteen then. I managed to pass my matriculation examination a few months later and was admitted to Surendranath College. (This institution, earlier called Ripon College, held a special place in my heart because Bibhutibhushan Bandyopadhyay studied here too.) My mind was set on getting a job, but in the vast unfamiliar city of Calcutta who would give a job to an unknown boy?

Now that the guardian who wanted me to stay away from literature was gone, I even sent a piece furtively to the college magazine. I caught the attention of fellow students and teachers on the strength of a piece of mine I read out at a literary gathering. One or two of my well-wishers began to harbour the idea that I would also excel at the coming Intermediate examinations. But disappointing everyone, I got an ordinary first class, after which I bid a final adieu to Surendranath College and went out broken-hearted to the street named after Mahatma Gandhi.

I wandered about desperately in search of a job, but there were countless obstacles. I knew no one who held a high post in this enormous metropolis of Calcutta, my clothes were dirty, and legally I was a minor. I hawked various goods on the street, and tried to sell things to shops under the guise of an order–supply business. One day I asked a stranger at a roadside tea shop on Canning Street, 'How do those who have no support survive in this city?' Smoking his bidi, he answered, 'There's not one man but two to rescue helpless middle-class Bengalis from their woes—the great Hahnemann and the great Pitman. For those who have no other options, there's either homoeopathy or shorthand.'

This valuable advice prompted me to take Pitman's name with reverence and immerse myself in learning shorthand. The advocate Girindreshekhar Bose, my late father's close friend, used to have a typewriting machine. An extremely kind man, he handed over his expensive machine to an amateur without hesitation.

To overcome my regret at having to give up my education, I used to read in various libraries and sometimes try to write weighty pieces. Thanks to the good offices of a generous neighbour, Bhabesh Chandra Gangopadhyay, one such piece reached Pranotosh Ghatak, the editor of the *Dainik Basumati* newspaper. Ghatak published it in the Sunday supplement. Other than in school and college magazines, this was my first officially published piece.

'They will probably pay you for the piece,' Bhabesh Da told me. I waited several weeks without having my expectations fulfilled. I sent another piece to *Basumati*, and this was published as well. This gave me the courage to send one to *Anandabazar*—this too was published on a Sunday. Even if I hadn't got an education, I consoled myself, my writing was being published in important newspapers.

Eventually I earned the title of a shorthand expert. May all of god's blessings be showered on you, Bibhuti Da, for taking me to meet the famous barrister Noel Barwell. It was thanks to you that a luckless, bewildered young boy from Howrah got a job with an English barrister, which changed the course of his life. God must have reserved for me the honour of being the last clerk to the last English barrister at the Calcutta High Court.

What did the Almighty have in mind when he dragged an inexperienced, scarcely educated, scrawny young man out of a dark lane in Howrah's Chowdhurybagan and brought him face to face with an Englishman whose learning was legendary, and who had built a formidable reputation for himself at the High Court? Of the two, one had never gone beyond Howrah for all intents and purposes, had a bulbous head attached to a scrawny body, and had never seen an Englishman in his life—while the other was an MA from Cambridge University, a retired army colonel, and a First World War hero with several awards.

Thanks to my English employer's indulgence, my new work life gradually revealed an extraordinary world to me. I had seen the enormous red building that houses the Calcutta High Court several times before, but I had no idea it was replete with such epic poetry and drama. I could not always fathom the significance of all the incidents myself, but first Bibhuti Da and later Mr Barwell personally patiently satiated all my curiosity.

Despite the busy life he led, the eternally amiable barrister would tell me various tales of the High Court. Having no experience at conversing in English, I was reluctant to talk. Guessing as much, Mr Barwell forced me to speak in English without fear, correcting my mistakes later over a cup of tea.

I remember him smiling at me and saying, 'Your English is excellent. It won't take you more than ten days to iron out the rough edges. The only people who can never be taught to speak English are the jute mill managers who have come here from Scotland.'

He sowed the seeds of self-confidence in his new clerk with small observations such as this one. My fear of speaking English vanished almost immediately.

Even though he was immersed in his legal work in the chambers on Old Post Office Street, Mr Barwell made it a point to discuss various matters with me, as though I was also well versed in the law. When dictating a complex letter or document, he would become especially alert whenever there was an incomprehensible Latin word or phrase. As soon as he was done dictating the paragraph he would explain the meaning of the Latin term to me.

Smiling gently even as he threw a sharp look at me through his glasses, he would say, 'Never type anything without knowing what it means. Until you know what they mean they are like rocks weighing you down, but once you understand these terms, they turn as light as feathers and become your own property.'

One day he used a complex term in his dictation—*uberrimae fidei*. I was taking it all down, but he stopped dictating to say, 'Well, you didn't ask what it means?' I was silent.

Mr Barwell would return home in the evening once he finished his work in court. Getting out of his clothes, he would wrap a lungi around his waist and sit bare-bodied in his drawing room. 'I was a Bengali peasant in my previous life,' he would say. 'I cannot keep clothes on my body.'

When I laughed, he smiled and said, 'What are you laughing at? The moment I have some leisure I'm going to write to Jawaharlal Nehru that India's national dress should be the lungi and gamchha.'

Then Mr Barwell looked at me and added, 'Don't laugh, my dear boy. Jawaharlal and I went to the same university, though I was several years his senior in Cambridge.'

Mr Barwell had known Nehru quite well, and not in happy times either, but when Nehru was going in and out of jail. I'm told that during the British Raj the CID had kept an eye on Mr Barwell at one time because of his close friend from his college days, Sarojini Naidu. He fought cases for the revolutionaries in court, helped the families of executed freedom fighters regularly with money, and met Mahatma Gandhi several times. His close friend Dinabandhu Andrews, another Cambridge alumnus, was also a constant source of discomfort for the British government in India.

Bibhuti Da told me that Dinabandhu Andrews had been to see my employer shortly before Andrews' death. And he had asked to meet his college friend again when on his deathbed in P.G. Hospital.

Before being taken in for surgery he had told Mr Barwell, 'I want to make a will, Noel.' My employer had prepared Dinabandhu Andrews' last will and testament according to his wishes. That was the end, Andrews did not come back from the hospital.

Waiting in his lungi for his cup of tea, Mr Barwell would tell me entertaining stories every day. He used to refer to Dinabandhu Andrews as Charlie.

'I was posted as a colonel in Fort William,' said Mr Barwell, 'in charge of the secret service. Secret telegrams came from all over the world about the whereabouts of a dangerous man we were keeping tabs on. His name was Charlie Andrews. I had only just arrived in India, how was I to know it was the same Charlie I knew back in Trinity College? Then I ran into him suddenly after some time, when I had left the military and begun practising as a barrister. I insisted Charlie join me at our residence on Middleton Street. We chatted for a long time, renewing our old friendship.

'Then I invited Charlie to our Cambridge annual dinner, where all the former students would gather. Charlie said, "I can't possibly go, Noel." "What's your problem?" I asked. Charlie answered gravely, "I don't possess a suit or even clothes that I can wear to your dinner." I said, "We don't meet at the Governor General's court, Charlie, you can wear anything you like. We won't object if you show up in a lungi and a gamchha."'

Mr Barwell's bearer Dewan Singh would bring in cups of tea while he told me anecdotes like these. The stories from the old days would get even more interesting over steaming tea. Then we would start work. Scanning his briefs, Mr Barwell would dictate notes and letters. I would take it all down in shorthand and type it up, while he would enter the forest of documents.

Having worked for some time in his chambers, I had acquired a modicum of confidence. I no longer made typing mistakes, and passed him the briefs and books he needed swiftly. Our discussions over cups of tea after returning to Spence's Hotel from the court covered a variety of subjects. It was easy to forget that I was a mere clerk and the person I was conversing with a storehouse of unlimited knowledge and experience. He had already taught me how to use cutlery the English way. To rid me of my hesitation, he told me, 'You Indians are born magicians. What you can do with just the five fingers of one hand is more than we can with both hands, ten fingers, and a dozen forks and knives!'

Was it really possible to develop such closeness with someone? I was overcome with wonder and gratitude. The scarcities and deprivation I grew up with, not to mention the heartless neglect I faced from relatives, had brought me to the verge of losing faith in people. After meeting Mr Barwell I said silently, 'Forgive me, O lord, I did not grasp the world correctly, my education was incomplete.'

It was truly a momentous experience, as though I had been nurtured in a well all my life and had suddenly been transported to the edge of the ocean. The unbelievable drama of human life was enacted in front of my eyes every day in the courts and in the barrister's chambers. I had never encountered so many different facets of people, so many problems, so many desires and agonies. And yet I had no trouble discovering and understanding this incredible world afresh, for Mr Barwell was always by my side to show me the way. I seemed to cover a long journey in a matter of months.

At times Mr Barwell and I would discuss literature. He would read W.S. Gilbert's *Bab Ballads* to me. Extracting a smile from a grim visage by reading out funny poetry made him extremely happy. On some days the sessions would be devoted to Wordsworth, Shelley, Keats and Byron. Mr Barwell would insist that I comment on the works of these poets. I used to be hesitant and embarrassed, but he wouldn't take no for an answer. Come on, he would say. These great poets didn't devote their lives to the pursuit of poetry so that they could be reduced to examination topics for university students.

I also remember what he would say with mock solemnity about Byron. 'I should warn you that I will not tolerate any innuendos about Byron's life and works. For he was my relative. Even if distant, there's still some Byronian blood flowing in here.' Then he would extend his right arm.

Mr Barwell got me into deep trouble one day. There was no one in the room, I was arranging things on the desk after completing the typing, all set to leave.

Suddenly my employer said, 'There's a complaint against you, Sankar.'

I would have been worried had I not noticed him smiling. 'Have I made a typing error?' I asked.

'I could have corrected it myself if that were the case,' he answered.

What he went on to say was enough to have me worried. 'Sankar, I have taken you to the cinema and to lunch and dinner, but you have never done the same for me. Tomorrow you will take me to lunch and to the cinema.'

Although ours was a master–servant relationship, this was embarrassing. You can imagine my financial situation at the time. I was barely eking out an existence in a semi-slum in Howrah. There was no question of inviting Mr Barwell home. But he had chalked out the plan himself. Lunch and a film. My head began to spin.

Now that he had made the demand, I would have to do something about it. 'Very well,' I said, 'since you've mentioned it, I request you to join me for a film and lunch tomorrow.'

Feigning seriousness, Mr Barwell whispered, 'No matter how greedy a man might be, how can he accept an invitation extended to him in this manner? You have to say, I'm terribly sorry, Mr

Barwell, you keep so busy all day that despite my ardent desire I have not dared to invite you before this. In case you have no other engagements, what about tomorrow? I beg your pardon for the short notice.'

Hiding a smile, I said as instructed, 'I'm terribly sorry, Mr Barwell, you keep so busy all day that etcetera. What about tomorrow? Do you have any engagements?'

Putting his hand on my shoulder with a flourish, Mr Barwell said, 'I am deeply grateful for your kind and warm invitation, my dear Sankar. Since you have extended a personal invitation to me, no work can be more important. I shall await your arrival tomorrow.'

Bidding him goodnight, I left with a smile, but then I began to worry. This was no ordinary guest, after all, taking him to the cinema and lunch was going to be expensive. I could hardly give him a cup of tea at Gyan Babu's shack on College Street and a simple Bengali meal at Bangalakshmi in Bowbazar.

Fortunately I had a secret emergency fund stashed away. I would have to dip into the Rs 40 I had hidden in an envelope behind the bookshelf for any unexpected family crises.

I arrived at the appointed hour on Sunday with the four ten-rupee notes. I was dressed in a dhuti and a panjaabi, the pleats of the former tucked into a side pocket of the latter. And in my breast pocket lay the valuable emergency resources.

'Good morning, my dear boy,' Mr Barwell greeted me affectionately. Then he added, like an actor declaiming his lines, 'I have been waiting impatiently for you, sir.'

Not knowing the finer points of social etiquette, I merely smiled widely without answering.

Mr Barwell said, 'I'm going to the bathroom, Sankar. There's a letter for you on the desk, take a look at it meanwhile.'

I was astonished when I opened the envelope. Instead of a letter, it held six ten-rupee notes.

Emerging from the bathroom soon afterwards, Mr Barwell said, 'I am ready to leave at once if you like, sir.'

'Let us proceed then,' I said.

Mr Barwell said, 'Many thanks for this invitation. I have no doubt that I will enjoy myself greatly in your pleasant company.'

As we were leaving, we ran into the intimidating figure of the head of a foreign company near the library door.

'Hello, Noel, how are you?' he said.

'Allow me to introduce you,' Mr Barwell said. 'This is the managing director of _____, Sir _____ _____, and this is my personal friend and assistant, Mr Sankar. Sankar has very kindly invited me to lunch with him today.'

The powerful Englishman probably did not approve of going for lunch with one's clerk. Still he said out of politeness, 'How do you do, very pleased to meet you.' Turning to Mr Barwell, he added, 'How nice.'

Many of Mr Barwell's peers did not like the way he had built relationships with Indians. But he didn't care for anyone's views on this. On one occasion I had suggested not taking me into the dining hall with him. In all seriousness he had answered, 'Your friendship is a thousand times more valuable to me than the company of those people. Don't say this ever again. I am old enough to know what I'm doing.'

So I didn't bring it up that day. We walked along the gravel driveway and stopped outside the gate. A taxi was approaching us from the west, we hailed it. I was about to open the door and get in, but Mr Barwell put his hand on my arm and whispered, 'I'm your guest, you must let the guest enter first.'

I had no idea of manners. Learning quickly, I held the door open and said, 'After you, Mr Barwell.'

At once he said, 'Certainly not, after you, Mr Sankar. And besides, you know I have become a little hard of hearing in my left ear, therefore I would like to sit on your left.'

We wandered aimlessly around the city that day in the taxi. Mr Barwell recounted several episodes of British history, along with stories from the old days. Occasionally he said to me with a chuckle, 'Many thanks for your hospitality.'

When I didn't respond to this, he poked me and whispered, 'The guest will be upset if the host is silent. You must say, not at all, sir, the pleasure of your wonderful company is mine.'

We ate lunch at a Park Street restaurant that day, and then took a taxi to Metro Cinema. I was about to walk up to the booking office to get matinee tickets, but Mr Barwell reminded me, 'Request me to take a look at the seating plan and ask what kind of seat I'd prefer.'

At once I said, 'What sort of seat would you prefer, Mr Barwell? Do take a look at the plan.'

My employer protested vociferously. 'Any seat will do, Mr Sankar, as long as it's next to yours. And please don't get very expensive tickets, the idea is to watch the film, not occupy expensive seats.'

During the interval Mr Barwell murmured, 'You haven't yet asked whether I'd like an ice cream or coffee. Haven't you noticed my glum expression?'

Realizing the lapse in my hospitality, I said immediately, 'An ice cream? Or perhaps a cup of coffee?'

My guest almost shrieked, 'An ice cream after that lunch! Do you think you've invited a monster?'

After the film, we went to the famous Park Street teashop Flurys, where the waiter deposited a number of pastries on our table. I was about to tell him we wouldn't need so many, when Mr Barwell whispered to me, 'No need to say anything to him, they'll charge us only for the pastries we consume.'

I didn't know this; I was worried they would charge us for everything they had served, whether we ate it or not. Instead of suppressing my doubts, I asked naively, 'How will they know how many we have eaten?'

'Subtraction,' Mr Barwell told me affectionately. 'They know how many pastries they brought, when they prepare the bill they will check how many are left.'

We talked about many things over tea. Once again Mr Barwell told me solemnly, 'The film was magnificent. Your choice was splendid. The hero was as handsome as the heroine was beautiful.'

It was time for the bill, which came to about four rupees and four annas. I put a five-rupee note on the tray. When the waiter brought the change, Mr Barwell signalled to me with his eyes to leave the entire amount there. Unaware of these instructions, the waiter offered me a mighty salute for the generous tip. Strutting out like the other affluent customers, I stood on the pavement and called out, 'Taxi!'

This time I made no mistake, and held the door open for Mr Barwell to get in first. Perhaps to please me, he obliged.

The lights were coming on when we returned. Getting out of the taxi, Mr Barwell said, 'I don't know how to thank you. I shall remember your hospitality and kindness for a long time.'

At once I responded, 'The pleasure was all mine. I greatly enjoyed your wonderful company.'

Patting me on the back, Mr Barwell said, 'Excellent response.'

Afterwards, standing in the foyer, he said, 'Unless you have some other pressing engagement, do give me the pleasure of your company at dinner. I apologize for this short notice, but our relationship allows me to invite you in this manner.'

I stayed back for dinner, enjoying myself greatly. We seemed to have played a new kind of game all day.

I didn't realize then the sheer effort Mr Barwell had expended all day so that a raw young man could become more refined. Recounting that incident all these years later makes it seem like a story—my eyes are moist for no good reason. This is a weakness I haven't been able to overcome despite all the unpleasant experiences in my life—the smallest things remind me of the ever-smiling Englishman with sparse hair who gave me the courage and the opportunity to meet the complexities of life head-on.

That night I lingered after dinner. The shy, troubled boy within me who had recently acquired a sheen of respectability grew bold. Mr Barwell and I had a heart-to-heart talk. I forgot I was a mere babu with brown skin, and he was a barrister who had sailed across the seas to India.

In the midst of amusing stories, Mr Barwell grew grave suddenly. 'I have something important to tell you, my dear boy,' he said.

We had been talking all day. What more did he want to tell me? I was a little surprised.

Mr Barwell gazed at me. 'I held you back so that I could tell you this,' he said.

I didn't normally see him so serious, although this was the manner he adopted when questioning witnesses in court. It wasn't an aspect of his personality I was fond of.

He said, 'I have been meaning to tell you this for quite a few days now, my boy. I'm getting on in years. I don't know how much of your life I will be able to witness, but you must never forget you are an exceptional person.'

His eyes lit up the very next moment, an impish smile spreading across face. 'It's rather late,' he said, 'you have to go home. And I have to leave for Madras tomorrow to argue a case. Before that, let me do one of those naughty things I did as a child. During my schooldays, whenever I felt the urge to twist a classmate's ears I would tell him, my dear John, to prove that there is no ill will between you and me, I will twist your ears.' And then he proceeded to twist mine, saying, 'This is to prove there are no ill feelings between us.'

Mr Barwell went to the bathroom. I felt a spark run through my body, as though I had been unconscious all this while because of some incurable illness, and had only just woken up under the healing touch of electricity. All the hairs on my body were standing on end.

The very next moment I felt deeply embarrassed, wishing I could sink into the ground. I imagined the orderly, Dewan Singh, had been standing behind the door, listening to everything Mr Barwell had said—that I was exceptional.

I pictured Dewan Singh laughing his head off in contempt. Saying, with a sneer, 'There goes an exceptional man. Lives in Howrah, with only an I-A degree by way of education, works as a barrister's clerk.'

But Dewan Singh was nowhere to be seen. Still I was squirming. I went out. I wanted to slink away quietly, but I felt as though I had been caught, that the reception clerks here had come to know. That one of them was telling the other, 'Someone jokingly told a babu he's exceptional, and look how he believes it.' And when they caught sight of me, they screamed, 'There goes an exceptional person.'

I walked faster, turning a deaf ear to all of this. But the Nepali gateman seemed to be laughing too.

I rushed northwards along Chowringhee Road. All the lamp posts seemed to be mocking me, well, laughing electrically, 'There goes an exceptional person.'

What should I do now? I wanted to get away from all of them. I began to run without realizing it myself.

Hurrying along Chowringhee Road, I turned left where it joins Theatre Road. The area wasn't very well lit those days, the Birla Planetarium had not been built either. There were many large trees. With darkness almost upon us, I stood beneath a gigantic tree and finally felt a little at ease. My eyes settled on the star-studded sky visible through the leaves. How strange it was, the distant stars were gazing at me calmly, they weren't mocking me at all.

Staggering up to a passing Howrah-bound bus, I jumped on to the footboard. There was no peace to be had even after returning home; I didn't get a wink of sleep. Late at night I climbed the narrow staircase to the roof in the darkness. The golden stars in the indigo sky talked to me that night. Far from taunting me, they were giving me hope and confidence.

As I looked at the sky, rapt, I didn't realize when dawn arrived.

On that sleepless night, believe me, a new 'I' was born within me. The I who had left with Rs 40 in the morning was not, believe me, the I who returned. The I who had awakened from slumber was brimming with self-confidence. This new self was saying, 'I will strive my hardest, I am determined to make myself worthy of my employer's faith in me.'

Mr Barwell left for Madras the next morning, where he unexpectedly passed away a few days later. Holding the shattering telegram sent by Dewan Singh from Madras, it seemed to me I had no one of my own in the world any more. I was all alone.

After the first waves of grief had receded, I would gaze at the immense river of people along Calcutta's streets, and remember mournfully that there had been at least one person in this heartless, indifferent, self-centred world who had loved me, who had believed in me. Who had considered me exceptional. Who had felt even a semi-educated helpless impoverished young man could give something to this planet.

Finding no other way to honour the memory of Mr Barwell, I began writing about him in an old notebook. What if my own memories betrayed me one day because I hadn't put them down on paper?

I got a job as a typist at the Bengal Chamber of Commerce, the Mecca of business in Calcutta's Dalhousie area. I'd tried my luck at the post office earlier, without much success. My regular companion during the lunch break at the Bengal Chamber of Commerce was Bhabaniprasad Ghosh, who kept track of contemporary Bengali literature. I read some of my pieces to him, and he said, 'Keep writing, it's going well.'

Those days in the Bengal Chamber of Commerce were not happy ones. The love I have received during my itinerant working life is unparalleled, but the lion's share of the suffering came during the Bengal Chamber of Commerce phase. Something did not add up—the contempt from some of my fellow workers and the cruelty of higher officers plagued me every single day.

Amidst all this there were two oases—the writer Mohanlal Gangopadhyay and my friend Bhabani Ghosh. Mohanlal held an important post in the Indian Jute Mills' Association, but he didn't believe in hierarchy. He would come up to my typewriter from time to time and whisper, 'We're going to the Coffee House today.' I had no money to waste at the Coffee House then, but he insisted on treating me to a chicken omelette, and discussions on literature.

Bhabani's desk was at some distance from my department—but to term it a haven of Bengali literature would be to understate the case. Even today I don't know why he offered me all that extra love. One possible reason was that I was a glutton for affection, trying to forget all my disappointments and everyday sorrows in his company. The taciturn but deeply affectionate Bhabani tried to encourage me in every way possible, even lighting a fire of ambition within me. He advised me to enrol in the evening BA section of Bangabasi College. Each of us who gathered there had our own problems to bear, but literature brought peace to us. It was at his desk that I acquired a comprehensive understanding of what common people expected from literature.

Meanwhile my miseries were multiplying. An Anglo-Indian at the Bengal Chamber of Commerce kept humiliating me for no good reason. I had to swallow it in silence. I had begun to realize that I had become an inmate for life in the dark prison of a clerk's life. There was the mortification of constant disdain at home, from relatives, and in the workplace. And I didn't even have the stamp of a graduate.

Every time I looked around me the world seemed to hold nothing but despair. I had no past, present, or future—and yet, just like countless others on this planet, I had harboured so many dreams. Things were so bad at the office that I would have declared independence if I could have and walked out of the door. In the middle of the night I would remember that there had been at least one person in the whole world who had loved me unconditionally. He had shown me images of the entire world in the arena of the courtroom.

But that too was a fragile memory—how long could it remain intact within an eternally aggrieved heart? And so, by the light of a lantern, I began to write more chapters about my earlier workplace at the High Court.

I was hesitant to tell Bhabani Babu about this. Instead, I showed some of the chapters to a colleague in the department. He was not even remotely enthused on reading them, telling someone else in confidence, 'Absolute rubbish, a complete waste of time.' The person he had confided in cared for me and offered some advice, 'Never ask someone you know their opinion of what you've written.'

Needless to say, I was even more unhappy now. The world seemed to be bent on destroying me, and there was nothing I could do about it.

That was when, one day, Bhabani Babu said, 'My friend the writer Rupadarshi will be here today.' I had not seen a flesh-and-blood writer other than Syed Mujtaba Ali before this. Rupadarshi was one of my favourite writers. Had it been up to me, he would have got the Nobel Prize by then for his books *Sketches*, *Circus* and *This Calcutta*.

Rupadarshi, aka Gour Kishore Ghosh, arrived late in the afternoon. It was delightful to meet him; he seemed like an old friend, someone I knew well. Fortunately my Anglo-Indian boss had gone home after lunch that day thanks to a toothache. (O lord, you are present in the Bengal Chamber of Commerce then!) There wasn't much pressure at work either, so I presented myself at Bhabani Babu's desk at four. Rupadarshi was popular with readers then, his column 'Speaking of Things' was published in the Sunday edition of *Anandabazar*. Many people had gathered to meet him. Bhabani Babu was extra considerate with me, saying, 'We'll chat more after work.'

Once the office closed at four-thirty, we went out. The idea was that we would chat some more, after which I would go to Bangabasi College in Sealdah. Very few people had Gour Kishore Ghosh's ability to turn strangers into friends in an instant. Even in the worst of times he could laugh and make others laugh.

And so he said a little later, 'No one has done the world any good by attending college regularly. Skip your classes today. If god is kind your boss's toothache will be worse tomorrow.'

Instead of college, I accompanied them to the Coffee House on College Street. The subject of a sailor he had written about in a piece published in *Desh* magazine came up in the course of conversation.

The piece had been accompanied by a memorable cartoon by Ahibhushan Malik, titled 'Temporarily Unfit'. I mentioned that I used to know a sailor as well, and he too had become unfit. I began my story about Nikolas Skinnus, a temperamental Greek who was determined to struggle uncompromisingly against injustice, even at the cost of personal ruin.

It was this story that turned my fortune.

'How many such characters do you know?' asked Gour Babu.

'Many,' answered Bhabani Babu on my behalf. 'This poor fellow has been to all sorts of places ever since childhood.'

Gour Babu said, 'Don't you want to write about these characters? If you don't, give me their stories. But it would be best if you wrote them yourself.'

'He did try to write,' said Bhabani Babu. 'But someone said something harsh and that made him stop.'

I could have died of embarrassment. Gour Babu said, 'What do you want to trade in second-hand goods for?'

'I've written a few chapters,' I said, but couldn't bring myself to add what my colleague Ramakrishna Mukherjee had said about them.

Gour Babu seemed to ponder over this. Then he said, 'Bring me what you've written one of these days.'

Sometime later, thanks to Bhabani Babu's kindness, I met Gour Kishore Ghosh again, this time at his Paikpara residence. He was having trouble with his eyes, and said, 'Start reading.'

I began. 'Gazing in wonder at the tall spire of the High Court, it occurred to me, so this is the High Court.'

'Stop,' Gour Babu commanded with his eyes closed. 'Bring that bit forward. Start with "So this is the High Court." It's high time Bangaals showed everyone else the High Court instead of being shown it.'

On the way back from Paikpara, Bhabani Babu told me in the bus, 'Good news! Gour Babu will introduce you to Sagarmoy Ghosh.'

'He knows Sagar Babu very well, doesn't he?' I asked.

In an effort to dispel my fear of editors, Bhabani Babu said, 'Undoubtedly a very stern man. But a great friend of Gour Babu's. Besides, Sagarmoy Babu is very keen to discover new writers.'

Still I was apprehensive. 'Don't worry,' said Bhabani Babu, 'your star is on the rise. Why do you suppose your boss's toothache is getting worse?'

My memory of the Burman Street office of *Desh* magazine remains unsullied. From the intersection of Harrison Road and Chitpore Road, I had to walk past the fruit market and various habitations to arrive at the magazine office. Sagarmoy Ghosh's office stood in a corner of the earth, beyond several impossible corridors.

I deposited my submission. There was no conversation to speak of. I left fearfully.

I had a strange dream that night. A dark lawyer's gown was floating towards me, saying, 'Get back, get back.' I woke up abruptly and began writing a new chapter the same night, titled 'Black Gown'.

A few weeks later it was back to Burman Street.

Sagarmoy Ghosh's face was suffused with a smile when he saw me. 'We'll run your pieces.'

He ordered tea. Sitting in the editor's office with him and drinking tea that he would pay for was like winning a mini Nobel Prize.

Then he asked, 'You want it to be published under your own name, don't you?'

'No,' I said, 'a pseudonym, though it's not exactly one. This is how Mr Barwell used to address me.'

'Very well,' said the editor.

And so my literary journey began. I don't know the first thing about literature, but I have learnt the final lesson from the life of the most unusual Englishman, which is to trust and love your fellow humans. All of us have infinite power within us—once a person is roused, there's nothing they cannot do, they can scale mountains and cross oceans effortlessly.

I cannot resist repeating an old story here. Mr Barwell would often say, 'I want to marry a Bengali girl in my next birth, Sankar.' Looking at me with amusement, he explained, 'Don't imagine it's because Bengali girls are so beautiful. It's Bengali mothers-in-law I'm interested in. You don't get such mothers-in-law anywhere in the world. Their generosity is unmatched, when the new son-in-law offers ten rupees with his respectful greetings, she gives him her blessings and returns twenty. After the wedding I will borrow millions, use it to greet my mother-in-law, and live happily ever after on the riches.'

I used to think Mr Barwell was joking, but later I realized nothing could be further from the truth. I had wanted to convey my respects to him through what I had written, but it was I who became the recipient of many people's respect overnight. Apparently I was a litterateur, a teller of truths, a real artist. Whatever I had respectfully submitted to him was redoubled and returned by him from the afterlife.

Sometimes I regret my foolishness. Why did I offer Mr Barwell no more than a rupee? If I had laid all I had at his feet, if I had worked harder to write about him with more attention and care, who knows what he might have given me in return?

Editor at Large

I HAD TOLD SAGAR DA THAT PIECES SPECIALLY WRITTEN FOR centenaries do not reveal the real person. On the contrary, it is our tendency to exaggerate that becomes evident. Lacking as they do a sense of moderation, Bengalis will target a person with incessant criticism when they're alive, and then, when their birth centenary arrives, sing endless paeans to them as a way of paying their fines with interest.

Every race will act as it is wont to, what can you and I do about it, Sagarmoy Ghosh had told me.

We had laughed about it that day, but I had never imagined having to reminisce on a birth centenary myself—or that one of the XL-sized human beings from an era of greatness would slip away silently, putting those of us wracked by his memories in serious trouble.

On to the account books. Sagarmoy Ghosh was born on 22 June 1912. His relationship with *Desh* magazine began in 1940. His commanding reign as editor over the rest of the twentieth century came to an end on 19 November 1999. He was eighty-seven then. He might easily have ruled into the twenty-first century had he so desired, but he seemed to have realized that the ways in which he had advanced Bengali literature over the last six decades of the old century would not match the rhythms of the new one, that it was wise to step down with full honours while there was still time.

One thing that Sagarmoy would often say towards the end was that the hardest task of the editor is to understand the times and prepare a literary menu in tune with them. It wasn't as though powerful editors from the next generation did not understand this, but, perhaps unknowingly, they ended up as oil-mill owners who hindered the flow of literary quality. Some of them may have considered writers nothing more than mustard seeds, to be added at will to the press for their oil to be extracted and put on the market. Sagarmoy did not possess such arrogance; he asserted repeatedly that writers are not mustard grains. I deal in rose petals, he would say, and my job is to carefully extract the essence of each and offer it to the goddess of learning. In other words, it was about providing a combination of encouragement, indulgence and assurance. And, especially, about ensuring some protection for the writer before publishing serialized pieces, so that stray cattle didn't gobble up the tender leaves just beginning to sprout.

I didn't understand the significance of any of this when it was happening in my own life. Only now, all these years later, do I realize that nobody but magnum-sized editors can fulfil all these responsibilities and serve both literature and writers in equal measure.

My first, second and third serialized novels all appeared in Sagarmoy's magazine. I used to nurture a small grievance before our initial meeting in *Desh*'s Burman Street office. I had sent him a short piece once by post, only to have it returned, also by post, a few days later. I was so heartbroken that I tore it into pieces and dropped it into the river from Howrah Bridge.

Gour Babu had said it was impossible to pass off rotten goods with Sagarmoy Ghosh. He cared for nobody—not his family, not his friends, not even the owners of the magazine. But at the same time he was on a frantic quest for new writers and new works. 'Because I wander all over the city,' said Gour Babu, 'I was known as "the kidnapper". I was duty-bound to inform him if I learnt of anyone who wrote well.'

Thanks to Sagarmoy Da's kindness and indulgence, my writing career began at a time that can be described as the golden age of Bengali literature. Think of the writers of the 1950s—Bibhutibhushan Bandyopadhyay, Tarashankar Bandyopadhyay, Manik Bandyopadhyay, Saradindu Bandyopadhyay, Banaphool, Jarashandha, Premendra Mitra, Sailajananda Mukhopadhyay, Bibhutibhushan Mukhopadhyay, Bimal Mitra, Syed Mujtaba Ali, Rajshekhar Bose, Achintya Kumar Sengupta, Ashapurna Debi, Premankur Atarthi, Narendranath Mitra ... not one but three entire Test teams. Now it seems as though Sagarmoy Ghosh was the maestro conducting an unmatched and unbelievable symphony orchestra of literature. If this metaphor isn't acceptable, what comes to mind is the full Kumbha Mela.

Although Bengali literature's Kumbha Mela was brimming over then, still the far-sighted editor kept wading into the water in search of new writers. Some used to think it was the editor's luxury—selling tickets in the black market despite having a full house in order to create a record. Sagarmoy never said anything explicitly, but he seemed to have apprehended the emptiness that descends on the Triveni Sangam soon after the Purna Kumbha.

Five long years passed between the serialized publication of *Kato Ajanare* and of *Chowringhee*. It was a trying time for me. Despite maintaining a low profile, I managed to earn the ire of some influential people. According to their judgement, I had written a successful book about life as an English barrister's clerk by fluke, and it would be best for me to remain a one-book author. Under their instructions I was completely isolated. My book wasn't reviewed, and no one asked me to write for them. Writers are of two kinds—potato plants and aubergine plants. The former have a crop just once in a lifetime, while the latter provide crops at regular intervals, filling the arena with words.

At this time I happened to come into contact with the editor of *Basudhara*, Charuchandra Bhattacharya, who was fortunate enough to have been in Rabindranath Tagore's good books. He said, 'Sagar is fond of you, he knows you're struggling to survive.'

I used to have sleepless nights in my efforts to overcome the stigma of being a one-book author. One day, as I stood in a flooded Esplanade after torrential rain in Calcutta, the sight of a hotel in the distance gave me an idea. Why not exploit some of my experiences to write a story about life in a hotel?

I had assumed Sagarmoy was no longer interested in me. One-book authors are always 'former writers'. One day I ran into him again in a Chinese bar named New Cathay in the Grand Hotel arcade. He said, 'Why are you avoiding me? Now that you're in the water you might as well try to net a large fish.'

I couldn't contain my despair at being a one-book author. Patting me on the back, Sagar Babu said, 'He who has no one has his pen.'

Sagarmoy had great faith in his writers. He didn't ask for the entire work to be submitted before serializing it. It was the practice then to have a few instalments ready, bow one's head in reverence to the unknown, and proceed to entertain readers for a year or two. All that Sagarmoy asked me was, 'Is it ready?'

There was no other supervision. No excessive enquiries, no attempts to be cautious about the subject, what it was trying to say, legal pitfalls ... All that he would warn me of from time to time was that the editor had some responsibility when it came to a writer's first novel, but none thereafter. 'I just rent out the stage, your future depends on how well you perform.'

Sagarmoy would remind us that this was how renowned works of Bengali literature like Bimal Mitra's *Shaheb Bibi Golam*, Syed Mujtaba Ali's *Deshe Bideshe* or Jarashandha's *Louhokopat* had been written. Sometimes he would be worried if the novel was inordinately long. To comfort him, the writer Bimal Mitra would say, 'I stay up nights worrying about the harm I will cause the editor if I die while writing a serialized novel. I should tell the lino operator or proofreader the end of the story in secret.'

Sagarmoy betrayed no anxiety, though, saying, 'The lord provides additional protection when someone is writing for *Desh*. In all these years, no one has left us unexpectedly in the middle of writing a novel for my magazine. And if anyone were to hatch a conspiracy to die just to get me into trouble, they will fail, no editor anywhere in the world in the past hundred years has been given the responsibility of completing unfinished novels.'

Bimal Babu wouldn't agree. 'You should get the end written in advance and seal it in an envelope. You know very well writing *Shaheb Bibi Golam* reduced my lifespan by five years, and now that I'm writing *Kori Diye Kinlam*, it will be reduced by another ten.'

For my second innings, Sagar Babu did not ask any questions about the novel or its theme, its characters or outcome. He would send some of the 'letters to the editor' every week to my home in Howrah. My mother was terrified of these letters from readers and would never give me the envelope while I was eating, lest my meal be ruined. 'What a strange system,' she would say, 'they won't run the letters of praise, only the criticism.'

Fortunately for me, my elders among writers would send encouraging letters to the editor. Syed Mujtaba Ali, for instance, wrote, 'Drop a brick every week, brother. Bat freely all round the wicket without a care for anyone.' He would follow this with suggestions for correcting one or two errors in my choice of words. Back then our elders had the rare ability to be affectionate to us, to discipline us, and to correct us all at the same time. But then not everyone was Mujtaba Ali. Two or three writers, men and women, informed the editor that this new writer didn't know the ABDC of hotels, he referred to bed-and-breakfast as bread-and-breakfast. 'I could have done a much better job if I'd been asked, I have been a guest at five-star hotels both in India and abroad five or six times.'

The editor had added a note to this letter. 'This is not to teach or correct you, just to deepen your experience. You must continue batting recklessly.'

This was Sagarmoy Ghosh. He knew how to ensure you remained fearless once you went out to bat. 'How will anyone write with all their heart if they're afraid?' He used to dismiss the fear of the police or of lawyers. If the writer did make a mistake, he didn't abandon them to the mercy of armed enemies. I had heard of Samaresh Basu's case. Sagarmoy Ghosh had informed everyone that he wouldn't hesitate to go all the way to the Supreme Court over the novel if need be. Samaresh Basu had also been embroiled in a criminal case for something he had written for another publication. It is said that the affluent owner-editor had claimed in court that he had not read the piece before it was published, thus ensuring his personal safety and leaving the poor writer to his fate.

The editor of *Desh* didn't suffer from such inferiority complexes. It was his nature to extend the security needed for literature and for the writer without being asked. 'I experienced life in jail before becoming an editor,' he would joke. 'To tell the truth, it was because of my sojourn in jail that I got this job in Ashok Sarkar's organization, therefore I don't lack the courage to tell the truth.'

I too got into trouble for a novel serialized in *Desh*. Criminal summons invoking several sections of the Indian Penal Code came soon after it was published as a book. The tasks of surrendering in court and getting bail were accomplished. Occasionally I had to visit the court and stand with my head bowed, along with the publisher and the printer. Rumours were swirling that the flames would spread further. With many powerful people apparently incensed by what I had written, there was even the threat of my literary future being destroyed. My defence was slender: Even if they want to, no writer can withdraw their words once they have been published in print. Even if they are omitted from future editions of the book, they will still find their way to readers.

Sagar Da met me when he was told about the case. He was concerned about something else—for some mysterious reason, his name had not been added to the list of the accused. And yet the novel had originally been published in the magazine he was editor of. 'Just as well, Sagar Da,' I said, 'you would have faced unnecessary harassment because of me.'

Sagar Da was not pleased by this. He said, 'A true friend sticks by you through thick and thin. I am being deprived of the chance to experience this trial by fire simply to make it easier to isolate the writer and cause them more agony. Whether we're defendants or not, *Desh* magazine will stand by you, you will get whatever help you need.'

I remember marvelling at his generous support and courage. Fortunately the help he offered was not needed, and in a dramatic turn of events, the complainants turned into lifelong friends. Extremely pleased by the news, Sagar Da treated me to chicken cutlets at Chung Wah.

He wasn't just a gatekeeper of his weekly magazine; he would cast his experienced eye over every piece at the proof stage. It was next to impossible to evade this eye. I used to work at an office on Free School Street at the time. One morning I was astonished to find Sagarmoy standing outside the lift.

Going up with me to the first floor, Sagar Da pulled out the proof galleys and said, 'You've used a communal and parochial invective. I know the word is used everywhere all the time, but I feel uncomfortable about it.'

I said, 'We need a word that hints at corpulence and wealth—we can change it to "jaggery trader".'

He was delighted. 'Excellent!'

I said, 'You came all the way for this? You could have changed it yourself.'

He said, 'As a writer for *Desh*, you have chosen a word after much thought. As an editor how can I change it arbitrarily? I'm nothing but a glorified proofreader here.'

All told, it would not be irrational to call Sagarmoy Ghosh the 'golden editor' of the golden age of Bengali literature. As an editor he was not exactly the guardian of great wealth or influence, nor did he have the ability to use the publicity machinery in a big way to draw people to a specific writer. Still, he attracted an unprecedented degree of loyalty from both writers and readers.

Contemporary observers could not fathom the secret behind this success. He had demonstrated that it was possible to establish a literary empire even without riches. Working within his limited means, the compensation he offered the writers of that age will astonish today's authors and readers. I've been told Bimal Mitra was paid only Rs 500 for his very long, serialized masterpiece *Shaheb Bibi Golam*, but this didn't erode his loyalty even a bit. The community of writers at that time considered *Desh* its very own magazine. There was one official editor, but he had at least ten satellite unpaid editors, who could inform Sagarmoy whenever they heard of a new writer. Many of them would even collect advertisements happily from people they knew for the special editions of *Desh*.

Sagarmoy was unmatched when it came to keeping writers under strict discipline, even as he indulged their quirks. He would never bind writers to certain themes or particular ways of writing or specific lengths. He trusted them implicitly. In subsequent years, when editors with their noses in the air tried to get too nosey and give too many instructions, they ended up with failed caesarean deliveries of what might have become their best creations.

In 1967 I had the opportunity visit the USA at the American government's invitation. Sagar Da was waiting for me at Dum Dum Airport that day in December when I returned. Seeing me into a taxi, he thrust his head through the window and whispered, 'First, take some rest. Then write whatever occurs to you.'

No fuss, but he had said what he had to. Just as I completed my first account of travelling abroad, the editor of a renowned film magazine came to my house in Howrah with a proposition involving big money. 'You won't get even one-tenth of this from anyone else,' he said. I needed money desperately at the time, but I remembered Sagar Da's face. Without a moment's delay I took the bus to Sooterkin Street and handed over the manuscript to the person I owed it to. This was the origin of the book *Epaar Bangla Opaar Bangla*.

Given the limited means at his disposal, Sagarmoy Ghosh would often be discomfited when the question of money came up. Perhaps he was hurt too. He had once sent Rs 15 by money order for a short piece by a rising star; the amount was returned. The editor was so upset that he didn't ask her to write again for years. When a writer from outside Calcutta tried to negotiate the payment for his novel, Sagarmoy told him bluntly, 'I cannot help you if you wish to auction your piece.'

His door was always open for young writers, however. He could spend hours chatting with them, share all sorts of jokes and anecdotes. Before I began writing *Chowringhee* he told me, 'Pretend you're a celibate monk this coming year, do not allow your senses to be excited.'

There were many impediments while I wrote, but Sagar Da handled all of them with great affection. I was told he had been kind enough to keep some of the criticism from me, so that I wasn't shattered. When I visited him to convey my gratitude, he said, 'Some manipulative readers can be ruthless. Someone has suggested we stop publishing this other piece we're serializing and pour cold water on the writer's head. People nowadays have no patience. For heaven's sake, the story has taken off and is flying beautifully, give it a chance to land. Far too many novels crash during landing.'

When he received the invitation card to my wedding shortly after I had submitted the final instalment of *Chowringhee*, Sagar Da remarked, 'Didn't we have an agreement you wouldn't excite your senses?' I said, 'But I didn't announce the wedding date until I finished writing.' Indulgently he replied, 'There are some signs of being in a hurry towards the end of the story, it needed four instalments more to be wrapped up properly.' But the almanac wouldn't have cooperated in that case, and the wedding would have had to be postponed by several months. At that moment Bimal Mitra rang. When he was done with the conversation, Sagar Da said, 'The writers' trade union supports you. They say physical and mental loneliness can have a very bad effect on writing.'

This, then, was Sagarmoy Ghosh, who saw the entire world and all of life from the editor's perspective. He was not interested in the least in anything that did not involve the betterment of *Desh* magazine. And there was punctuality. He would explode in anger if a piece were not submitted on time. On one occasion he rang me to say, 'You've become a great writer, is it? My relationship with you is at an end unless you submit your piece by tomorrow.' Then he disconnected the call. I stayed up all night to complete the piece. The following day Sagarmoy came to my office. 'You wrote so well on the night shift that I came over to congratulate you.'

Towards the end of his life our Sagar Da may not have been particularly happy despite occupying the throne of his realm. Some loneliness somewhere, and a sense of hurt too. In private he would ask what it might be like to declare his innings. Sometimes he would slip up too. On one occasion he scolded me with great annoyance, 'You will never learn, you haven't yet submitted your novel for the Puja special. Writers like you will be responsible for my death.' I said, 'Sagar Da, you didn't ask me to write this time.' He said, 'I didn't?'

This editor with the golden touch had the rare ability to offer his writers discipline and indulgence, regimen and freedom at the same time. One didn't have to make an appointment to see him. On the contrary, he would be upset if we didn't drop in on him without being invited. He did not believe in imposing any kind of restraint on the pen. He didn't write those modern two-line letters which say, 'You must limit your piece on such and such subject to nine hundred and seventy-five words only and it cannot be published unless received by the twenty-fifth of the month.'

Editor Sagarmoy Ghosh could probably hear the footsteps of this coming age. It must have caused him pain, but he never expressed it. All he said was, 'I am no one special. I have nothing to give, and nothing to receive either.'

The Leaf Is Not the Tree

I KEEP REMEMBERING MA. IN SPITE OF ALL THE WEEKS WE SPEND in their bodies, with a close inside view, few of us really know our mothers well.

Once upon a time I used to think I knew my mother. But all these years later it often seems to me that I didn't try to understand her properly while she was alive. I squandered that period calculating what I had got from her and what I hadn't, but I never concerned myself with what she should have got but did not. Before I leave this world I must leave a record of her life in my words; everyone must know the goddess Durga doesn't come to live with us just four days a year, that she also occupies every home in the form of the mother who gives birth to children. It is our misfortune not to have recognized this Durga. Our judgement and conscience frequently shrink under the onslaught of pettiness in this world; we simply cannot imagine that the ten-armed goddess lives amongst and within us, that she has no mission other than ensuring our well-being.

I should write about Ma not just to salve my own conscience. How a mother of eight minor children who was plunged into an extreme financial crisis after the untimely death of her husband protected her family like a veritable ten-armed Durga is something that the wretched of the coming generations should know of. Perhaps it will boost their confidence in their own battles against misfortune.

My mother never went to school. All her understanding of the world came from Bangla books—she mastered the language with her own efforts. After my father died suddenly, she told me calmly when I turned fourteen, 'You must make some money. I do not know anyone in this city. You must find your own way to a job.'

Taking her blessings, I went out from Howrah to pound the streets of Calcutta in search of a living. All I had by way of resources was her exhortation, 'You must be unbeatable in whatever you do.'

As a child I did not understand how courageously she kept the perilous demon at bay to bring us up. Now when I hear the chanting for Durga, the goddess who overcomes all predicaments, I see no difference between her and my mother.

When I close my eyes it is my mother I see in the form of the ten-armed Durga. The only difference is that the clay idol is dressed in red, resplendent in bright colours, whereas my mother was the embodiment of melancholy widowhood. Dressed in nothing but a plain white sari, she used only the two arms she was endowed with to protect us from all dangers with the might of the weapon-bearing ten arms of the goddess.

Perhaps it is wrong to imagine Durga in the garb of a widow, but not all my best efforts will allow me to discard the image of the ascetic figure in white. What I had read long ago in the writings of a monk with no experience of being a householder, but never understood, torment me during the four days of the Durga Puja celebrations. 'Where is she, graced with glory, who gave me my body? Where is she, who bore me in hers for nine months? Where is she, who is ready to lay down her life for my sake? Where is she, whose love for me is unbound?'

I will add to the burden of my sins if I do not admit that I did not acknowledge the importance of her role in protecting eight young children like a ten-armed goddess after her husband's untimely death, despite having no formal qualifications or any resources. While she strived to achieve the impossible on the battlefield of daily existence, we kept thinking it was all quite natural—who would look after children if not their mother?

The years went by thus. But selfless and altruistic as she was, my mother was not constantly forgiving towards her children. She was adept at disciplining too—many's the time that she scolded me even when I became an adult.

I did not gain proper understanding of my mother's actual role until an unexpected meeting with Subodh Roy. I have no doubt he will arrive again during Durga Puja this year. He has 'shuffled off the mortal coil' a long time ago, but that makes no difference. Those who have gone a long way away all visit me during the Durga Puja celebrations, transporting me to the times I have left behind, surviving which was by no means easy. I do not go out much during Durga Puja, nor do I allow large crowds to gather at home, so that those who are far away can visit me in peace.

I had not met Subodh Roy of Chinsurah before *Kato Ajanare* began to be serialized in *Desh* magazine. A new instalment was being published every week; friends and acquaintances were encouraging me. For the first time in my life I had gained some confidence. It was a pleasurable moment of recognition for my work.

Where we lived, at the far end of the unbelievably serpentine Chowdhurybagan Lane in Howrah, it was impossible to locate anyone on the strength of the address alone. There was a furious rattling of the doorknob one searing Saturday afternoon. Needless to say, we didn't even have electricity, leave alone an electric bell, at home. Pausing my writing at the loud rattling, I opened the front door to find a small, frail old man standing outside. He was dressed in half-dirty clothes and heavy shoes. His hair was closely cropped.

Tucking his umbrella beneath his arm, he asked in a grave tone, 'Is this house number such and such and does such and such live here?' When I told him I was the such and such in question, he sprang inside and sat down on the cot without bothering to take his shoes off. I could see how profusely he had perspired in the sun.

With a brief glance at me, he said, 'I had to go to great trouble to extract your address from the *Desh* magazine office.'

Then he issued a threat, 'Is your mother at home?'

'She's in the kitchen,' I said.

'Fetch her,' came the instruction at lightning speed.

I went to the kitchen. 'A peculiar man has come, he's asking for you.'

Returning to the front room to inform the guest that my mother was doing the dishes, I discovered a horrifying situation. The stranger had taken ill, possibly with sudden chest pain.

I didn't know what to do. Still in the throes of agony, he said, 'Where's your mother? Ask her to come here.'

This time my mother did come. Quickly making the man take off his panjaabi, she propped his head on a pillow. Then both of us began fanning him vigorously with handheld fans. A little later my mother brought him a glass of water. He took a few sips and then signalled to her to stop fanning him, but that I should continue.

About twenty minutes later he seemed to have recovered somewhat and sat up. After throwing a sidelong glance at my mother, he jumped to his feet and bent down to touch hers in respect.

'My name is Subodh Roy,' he said. 'I live in Chinsurah. When I read what he's written I went straight to the *Desh* office on Burman Street in Chitpore. From there I rushed here to Howrah. It took a long time to find the house.'

We learnt that this unknown admirer of mine had a dilated heart, high blood pressure, unstrangulated hernia, and various other ailments.

My mother had gone to get some batasha and more water. Now that the visitor had recovered, I assumed he would discuss literature with me. But Subodh Roy showed no such interest—he was eager to talk to my mother.

She came back into the room. 'Sit down here, Ma,' said Subodh Roy. 'Your son is under the impression I've risked my life in this unforgiving heat and come all the way to Howrah because I want to meet him. There's no point meeting writers, you can get to know them through their writings. When I saw the leaf I felt the urge to see the tree itself, that is why I'm here.'

Subodh Roy settled down for a chat with my mother, releasing me so that I could go back upstairs and continue writing if I wished.

But I was sent for again a little later. Subodh Roy said, 'I'm too intelligent to be satisfied by the leaf, I examine the tree whenever possible. My wish has been fulfilled, I shall go now, I have a train to catch.'

My mother kept in regular touch with this aged, ailing but lively aficionado of literature. Subodh Roy of Chinsurah paid no attention to me on his visits; he conducted all his discussions with the tree before leaving. He used to say, 'Those who claim you must know everything about the writer's life to get the full taste of a book are fools. If you really want to understand the book, get to know the author's mother.'

My mother and Subodh Babu had a cordial relationship that lasted several years. I have a bad habit, which is that I never allow anyone to read an incomplete manuscript. It embarrasses me for some reason and makes me uneasy. I was writing *Chowringhee* at the time, and it was taking rather long. Months were going by without much progress. Subodh Roy visited from time to time, asking how it was going. One particular year he dragged his sick body all the way from Chinsurah on the first day of the Durga Puja celebrations.

He and my mother had a conversation, after which she told me, 'Subodh Babu is very ill. He has travelled a long distance although his doctor instructed him to stay in bed. He said, ask your son whether he will let me read at least a chapter of his new book.'

I couldn't disobey my mother. I fetched the unfinished manuscript of *Chowringhee* and went downstairs to the front room. My expression may have betrayed my irritation. Subodh Roy was lying flat on his back with his head on a pillow. Next to him was a plate of sweets.

My mother said, 'You can read what he's written. But eat your sweets first.'

Subodh Roy roared, 'Ma's sweets first, writer's manuscript afterwards.'

He began to read a chapter with close attention. I couldn't stand this intolerable situation and went upstairs.

My mother called me downstairs after some time. I entered the front room to find my manuscript where Subodh Roy had been lying. 'What have you written?' my mother asked. 'Subodh Babu wept for a long time when he finished reading. Then he prostrated himself on the floor before me and left with his umbrella. Didn't even ask to meet you.'

Subodh Roy never came to our house again. When *Chowringhee* was published he was no longer with us.

Whenever I think of my mother I am reminded of Subodh Roy. When the world is flooded with happiness during the coming Durga Puja festivities, and I will enjoy my own company with the prospect of uninterrupted reading for four days, Subodh Roy will visit me again and, unwilling to content himself with the leaf, will enquire about the tree.

Investigating Vivekananda: The Beginnings

Despite studying at Vivekananda School and being in the company of prominent monks subsequently, for a long time I had not dared to write about Vivekananda. All the writing on the subject was done by Shankariprasad Basu during my schooldays. I had assumed his was the last word when it came to the quest for Vivekananda. But we decided to write a book jointly for Swami-ji's birth centenary. I had no desire to write a formulaic, devotional piece. My contribution to the volume, titled The Conscience of the World, *is no longer easily available, which is why it is reproduced here.*

Secretary: Sir.

Great Man [annoyed]: Now what? Is someone here to see me? Haven't I given you standing instructions … now what do they call it in Bangla? Damn it, having to do everything in Bangla is difficult.

Secretary: Orders to be followed, sir.

Great Man: I know, I issue them by the dozen every day. The problem is with the standing. For years in school I didn't just have to stand, but also stand up on the bench. Given the chaos everywhere are you making my orders stand in the corner too? How many times have I said not to let things lie? Carry out instructions as soon as you receive them.

Secretary: Standing, meaning permanent.

Great Man: Exactly. I have given permanent orders that I will not meet anyone and everyone without notice, only by appointment. I don't have more than twenty-four hours after all. Time is short, but art is long. I don't have the time to listen to everyone in the country chatter away.

Secretary: I've made a note of that already, sir, and accordingly …

Great Man: What! Have you sent people away accordingly? I don't trust any of you, for all I know you've turned away someone important like last time. The bureaucracy is perpetually trying to put up what you call a wall in Bengali between the public and us.

Secretary: The person I didn't allow in last time is known as Haru the goon; he's been to jail two or three times.

Great Man: Mahatma Gandhi went to jail too, and so did Jawaharlal Nehru and Subhas Chandra Bose. So did I. Only two people didn't go to jail, and they're the ones everyone's been celebrating these days—Rabindranath Tagore and Swami Vivekananda. Haru's real name is Haradhan Tarafdar, he's an oppressed patriot. It's true many members of the public call him a goon, but our democracy cannot run without them. They're an essential pillar of democracy—just like what you call freedom of speech in Bangla, just like newspapers, education, etc. Without the Harus of the world we would have to pack away whatever hold we have on the public into our holdalls and buy train tickets at the station and vanish. I really don't know what you people are up to! Did you go and insult Haru again?

How many times have I told you not to stop him even if I'm in conference with God himself!

Secretary: No sir, he wasn't here, he only telephoned.

Great Man: And who gave you the power of attorney to keep me from taking a phone call meant for me?

Secretary: You were on a trunk call with the capital, sir, about Mr Bhogilal's licence. You took three extensions and talked for a total of thirty-two minutes and fifteen seconds.

Great Man: Never mind that, what did Haru say?

Secretary: He wanted to remind you of tomorrow's ceremony for Swami Vivekananda's centenary. A dawn parade—

Great Man: I've been on hundreds of dawn parades before Independence, I can't do it any more. Why do people forget we're too big now for these dawn parades! Besides, I can't even get out of bed before eight-thirty nowadays.

Secretary: I've told them as much.

Great Man: What! Have you let slip that I'm a late riser? Isn't it officially top secret? Do you know you can be prosecuted under the Secrecy Act? Besides, just the other day I told *People's Pulse* that I follow Swami-ji's ideals and rise when it's still dark. They've even published a photograph of me reading the scriptures before dawn.

Secretary: Don't worry sir, I didn't reveal anything like that. I said it's impossible for you to join the dawn parade because you have a meeting scheduled at the time.

Great Man: Excellent! Really, you are very intelligent. What's happening to your promotion? I made a strong recommendation to give you the Selection Grade. Put up an extra-strong recommendation if necessary, I'll sign it.

Secretary: Your kindness knows no bounds, sir. Mr Tarafdar said …

Great Man: For heaven's sake, how many times do I have to tell you it's Sri, not Mister. Even Rabi Thakur himself was never Mr, only Sri Rabindranath Tagore. Nagen Pal told me he even dropped the Sri later in life. Who knows what will happen when Sri is dropped from the entire country. But then Vivekananda has nothing to fear in that respect, he's neither Sir nor Mister, neither Sri nor Raibahadur, he's Swami Vivekananda.

Secretary: Sri Tarafdar wanted to remind you that you are the president of the Vivekananda centenary celebrations tomorrow evening. Bhogilal-ji is the chief guest, and Sri Tarafdar will inaugurate the programme himself.

Great Man: What! He's right, I completely forgot. A group of young men did come the other day, the We May Be Poor But We Endure Society. It was Haru who recommended them. I had no idea I'm their patron. Not their fault, all idealistic school and college students. They printed my name on their pads on Haru's instructions. But he didn't inform me. I was furious at first, but it's no use being angry with Haru, he controls legions of people—volunteers, we call them.

Secretary: What now, sir?

Great Man: Now we're in deep trouble. It was a huge mistake not to put it down in the appointment diary.

Secretary: Why should you be in trouble, sir? You keep going to meetings, what's another one? You're going to the Abanindra Fine Art Centre, then to the annual conference of the Bhatkhande Music Society, and afterwards to the quarterly dinner of the Indian Society of Philosophers.

Great Man: You don't get it, my speechwriter Debidas Roy has let me down. I've gone and given him leave. He put up drafts of all my other speeches before going. But Vivekananda. What to do now? Get Haru on the line if you can.

Secretary: Very well, sir.

Great Man: Hello, Haru my friend … you rang for me? Yes, of course … Swami-ji's birth anniversary after all, and then a programme of the We Cannot Endure Society … oho, very sorry, slip of the tongue, the We May Be Poor But We Shall Endure Society. A chance to be the president at their programme. But the thing is I've not been feeling too well … What?

[Covers the receiver with his hand so that he cannot be heard and addresses his secretary]

Driving me mad. Says cancel everything else, especially the Bhatkhande Music Society programme. But that's where Chitra Debi will be coming. Sohanlal-ji is the president, I'm the chief guest, and Chitra Debi will inaugurate. I met her last at the banquet, she promised to ring me, must have forgotten, or maybe someone like you didn't put her through, I must ask her tomorrow.

[Uncovers the receiver.]

Hello, hello, there's some disturbance on the line, Haru. Don't mind, we have to use the vernacular from now on. No, no, there's no need to ring Chitra Debi and apologize on my behalf … it won't be proper. And besides, they've already announced my name … The radio people will be there, newspaper people too … Yes, I know you've made all the arrangements and that my name will be in the papers tomorrow … But I've not been keeping well … Swami-ji said be brave, will he appreciate this ritual of devotion from someone who's ill? … Hello? No, no need to ring Chitra Debi, since I've promised I'll be there even if it means dying … Is she coming too? I thought not … There was a proposal before the committee to invite her, but many of the members didn't want to … No, you're wrong there. Swami-ji, Thakur Ramakrishna, they used to maintain relations with actors and actresses … Hello, hello, no don't say anything, I'll go to your programme too, I'll get the doctor to prescribe something strong.

[Puts the phone down.]

Intolerable, but I have to go. That's democracy for you. An extraordinary man must follow an ordinary man's instructions without protest. We didn't have these problems under monarchies or dictatorships. Nobody would have dared drag me to a meeting. I must tell Nagen Pal, he's writing my autobiography after all. He must include this. But in the second volume, which will be sealed now and will be published ten years after my death.

Secretary: Excellent idea, sir.

Great Man: You never know, this observation could become another centenary sensation. If I live till ninety, I don't wish to live beyond ninety, add ten, that's the centenary year, what you people call depletion of hundred years.

Secretary: I think it's completion, sir.

Great Man: Same thing, a prefix here and a prefix there.

Secretary: I'd better note down the Vivekananda centenary celebrations in the appointment diary, sir.

Great Man: Don't disturb me. I'm thinking of my speechwriter. Why did Debidas Babu have to take leave right now!

Secretary: He hasn't taken a single day's leave in the past two years, sir.

Great Man: How do you people expect him to get leave in Rabindranath Tagore's centenary year? And really, what were all these great men thinking? Did Vivekananda have to be born at the same time as the others?

Secretary: He would never have got leave if not now.

Great Man: What do you mean? Are there more centenaries?

Secretary: That's what Debidas Babu was saying. Three great men were born in the same decade—Tagore, Vivekananda, Gandhi. And Sri Aurobindo soon afterwards.

Great Man: What! Would the world have come to an end if they had spaced it out a bit? Still, it's a good point for tomorrow's speech. The golden womb of Bengal—three world-conquering offspring in the same decade.

Secretary: Don't you mean India, and not Bengal, sir?

Great Man: Don't you know it's a gathering of Bengalis? I would have said India for the benefit of a different audience, but here it's got to be Bengal.

Secretary: But Gandhi, sir? He was born in Gujarat.

Great Man: We cannot say anything constructive, this is our problem as a race. No wonder Swami-ji bad-mouthed you people and extolled south Indians. You destroyed a beautiful idea. Nothing but destructive criticism.

Secretary: I'm sorry, sir.

Great Man: It won't do to apologize and slink away. Now that the speechwriter isn't here we have to do it ourselves. Don't just stand there, draw up a chair. Now the thing is, we have to dig out what Vivekananda did for the country. The greatest problem is that he never went to jail. I faced the same sort of trouble during Rabindranath Tagore's centenary. But there's no chance I can say it out loud, for there will be editorials in all the newspapers at once. The editors are just waiting to gobble me up.

Secretary: Indeed, sir.

Great Man: It's clear he was born in 1863, or else his centenary would not have been observed this year, in 1963. This is what Bengalis call common sense. I may not have direct information, but I pieced it together from circumstantial evidence. Swami-ji must have had this extraordinary ability too, or he wouldn't have become a great man. And his fame isn't limited to India—by God's grace I have a good deal of it too. But abroad? All those white people swooning over 'Vaivekanand', you need something up there to achieve this.

Secretary: But of course, sir.

Great Man: What should I say about Swami Vivekananda? That's the problem now. Young Debidas would have prepared something in a jiffy. I break out in a cold sweat when I have to think it up for myself. Still, when I see what he has written, it's exactly what I wanted to say. But my thoughts are so constipated now they refuse to emerge.

Secretary: You're a busy man after all, sir …

Great Man: Yes, you can see for yourself, can't you? I have to oblige so many people. Not just the living, but also those like Vivekananda who died a long time ago.

Secretary: Then, sir, I'd better …

Great Man: Go through the biography files and put up a note on Swami Vivekananda immediately.

Secretary: The biography files only have details on the living, with whom we have dealings.

Great Man [annoyed]: No excuses. Get the note ready or be ready for a chargesheet, it could even be a suspension. You people may be on top of the law, but we understand a few things too. Let me tell you that great men never die, they live forever, which is why they're called immortal. Surely we have not stopped our dealings with these immortal figures. You should have maintained a file about them.

Secretary: Should I prepare a brief biography from the last few days' newspapers?

Great Man: You people are not worthy. I really don't understand how the country will survive a crisis with people like you. Ordinary people can quote from the newspapers, but we cannot, whatever we say will be considered the official view. So no matter how great the personality, we have to be careful about what we say about them. Our words will spread far and wide, you never know, they could lead to an international crisis. Any gazette notifications about this gentleman?

Secretary: No sir.

Great Man: Then ring the police and ask for a report immediately.

[Secretary leaves. The phone rings.]

Hello ... speaking. Don't ask, I'm caught up completely in this Vivekananda business. Swami Vivekananda, you must have heard of him, a great reformer ... Hello ... no, no connection with land or excise reforms, you're making a mistake, he was a plain and simple social reformer. I've spoken to the Centre about that matter of Bhogilal-ji's, it isn't safe to discuss it on the phone. See me at home later, it'll be done as you want. Remind him of the donation to our fund ... And Narendranath Roy, my youngest brother-in-law, note the name in your diary, he'll probably meet you tomorrow. Get him to meet Bhogilal-ji. All right, we'll talk later.

[Secretary enters.]

Secretary: Got it. Found it, sir.

Great Man: Got what? Even getting an import licence doesn't make people so happy. Vivekananda himself didn't feel this kind of joy on finding God.

Secretary: There was a list of the main events in Vivekananda's life in Debidas Babu's drawer, sir. He must have noted them down on the assumption he would need them for a speech in the future.

Great Man: Saved! Saved from ringing the police too.

Secretary: According to this note he was born on 12 January 1863. He came into contact with Sri Ramakrishna in 1881. Ramakrishna passed away in 1886, and Vivekananda established the Ramakrishna Monks' Association immediately afterwards. And then he went on his tours.

Great Man: Do you see how important tours are? Those who are opposed to tours disrespect Vivekananda.

Secretary: It says here he went to America in 1893.

Great Man: Excellent!

Secretary: He represented India at the World Parliament of Religions when he was just thirty.

Great Man: But how did he manage the foreign exchange? Remember to investigate this point later.

Secretary: It was when he was abroad that he became world famous.

Great Man: Naturally, no one gets ahead in life unless they go abroad. Look at Rabi Thakur, look at Gandhi, same story everywhere. Anyway, never mind the fame, when was his golden jubilee observed? Debidas had referred to Tagore's golden jubilee in a speech.

Secretary: Can't locate it, sir.

Great Man: Debidas isn't very thorough, doesn't write down all the particulars. And yet expects to be in the Selection Grade.

Secretary: The notes end in 1902.

Great Man: He didn't bother to write any further. Lazy chap.

Secretary: Just a minute, sir. It says here Swami Vivekananda passed away at just thirty-nine.

Great Man: Oho, what a sad loss. It's just that we were under British rule then, or I'd have shut down all government and private offices for the day.

Secretary: What should I do now, sir?

Great Man: You seem to be in a hurry to go home. And yet think of Vivekananda, he left home altogether for the sake of the country. Why did they have to destroy their own lives for ordinary people? Anyway, ring the organizers if you can. I was told they've been thinking of felicitating me, they can do it at tomorrow's meeting if they like. It'll make things easier for them. After all, we're doing what Vivekananda wanted to accomplish but could not. You know what he had said, humans are the truth above all, nothing else is truer

Secretary: Er …

Great Man: What are you erring for? You don't like it because it's so progressive, isn't that so? The lord alone knows how we will create a socialist nation with such people.

Secretary: That's not what I am saying, sir.

Great Man: Never mind your that's not what I am saying. We can't even get the middle class to our level, and Vivekananda went and said, 'the cobbler and the toilet cleaner are your blood, they're your brother'. To tell the truth, this is most irresponsible. He said what he had to and disappeared from the scene, now we have to bear the brunt.

Secretary: I was saying, sir, that it was probably Chandidas who said that thing about humans being the truth above all.

Great Man: What! I've passed it off as Vivekananda's at not one but two meetings. Still, both meetings were in the suburbs … may not matter.

Secretary: And besides, great men think alike. You've said the same thing yourself.

Great Man: You've saved my life. I'm definitely going to arrange for an advance increment for you. Don't worry about your nephew either. I'll do something for him as soon as things are worked out for my youngest son-in-law's friends. What I was saying was, since there's a bit of time, I'll make a quick visit to the racecourse. When we were students, Swami-ji's birthday used to be celebrated at school every year. If only I'd listened closely to the speeches … But we were more interested in the food, we'd hover near the snacks. If I'd paid attention then I wouldn't be regretting Debidas's absence. I was thinking, look through his drawers, you might find some quotations, that's all I need.

[Secretary leaves. The phone rings.]

Hello, is that Nagen Babu? Not at all, I wouldn't feel disturbed if a writer like you rang me every hour. I've received your books.

They're very well written, I will certainly read them if I can make the time. Why don't you write a novel about Vivekananda? All right, if that's difficult, how about a poem—I'll give instructions to include it in all the textbooks. And yes, write extensively about Vivekananda in my autobiography, his speeches and collected writings have influenced my entire life. If I were hanged I would go to the gallows with a copy of his book … Hello? No need to thank me, it's our job to encourage and inspire artists and writers.

[Secretary enters.]

Secretary: You were right, sir. I found a compendium of quotations in Debidas Babu's drawer. His schoolteacher Radhakanta Babu had collected them in a notebook.

Great Man: People have such strange whims. Teachers don't understand the value of time—instead of attending to their students' education they waste time collecting autographs. Still, it's going to prove helpful for me. What does it say there?

Secretary: Many quotations.

Great Man: You people are so inefficient. If only you had a file on every great man, I wouldn't have been in trouble at the eleventh hour. Anyway, tell me some of what he said, it's a public meeting after all, without a couple of quotations it doesn't … But not that one about toilet cleaners, it's rotted by now.

Secretary: Some others then?

Great Man: Yes.

Secretary: Swami-ji said, 'Wherever there is struggle, wherever there is rebellion, there are signs of life.'

Great Man: Oh my god, this is problematic. We can't get into such controversies.

Secretary: He also said, 'Do not repose faith in well-known or highly ranked or rich people.'

Great Man: He was right about the rich. We don't get half the donations we expect from them. But well-known people? How will the country progress if you don't repose faith in us?

[The phone rings again.]

Hello … Oh Jhunjhunwala-ji, how are you. Yes, this year the All India Poor Conference is being held here, you must be one of the sponsors. All the big fish of the Centre are behind it. A contribution of Rs 25,000 … no, being a poor man is not an excuse. Don't forget this is an association of the poor, who will contribute funds if not poor people like you.

[Puts the phone down.]

No, that quotation won't do. Businessmen will be furious if it's reported in the papers. No programme can be conducted without their funds.

Secretary: Swami-ji also said, 'Tolerance is infinitely better than action.'

Great Man: He was never involved in politics, how did he manage to get this right? Take these positions we occupy, we're here to tolerate, that's far more important than action. But we can't tell anyone this, they will misunderstand.

Secretary: Then what's to be done, sir?

Great Man: Check for more quotations. Swami-ji himself has said, 'Seek a hundred times if you cannot find it the first time.'

Secretary: It says here, 'All those peasants and weavers, the insignificant people of India, vanquished by foreigners and reviled by their own people, the lower castes, are the ones who have been toiling in silence since time immemorial without reward. All you forever-oppressed labourers, I salute you.'

Great Man: Do you people want to ruin me? Why did he have to say all these things that incite labourers? You should be speaking about increasing production, but no, it's the forever-oppressed. And I can't trust Debidas either, imagine being my confidential assistant and writing these things in his diary. Get a photograph and send it to the police immediately. Who knows where the fifth column is in action!

Secretary: Should I go on, sir?

Great Man: Do I have a choice? There's no respite from the meeting tomorrow. If I'd known this is the kind of thing the gentleman has said I would never have accepted the invitation. Did he say nothing that's good?

Secretary: Here he said, 'The efficiency and sincerity these peasants and cobblers and corpse-bearers show is far greater than those of you useless people. You have persecuted these tolerant lower castes for all this time, they will take revenge now, and you fools will keep chasing employment and go extinct.'

Great Man: Stop, stop, I don't want to hear any more! Useless, fools—what is this language? Here we are advertising on public transport asking people to be polite. And there's something else I'm forced to say, this is nothing but destructive criticism, like the leader of the opposition, not a single constructive word.

Secretary: 'How will you get your clothes and food if this set of people stop work? Lamentations are heard if the toilet cleaners don't work for a day in Calcutta—if they stopped work for three days none of you would have a stitch to wear or a morsel to eat.'

Great Man: Which book did he write all this in? I don't understand what the police is doing. Why have these books not been confiscated yet? The man is inciting toilet cleaners. He's advising essential-services people to go on strike—this is illegal.

Secretary: What should I do then, sir? Should I send a note to the Home Department? Shall I get my notebook?

Great Man: Yes, but first ask them whether they have a file on this man. I'm beginning to suspect [hesitates], this is top secret, but no harm telling you, was he a member of a political party?

Secretary: Monks have no caste, leave alone party affiliation.

Great Man: Oh please, we've heard enough of such dialogue. Now find out the context in which he's trying to inflame passions.

Secretary: He said, 'The lower classes are going on strike these days, the upper classes cannot suppress them any more no matter how much they try … That's why I say, all of you should get involved in ensuring that education flowers among the masses. With your empathy they will become a hundred times more enthusiastic and efficient.'

Great Man: I see. It's a well-planned conspiracy, it's clear as daylight now.

Secretary: 'Reforms will not come from a superficial involvement, you must enter within.'

Great Man: This is what is called infiltration nowadays.

Secretary: He has also said, 'Light the fire at the base, let the flames rise.'

Great Man: Not so simple, the institution known as the fire brigade has not been wound up yet. We know the technique for dousing a conflagration. Send a top secret note to Kulada Babu, every single quotation should be investigated. We spend millions on them every year, what do they do?

Secretary: Maybe this line will prove useful. 'I want to tell the reformers that I am a greater reformer than they are.'

Great Man: Shameful, the man didn't have a modest bone in his body. I too know there is no greater leader than me, but do I say it out loud? You've typed so many of my speeches, have you ever seen any mention of this?

Secretary: You don't have a trace of vanity, sir.

Great Man: And yet not one of the blasted editors published this on my birthday.

Secretary: He was probably not a votary of peace either, sir.

Great Man: What, really?

Secretary: He said, 'If someone slaps you once, it's wrong not to slap them back ten times.'

Great Man: Be very careful! These things must remain confidential. Fortunately our public doesn't read very closely. There will be murders on the streets if these things get out. We'll have to increase the police budget five times.

Secretary: He's brought up fire again. 'You must be ready to jump into the flames if you want to accomplish anything.'

Great Man: Put the quotation in the fire brigade file. I can use it if I have to go to their meeting. Hurry up, after this I have to meet Mrs Hazra and Mrs Swaminathan. A meeting of the beauty contest subcommittee. Their motto is 'Satyam Shivam Sundaram, Beauty Is Truth'.

Secretary: Was Sita very beautiful, sir?

Great Man: Considering the trouble Ram went to in order to marry her, she must have been beautiful. But the lady had no personality to speak of, she endured Ram's torment without demur. You know what Mrs Hazra says? What's the point of going underground? Protest, raise your voice. If divorce is embarrassing, ask for judicial separation at the very least. That's what Mrs Swaminathan says too.

Secretary: But Swami-ji has said, 'Indian women must follow in Sita's footsteps. This is the only way to arrive at a better station in life.'

Great Man: You're a lifesaver. Chitra Debi has a weakness for Vivekananda, I'll quote these lines to her.

Secretary: Swami-ji has said more about women. 'I need some followers, intelligent and intrepid, who can look death in the eye, who can swim across the ocean. I need hundreds, both women and men. I need women as well as men, there is no difference in their souls, I want power to flower.'

Great Man: Marvellous! A ruinous plot. He wants to send our goddesses out of home into the jaws of death.

Secretary: But he did love people. Here he says, 'To all of you I offer my sympathy and utmost efforts as my duty for the poor, ignorant, and oppressed. Go at once to the temple of Krishna, who was the friend of the poorest people of Gokul, who did not hesitate to embrace the low-caste Guhak Chandal, who, as the Buddha, spurned a royal invitation to accept instead the invitation of a prostituted woman—'

Great Man: No need to read any more, I'm feeling nauseous. So it comes down to accepting the invitation of a prostituted woman.

Secretary: Krishna delivered her from her plight by accepting the invitation.

Great Man: Oh please, everyone says such worthy things. There'll be plenty of young men at the gathering tomorrow—in these times of moral decay I cannot incite them further. Besides, my wife will raise hell if she hears.

Secretary: I think he was talking of romantic love. In this letter he says, 'In romantic love there is no difference between Bengalis, Aryans, heathens or lower castes. Love unites all.'

Great Man: You bet it does. They're uniting dozens at the marriage registry offices every day, while innocent parents beat their breasts and weep. I may not be able to say it in as many words, but this is not at all a good thing.

Secretary: The context in which he said this was, 'No great task can be accomplished by trickery. Everything is achieved with the help of love, genuine devotion and great courage.'

Great Man: I've heard this nonsense many times.

[Secretary leaves. The phone rings.]

Hello? Speaking. Oh, I can't believe I'm talking to Chitra Debi. How fortunate I am to receive a call from you. After our last meeting at the trade show for your new film I've been thinking of ringing you to congratulate you. I haven't seen such a performance in a long time. Hello? My programme tomorrow is packed, don't ask. Things are even worse for public men than public women. About a dozen committee and subcommittee meetings in the morning. Then the annual meeting of the trade association and cocktails and lunch at Ganges Club. The racecourse in the afternoon, you may have seen it in the papers, I have to give away a prize. It's counted as a sport these days; we have to encourage it. Then an important meeting about the Miss Calcutta contest at the Imperial. After that there's a spot of trouble. Don't ask, it's Swami Vivekananda's birth centenary, I'm the principal speaker. I have to be there whether I want to or not. Hello? Oh, I didn't know you share a birthday with him. Yes, I'd love to be at your dinner and cocktail … I'm sending advance wishes … no please, Chitra Debi, don't cut off relations with me if I can't make it. I promise to be there. I'll give a short speech early on in the meeting and then come directly to your place.

[Radio news]

Swami Vivekananda's one hundredth birth centenary was observed with great solemnity and enthusiasm today. The Great Man ______ was present at the ceremony organized by the We May Be Poor But We Endure Society despite his physical illness. He issued a full-throated call for every citizen to be inspired by Swami Vivekananda's holy ideas, reminding his audience repeatedly that the voice of the conscience is our greatest source of dependence in the dark times that the nation is shrouded in. He said that as long as Vivekananda's words live within us, we shall not die, we shall be immortal.

The Kingdom of the Dead

THE WRITER WHO WIELDED ENORMOUS INFLUENCE OVER OUR family by virtue of his birthplace was Bibhutibhushan Bandyopadhyay. His wife was, like us, a resident of Bongram before marriage, and knew my mother as a result.

I saw the writer of *Pather Panchali* many times from a distance, and heard many personal stories about him from my stepbrother Gaurishankar. My brother would sometimes visit him at a boarding house on College Street for a chat.

Bibhutibhushan was no longer alive by the time I got a break as a writer at an early age and earned the right to frequent Boipaara, the concentration of publishers and bookshops in Calcutta. He died on 1 September 1950. I was, of course, present at the huge memorial meeting held for him, not as a fellow writer but as a former resident of Bongram.

I made my maiden appearance in the pages of a major newspaper some three months after this. The relationship that began in the offices of *Anandabazar Patrika* on Burman Street in Chitpore remains unbroken even now, several decades later. In a land of writers who die young, this is probably something of a record.

Writing for the Sunday pages brought a number of privileges. Such as arriving overnight without notice at the drawing rooms of thousands of readers, and knowing that before they sold it off as scrap, thrifty middle-class readers would not leave unread a single word in a newspaper they had spent good money on. And as a bonus, there were the homemakers. The television had not yet infiltrated their daily lives.

Being able to attract hundreds—maybe even thousands—of readers of the Sunday pages was about to give me a swollen head. There was a serious dearth of potable water in the blind lane in Chowdhurybagan in Howrah where I lived. There was usually a long queue at the single public handpump in the area, and it took nearly forty minutes to collect two buckets of water. Being published in the Sunday pages meant unbelievable benefits.

One day, our neighbour Sudhananda Chattopadhyay said, 'You write for the papers, you mustn't waste time this way. Take as much water as you like from the private handpump in our yard.' This incredible change of fortune arising from a single published piece, not to mention a payment of Rs 10 through a money order, was beyond my wildest dreams.

I grew bolder and began to investigate ways to win the heart of the editor of the Sunday pages. My research revealed that interviewing famous personalities might be helpful, but unfortunately I didn't know a single such person. Eventually I gathered courage in my hands and interviewed one of the senior bulls on Calcutta's streets, titling the piece 'Calcutta's Bull Culture'. To my own surprise, it was published, and it drew the attention of Parimal Goswami, a journalist with a sense of humour.

Instructed through a postcard to meet him, I obeyed. He asked how the idea had occurred to me. I told him that I personally knew each of the bulls in Burrabazar whom I met on the way to Surendranath College in Sealdah. Their disciplined adherence to rules was inspiring. They were never annoyed when followed for hours by a human with a notebook and a pencil. Parimal Babu was particularly pleased to learn that many of the bulls of Burrabazar obeyed traffic signals when crossing roads. 'Will you write about dogs next?' he asked.

'I'm tempted to, but I dare not. Street dogs are particularly bad-tempered. There'll be trouble if they bite. The payment for the piece is only ten rupees, but I'll have to take twelve injections.'

'Are you giving up writing?'

'Certainly not. Swami Vivekananda has told the youth—draw on your courage, O bold legions.'

'Is it necessary to accept everything he said as one hundred per cent correct? He had written—arise, awake. For heaven's sake, it's not at all safe to get out of bed when you're drowsy. You have to be awake before you arise.'

'There was no scope for arguing with him at Vivekananda School,' I said. 'At most we could sidestep him with bowed head and then do as we pleased. This, of course, demands great application of the mind, which I have attempted. The manuscript in my pocket at the moment is titled "Memsahibs' Dogs". They are sweet creatures, never biting without orders. And even if they bite, injections are not necessary. On the contrary, if one is lucky, one might get a job in the lady's husband's office. Someone I know has had his fortune transformed in this manner.'

When he had read the piece the editor said, 'But you haven't written about your friend getting a job.'

'How could I? Swami Vivekananda said mortification at the success of others is one of the greatest flaws of Bengalis. He repeatedly warned us not to be envious.'

'It's impossible to be a satirist without some negativity.'

'I have vowed not to tread on that path.'

'Vowed to whom?'

'To Shibram Chakraborty.'

'Do you know him?'

'I don't. I was bold enough to visit him at his boarding house with a friend. It was he who told me, "Don't you dare become a satirist. Tell everyone they'll have to cry in the same proportion that they make people laugh." I said to him, "Give me a solution, sir, I promise to read nothing but your stories about Harshabardhan and Gobardhan over the next five years." He asked, "Not even Rabindranath Tagore?" I said, "I'll avoid him like beef. It's no use reading him, he's impossible to copy." After some thought, Shibram said, "People misunderstand everything I say, which is why I have stopped dispensing advice. But you are a citizen of Howrah. This payment of ten rupees is so important to you that instead of a romance with your cousin you are intent on sacrificing yourself to writing. So listen. Make your readers weep as much as you can. They are the ones who will bring a smile to your face. They will send so many postcards to the editor that your payment will be increased by twenty per cent to twelve rupees within a year."'

All of this, of course, was a long time ago. Parimal Goswami forgave me for suppressing the story about the harmless bite of a pet dog leading to a job for the victim. 'This is the obstacle to creating literature in our country,' he said. 'So many things have to be concealed under the pressure of the environment. Only an epochal personality could have used such dazzling language to hint at the change in fortune arising from a dog bite. Behind every joy there is suffering.'

Parimal Goswami of Faridpur was with us for another twenty-five years. In this period someone had described me as a 'ticketless' entrant to the precincts of literature. It was Parimal Babu who had encouraged me then. Some are given invitation cards, some have to buy their own tickets.

I began to frequent Boipaara more often after becoming an author. Shibram Chakraborty was to be seen there quite often. With great affection he would tell me, 'Why are you wasting your time here instead of spending it in the joyous company of your cousin? What will you see here anyway besides mountains, peaks and forests that are named Achintya, Manik, Tarashankar, etc.?'

It was truly that all-too-rare golden age of Bangla literature. At no other time in two hundred years of history have so many blessed children of Bengali letters been seen together. Fiction or essays or humour or travel writing—College Street was a veritable confluence of many greatnesses. Surprisingly, it has not occurred to anyone that there has not been another age such as that after the deaths of Saratchandra Chattopadhyay and Rabindranath Tagore.

Consider some of the names. Among the formidable Bandyopadhyays were Manik, Tarashankar and Saradindu; the Mukherjees included Sailajananda, Bibhuti, Ashutosh, Banaphool and Jajabar; in the ranks of the Mitras were Premendra, Bimal and Narendranath; the Basus included Rajshekhar, Buddhadeva and Samaresh; the Gangulys were represented by Narayan and Sunil; the Ghoshs by Subodh and Santoshkumar. There were countless others. Abanindranath Tagore, Ashapurna Debi, Satinath Bhaduri, Pramathnath Bishi, Jarashandha, Prabodhkumar Sanyal, and, of course, Syed Mujtaba Ali, who was no less than the Qutub Minar, with nothing coming before or after when it came to sheer quality of writing.

Talking of essays will bring up names we bow to in reverence—Sunitikumar Chattopadhyay, Kalidas Nag, Niharranjan Roy, Sukumar Sen, Nirad Chandra Chaudhuri. And last but not the least, coming at the end of the batting order: Satyajit Ray, who astounded everyone.

This list is, of course, far from complete. Supplying forty-eight names for four Test teams is a simple matter for the guardians of Bangla literature. And I have mentioned only prose writers, without even approaching the special place reserved for poets.

It was hard to believe that even while all these supremely gifted writers were publishing their memorable works almost simultaneously, no one was talking about the golden age of Bangla letters that seemed to have begun. An audit of how and why such neglect was possible, and the extent of permanent damage done to our literature as a result of this, has not yet been conducted. And to think some people now claim that nothing significant has ever been created in Bangla literature!

At times one is tempted to observe that this is in fact the sign of a jealous race that cannot celebrate the joys of others. Everyone is sunk in the gloom of deprivation even when they have a wealth of possessions. But even if they do not get it, what writers and artists consider oxygen is appreciation.

It is time to examine the factors behind the Bengali reader's recent love for dead authors. Those who had labelled Bengalis 'a race that has forgotten its own identity' are treading with caution now. Many claim that living writers are unable to meet expectations, forcing readers to turn to their dead predecessors. One more cruel truth has emerged—people are concerned with books alone; they couldn't care less whether the authors of those books are living or deceased.

Then again, some people are of the view that the Bengali writer's work is like a 'whole-life' life-insurance policy. Even if the premium is paid regularly, no one will check the file before death. A favourite writer of mine, now dead, used to say, 'We can expect nothing but reimbursement for our expenses while we're alive.' Of late the literary community has trained its eyes on the works of Sunil Gangopadhyay to assess whether his posthumous popularity surpasses the level it had reached when he was still alive. This is the dearest wish of far-sighted Bengali writers. The possibility of more glory in the afterlife than in this one keeps their creativity flowing unhampered.

It is necessary to return to my own story now. Once, as I was about to enter a publisher's office, Shibram Chakraborty introduced me to the memorable writer Achintya Kumar Sengupta, who was rather worried about my having become an author at the age of twenty-two. He said, 'You've started far too early, my boy. Your health and heart and pen will break under the burden of a lifetime of writing. Neither your heart nor your stomach will be full. May the gods ensure your well-being.'

My Howrah

IN ALL THESE LONG YEARS THAT I'VE BEEN ALIVE I'VE NEVER heard anyone powerful say 'my Howrah' or 'our Howrah'. The slogan I've often heard from various processions proclaims how everyone's naam or name, yours as well as mine, is in fact Vietnam. All that chanting paid off, Vietnam's luck has been looking up. But across the river from Calcutta, there has been no improvement in Howrah, which is everyone's shame, yours as well as mine, Bengal's as well as India's. Howrah has kept falling behind in full view of helpless citizens. It's retreated so much that it cannot go backwards any more.

In such a situation it's sensible to ignore the very existence of Howrah. This is what has happened. Over the past decade no powerful person in Delhi or Calcutta has included Howrah in their wise sayings. There is no difference of opinion between political parties on the left and on the right, above and below, on the subject—it's best to hide this enormous urban habitation behind a screen of fog and smoke, like an eternally bedridden relative.

Howrah is an astonishing case study for those who are under the impression that such brazen denial of existence is impossible in a democracy, that the ever-active mass media will pounce on the issue whenever they see injustice and bring about a resolution.

Colossal decay and deterioration is taking place under the nose of one of the world's largest metropolises, and yet this has escaped the eye of every alert investigator.

The geographical advantages that can make a city claim the status of a metropolis were present to a far greater degree in Howrah than in Calcutta. But, driven by some short-term, distorted thinking, the British crossed the river Hooghly and established their capital where Calcutta stands today instead of in Uluberia. It is difficult to justify this. And it is not just the British. We too have displayed the same lack of foresight—instead of integrating the burgeoning city of Calcutta with Howrah and advancing towards the mainland of India, we lavished millions on a saline lake. Now, cursing the traffic-jam-inflicted Calcutta, the Hooghlys and Medinipurs and Bardhamans are rushing to the government offices in Salt Lake. But Howrah remains in eternal darkness.

No one spoke of change in step with time, for there was no one to think about the future of Howrah. And so its formal name was the 'Birmingham of Bengal', while its nickname was 'Coolie Town'. There is no major minister from Howrah, no chief minister has passed a single night in Howrah, not even inadvertently.

Whatever Howrah can be proud of is accidental. The address of the first and probably all-time bestselling Bengali poet Bharatchandra was in Howrah. Only Saratchandra Chattopadhyay could have explained why after leaving Burma in the early twentieth century he chose to live in, of all places, the notorious red light area of Gholadanga in Howrah, and subsequently created his finest work in Baajeshibpur. Still we are hurt by the fact that the city of Howrah did not appear in his works. There was one other far-sighted person who chose Howrah voluntarily. He declared with pride that Ramakrishna would live in Belur, Howrah, for the next fifteen hundred years, that the monastery was his body. That Swami

Vivekananda left his mortal body behind in the same Belur proves that it is the humiliated, the neglected and the ignored whom he loved the most.

The people of Calcutta have given Howrah only one gift of love—they have not objected to the name of Howrah Bridge. Citizens from the next era were much cleverer, however. Writing of the life of a rickshaw-puller from the infamous Pilkhana slums of Howrah, a French writer named his book *City of Joy*—and the authorities in Calcutta promptly appropriated the moniker for their city. No one protested. A bunch of young doctors who studied abroad proved much more generous. They built a hospital in Howrah and called it 'West Bank'. After all, new age business ventures must have a glamorous modern touch.

It's worth pointing out that Howrah is now a city of Bengal, not of Bengalis. Like a bountiful mother, Howrah keeps its doors open for everyone, which is why the population here keeps growing. This Howrah is my Howrah. I took shelter in the most dilapidated house in its narrowest lane in the dim distant days of my childhood, clutching my fortune-seeking father's hand. I have encountered various sorrows here, by day and by night, but never have I had to halt in my tracks. That humans can still love one another has been proven to me in this very same strange city. Seven decades have passed describing some of this in literature. It hurts greatly when anyone but me is critical of Howrah.

Rama Prasad Goenka

I met the industrialist Rama Prasad Goenka for the first time in December 1984. That was when, in partnership with an associate, he acquired a famous tyre company whose head office was on Calcutta's Free School Street. Fearful of being unable to work with the new owners, I expressed my desire to pack up and resign. Sending for me, Rama Babu got straight to the point and said in perfect Bangla, 'Didn't you become famous with your novel about the High Court? Does the hanging precede the trial there? You have to try me first.'

Far from 'trying' him, I found myself enchanted by this unusual man. Three decades of a wonderful relationship ensued. The up-close and intimate view I had of this millionaire who shook the land from the mountains to the seas with his intelligence and acumen, all from his Calcutta address, would probably make for an entire novel which will include the courage of the world conqueror, rare battle strategies, and that all-too-rare ability known as negotiating skills.

From humble beginnings, Rama Prasad demonstrated the temerity to acquire a succession of well known companies, which many mistook for the arrogance of the wealthy. Some labelled him a 'takeover tycoon'. But this gentle man was not one to usurp anyone's property against their will. He would often say, 'I never forced myself on anyone in any of my acquisitions.' Once, he had attempted a hostile takeover of a car company in Bombay, but Indira Gandhi had drawn him aside and asked him to desist. On another occasion, an agreement was signed in secret for the acquisition of another Bombay-based company. But the patriarch of the family that owned it said ruefully that his son was objecting strongly to the deal. Rama Prasad let go of the company.

I often feel a sense of pride about Rama Babu, who was a Bengali in heart and soul. At a time when big businesses were deserting Bengal in the decades after Independence, he acquired large companies and enhanced our prestige. He spoke Bangla fluently. Beginning his education in a Bangla-medium school, he went on to graduate in history from Presidency College. He commuted by bus or tram to College Street from the family home in Muktaram Babu Street where he was born, and joined the endless Coffee House addas. His favourite sweetshop was Putiram, and his favourite professor Susobhan Sarkar. Another favourite was Professor Taraknath Sen.

Rama Prasad did not choose to restrict himself to the company of wealthy businessmen. He had extraordinary relationships with a number of people, some of them journalists, some politicians, some singers. He would often say that once his burden of work was lighter, he intended to invite a well-known author or researcher or artist home every week to felicitate them and spend some time with them.

He had a special weakness for the Nehru family, and even acquired the sobriquet of 'Poster Goenka' for having posters of Indira Gandhi printed during the elections one year. His supposed 'obsession' with Indira Gandhi had earned him something of an unsavoury reputation within the joint family of the Goenkas. After her downfall he even had to spend a few days in jail in Nainital.

His residence was also subjected to searches several times. Indira Gandhi herself had secretly visited his house in Delhi during those troubled days to express her regret at his having to pay the price for supporting her.

But Rama Prasad was irked by no one. He would invite in the sleuths commissioned to keep him under surveillance. 'How long can you stand in the streets?' he would tell them. 'Come in and have a cup of tea.'

He had acquired the Bengali's love for stories and anecdotes. 'My father didn't have much faith in me,' he would say. 'Once, after I went off with my grandfather to a wedding in Deoghar without taking his permission, he was so angry that he made me the telephone operator at home.' A significant incident in his life was his mother's untimely death in an air crash abroad. This loss left a deep impression on him. He would often look up astrological predictions.

Rama Prasad's grandfather was Sir Badridas Goenka, the chairman of Imperial Bank. He was a constant source of inspiration for Rama Babu. When he went to meet his grandfather on the day he was to join the family firm Duncan Brothers, Sir Badridas advised him affectionately, 'Never hide your troubles from your doctor and your bank. And remember, your word is worth more than any document, no matter how heavy the loss.'

Rama Prasad's ability to draw people to himself was unparalleled. He would introduce me to everyone with these words. 'This is Bengal's favourite writer. He helps me now and then in his spare time.'

When it came to food he was a globetrotter across Calcutta He would send for beguni from College Street, kochuri from Putiram, shingara from K.C. Das, or moghlai porotha from Anadi. And sometimes, for shondesh from Nakur. During his final illness, he expressed a desire for vegetarian Bengali food. After my wife's death my home was a veritable desert. I rushed to Bapi Barik of Bijoli Grill, the restaurant and catering services firm, and sent a gourmet vegetarian Bengali meal to the Goenka residence at just a few hours' notice. Rama Babu was delighted.

He would often ask me about the Dhakai porotha.

Rama Prasad would say, 'I have suffered as much failure as I have tasted success. I couldn't acquire Balmer Lawrie, I couldn't acquire Premier Auto or Bombay Dyeing, I couldn't hold on to Dunlop, I had to let go of Remington after acquiring it, I couldn't keep Haldia Petrochemicals. But I have no regrets. I have observed that I make big gains immediately after small losses. I believe God ensures that whatever happens is for the best.'

Rama Prasad was a member of the Rajya Sabha. He was present, unafraid, in Parliament when terrorists attacked in December 2001. Unless you are fearless and resolute, unless you can repose your trust and faith in others, you cannot discharge your responsibilities in the project of life. This was what Rama Babu had conveyed with his characteristic calmness that day. I have not heard anyone else say anything like this in my entire life, and I cannot but offer my humble respects to such a man.

Had he lived, Rama Prasad would have been ninety-three on 1 March 2023. I would like to remember him not just as an industrialist with great accomplishments but also as a memorable personality.

As far as I remember, the first time I saw him was on a flight from Calcutta to Delhi, devoutly clutching a book, possibly the Gita, during take-off. I was a little surprised at the sight of an internationally reputed industrialist being so dependent on the Gita, but later I heard of his young mother's untimely death. The accident had scarred her eldest son for life.

My colleague and fellow passenger had said, 'This is none other than Poster Goenka, Indira Gandhi's supporter, who gets hundreds of thousands posters printed free of cost from Calcutta for her.'

I had had a mild run-in with his grandfather Sir Badridas Goenka over my novel *Chowringhee*. The novel begins in front of the bronze statue of Sir Badridas's elder brother Sir Hariram Goenka. The chairman of Imperial Bank had not been able to make out whether the scene was respectful or satirical. To protect myself I said that readers evaluate characters according to their own mindset—some consider them good, others bad.

Several years after this sighting, a rumour began to float that the tyre company where I worked was about to be acquired by the Goenkas. My horoscope had also said there was a possibility of change of employment after middle age. As it turned out, far from leaving the job, I went on to become involved with the Goenkas' other companies too.

Rama Babu was adept at telling stories as he worked. He told me about his first day at the family-owned business, when he wasn't allowed into the lunchroom at Duncan House because he didn't have a tie on. There were two separate benches for visitors outside the office of the Englishman who headed the company—one for white people and one for Indians.

He told me about the diploma he had acquired from Dundee in jute-weaving. And about the time, some years later, when a temple was scheduled to be inaugurated on the premises of a jute mill. The workers were on strike that day, but being religious people, they thronged to the temple and asked for proshad. Rama Prasad was embarrassed, for no arrangements had been made. Before getting into his car he humbly asked everyone to come back the next day. It was a mammoth task for the managers to procure several thousand laddus overnight, but Rama Prasad would brook no obstacle.

On a subsequent visit to the mill, he was unhappy at the size of the snacks available at the workers' canteen, and halved the price on the spot. Later, as chairman of the Indian Jute Mills' Association, he felt the wrath of his fellow jute-mill owners. The conflict over the demands made by lakhs of workers was finally escalated to the prime minister, Indira Gandhi, for arbitration.

Rama Prasad was a blind devotee of Indira Gandhi's. Before the tripartite meeting, she sent for him and asked, 'The unions have demanded a certain amount, the owners want to pay less than that, what can I suggest that will be acceptable to both sides?'

Astonishing her, he said, 'You are Indira Gandhi, suggest an amount larger than both.'

Indira Gandhi did as much, creating a sensation. It is said the other industrialists were so unhappy they deposed Rama Babu as the chairman of their association.

After his release from jail, Indira Gandhi had apparently wanted to appoint him as the high commissioner in a foreign country, but he could not accept the offer because his business needed him. It is said that when Indira Gandhi had insisted on giving him a position of his choice, he had asked for a directorship at Tirumala Tirupati Devasthanams.

Once, a major foreign company slipped out of his grasp because of political concerns. The famous person who beat him to acquire the company was killed by an assassin's bullet during an inspection of the premises. Rama Prasad would say, 'Losing out proved beneficial for me.'

At one point Rama Babu became interested in Haldia Petrochemicals. I accompanied him to Writers' Building to meet Jyoti Basu, who was then the chief minister of West Bengal. I was wondering how he would bring it up. Rama Prasad said, 'I am not a science graduate, but I have learnt chemistry so well that the Gujarat government offered me a chairman's position on a salary of Re 1. However, I don't hold that job any more.' Jyoti Basu read between the lines and asked, 'Are you interested in our Haldia Petrochem?'

There was great activity around Haldia Petrochem for several years. Eventually Rajiv Gandhi came to lay the foundation stone, but Rama Babu was not invited to sit on the stage. I suspected then that something was wrong.

Soon afterwards, Jyoti Basu replaced the Goenkas with the Tata Group. An unexpected blow. Rama Prasad told me, 'Use the pen with which you write your books to draft a statement that will let me exit with my head held high.' Some suggested suing the state government. Rama Babu's response was, 'You cannot fight with crocodiles in the water and the king on land.'

Even when absorbed in work, Rama Prasad had a penchant for making interesting observations. He loved to bury himself in books. One day he told me, 'I've learnt a lot of things from the book written by Mao Zedong's doctor, I've found out personal information about John Kennedy too, now you must extract some details about Karl Marx from his followers.'

I managed to locate a book for him. He told me, 'If my professor Susobhan Sarkar had been alive I could have rung him to find out.' I had only recently come to know that Susobhan Babu and his leftist friends would use some of the volumes available at Oxford Bookstore on Park Street to exchange secret information away from the prying eyes of the police. On hearing this Rama Babu visited Oxford Bookstore immediately and showed me the thick books that didn't sell at all. He couldn't stop himself from buying dozens of books whenever he went to a bookshop.

We were chatting about College Street. He told me his monthly pocket money when he commuted from the family home on

Muktaram Babu Street to Presidency College by public transport was Rs 50—including the fare. But at the Coffee House his friends would say, 'You're a Goenka, how can we possibly pay the bill when you're with us?'

'So my pocket money was under severe pressure, but the accountant wouldn't increase it. Finally I hatched a plan—economics was proving difficult to understand, I needed a tutor. The elders of the family held a meeting to sanction the expenditure. I took the money and visited a teacher at home occasionally.

'Arriving with a box of sweets and snacks, I asked, "How are you, sir?" As he ate, the professor brought up economics. "Are you following the chapter on Keynes?" Then he would explain it himself, with the question of fees never coming up. So I had a lot of extra money. After some time, there was turmoil in our Muktaram Babu Street home. The family elders were convinced I had gone to the dogs, that I had even given up going to college. The fact was that I had so much cash from the amount allotted for the private tuition that I had forgotten to collect my pocket money, leading them to believe I had dropped out.'

Many years later, when he became the president of the alumni association of his college, Rama Prasad would sometimes take me along for meetings. On one occasion he led me on to the stage. Being an obvious misfit, I was deeply embarrassed, and had no choice but to tell the renowned IAS officer sitting next to me that I had gatecrashed. Laughing, he said, 'Not gatecrashed but goencrashed.'

Rama Babu was swept away by old memories on the way back from the alumni meeting. 'It would be a crime to have come here and not paid a visit to Putiram's sweetshop,' he said. He also made enquiries about Kalika's world-famous beguni shop, just down the road from Putiram, asking how long it might take to get the freshly fried fritters across to Alipur from Surya Sen Street if the traffic police were to cooperate.

Rama Babu nurtured a lifelong interest in Calcutta food. Once, he sent word from Europe to ask who had discovered the sweet known as 'Abaar Khabo' or 'I want one more'. On another occasion, he was deeply upset at being unable to get the chholar daal and luchi that Dwarik was famous for. He also asked me to compose a note on the decline and fall of the Dhakai porotha. Another time, he expressed a desire for a clandestine taste of the moghlai porotha at Anadi's Cabin. As he ate, he declared that food which wasn't on the forbidden list could not cast a magic spell over him. One day he requested a paean of praise to the tiny shingaras created by Bengali cooks, and declared the Bengali shingara available in winter the best in the world, unparalleled anywhere. Muri was equally incomparable, he felt.

Alongside food, Rama Babu was also deeply interested in Bengal's vanishing textile industry. He used to say that the Goenkas' business expansion came from marketing the Manchester saris manufactured by Ralli Brothers. One of their famous dhotis was branded 'Poromshukh' or 'Extreme Bliss'. When studying history, said Rama Babu, he had discovered that the famous muslin of Dhaka, which had become all but extinct, had the same name.

Later, after getting more details from a journalist friend, he gave me instructions to locate a muslin weaver. He would hold discussions with this person, ordering special muslin turbans (for the prime minister), and saris, dhotis and kurtas for family and friends.

Rama Prasad was particularly interested in reading about the food habits of Bengalis from an earlier era. When he had recovered partially from what turned out to be his final surgery, Rama Prasad went to his office in Esplanade on a wheelchair, surrounded by nurses. In a faint voice he asked if the doctor would allow him to order Bengali food from a restaurant.

Bengali cuisine had reached Himalayan heights long before the birth of restaurant culture. With no one to cook at home, I rushed to a well-known caterer, who dispatched a few famous vegetarian dishes cooked with the help of his family. Rama Babu rang at night to tell me they were delicious, the dhoka would have to be repeated soon.

The opportunity did not arise, for his health deteriorated sharply afterwards.

Towards the end of his life, alongside Bengali food, Rama Babu developed an interest in Saratchandra Chattopadhyay. Sometime earlier he had been charmed by the Hindi film version of *Devdas* and had asked me to send the complete works of Saratchandra to him in Delhi. He was so enchanted by the books that he immediately sent his car to fetch a Bengali friend. And then he rang me. 'I have a huge complaint. We've talked about so many things, but you've never told me about the Saratchandra who wrote *Devdas*. I was told he had left the manuscript in his trunk. Let me know immediately how many such rejected works of his there are.'

My late wife, Bandana, would sometimes ask me, 'When do you work? All you do is chat with the owner.' There was no need to answer this question.

Rama Babu had once invited an Indian prime minister home. When introducing me, he said, 'This full-time Bengali writer who loves Saratchandra helps me out in his spare time.'

Since Rama Babu came into my life, this is the first time that I shall not be meeting him on his birthday, 1 March. But rummaging through the memories of him in the crevices of my mind will occupy me for a long while yet.

Chowringhee at Fifty

MY NOVEL *CHOWRINGHEE* TURNED FIFTY ON 10 JUNE 2012. My Bengali publisher, Dey's Publishing, in association with my principal English publisher, Penguin Books India, organized a ceremony at the South City Starmark auditorium, for which I am deeply grateful. I had to say a few words on the occasion.

Fifty years ago, the venerable authors, publishers, readers and intelligentsia of the time had not realized that that was the golden age of Bangla literature. I would like to begin this momentous day by bowing in reverence to the unparalleled creators and the departed and forgotten Bangla writers of this golden age who have conquered death.

The reputed writers of those days were opposed to self-publicity and also overly self-conscious. Almost all of them were against the idea of projecting themselves, which is why it was not a measure of good taste to be present at the 'launch' of your own book. Times have changed, and I am present on the occasion of my own novel completing fifty years in print—not because I want to hear good things being said about me, nor to publicize my own book, but only with the thought that the Bengali novel does not always have a short lifespan after all. That some books are in fact fortunate enough to survive the ordeals of time and even display the temerity to vault over the barbed wire fence of recognition.

Even if not in large numbers, said my normally laconic publisher Sudhangshusekhar Dey to dispel my doubts, a handful of Bengali novels and short story collections have in fact continued to enhance the pleasure of readers even after half a century, but the additional pleasure in this case was that both *Chowringhee* and its author had gone past fifty and were here with everyone.

Many years earlier, sceptical of my chances of living long, a life insurance company had demanded extra premiums. My family history had given them no cause for confidence, but I am still alive today on the wrong side of seventy-seven, and even now quite enjoy filling my fountain pen with ink and pages with my writing.

Many of our venerated litterateurs have of late continued to live beyond seventy. Still they could not be present at the fiftieth anniversary of their memorable works, for many of them did not exactly begin their literary journeys when still young.

The word my mother would use when particularly irritated with me refers to someone who has ripened early. This precociousness is both my strength and weakness. I was thirteen when my father died unexpectedly in Howrah in 1947. A cruel battle for survival started immediately afterwards. I began to earn from writing at the age of seventeen. I was first published in the Sunday section of *Anandabazar Patrika* in December 1950, and the relationship has continued over subsequent decades. The magazine *Desh*, published by the same group—it, too, was born in 1933—has been my companion in creation since 1954. Becoming famous early is not always good for a writer's physical and mental health. It has led to no little trouble, but finally it has yielded a pleasant outcome—it has enabled my physical presence at the celebration of fifty years of *Chowringhee*.

What can I say on this occasion that has not been said already? What I have experienced personally over this long period of time is that the pilgrimage of a writer with limited financial means is especially lonely here in Bengal. Those who gain unexpected recognition for their very first step in the world of literature after withstanding all manner of hardship in life are both fortunate and unfortunate. There is the apprehension of losing something after it has been gained. My first book, *Kato Ajanare*, received the kind indulgence of readers as soon as it was published. I had mailed a copy of the book to the respected writer Annadashankar Roy, who wrote back with his blessings, 'May the first success of your life not be your last.'

At about the same time, those who ruthlessly controlled the ups and downs of the stock market of Bengali literature put their foot down. They paid no heed to my youth and my relentless struggle for survival. Deeply concerned by the sudden and unexpected success of an unknown, almost unidentified, young writer, they issued a fatwa—this lawyer's clerk may have won a lottery by cashing in on his own experience, but Barrister Barwell's babu was 'nothing more than a one-book author'.

It was amidst great anxiety that I embarked on gathering the ingredients for *Chowringhee*. My only prayer to God then was: I don't seek money, I don't seek recognition, I don't even seek a long life, only free me from the agony of being a one-book author.

I bow to the Almighty a thousand times—*Chowringhee* did in fact release me from this stigma. But I have never been free of uncertainty, loneliness and worry. Readers of various languages from different parts of India, beyond the borders of Bengal, have encouraged me and reassured me, and with my mother's benediction I feel as though I have somehow escaped an untimely death. I bow today to all these well-wishers who have read my books, familiar faces and strangers alike. To them I want to say that writers have no fixed address, every reader in every language is someone I call my own. My mother would laughingly say, 'Your readers in Bangla only write long letters to you, but the unknown reader in Hindi who has not revealed his address and yet sent you sweets from Agra by registered post is actually your best reader.'

That I had managed to even get on the train in this one life and then halt at every station from Howrah all the way to Asansol was no small gift for a writer like me. This was what I had told myself. Then a young reader translated *Chowringhee* into English on his own initiative; Sudhangshu Babu stepped up to offer him a small fee, but that was as far as matters progressed. A long time passed this way, which can be attributed to the unforgivable self-respect or impudence of Bengali readers—if anyone needs anything of mine, they must come to me; a writer from Bengal, be they ever so significant, will never knock on anyone's door.

Encouraged by the world-famous writer Vikram Seth, the Penguin India train, even though delayed, finally took me from Asansol to Delhi, and from there to all the cities of the new India, to the homes of readers who love books written in English. And then across the seas to England, where Atlantic Books took it to different cities. After this, Italy. Then France, Spain, and, the source of greatest joy, China. For modern Indian literature to reach China on the Beijing Express is a matter of distinct happiness. It was so many years ago, in the thirties of the past century, that Rabindranath Tagore arrived in Shanghai with his friends. I have long been interested in China. Ever since the Buddhist era, China has been keen on learning about the literature of India, some of which has to do with the all-but-forgotten Bengali writer Atish Dipankar. I have even written a book on the subject. But today's China has turned away from our contemporary literature. We don't keep ourselves informed of Chinese literary trends either. Our only hope is the immortal bridge named Tagore—even today we are far too dependent on him.

People talk too much as they grow old—it is this dread that makes me want to apply the brakes well in time. The novel that is being celebrated today has given me a great deal.

This day, 10 June 1962, is memorable in my life for another reason as well. I was married on the day *Chowringhee* was first published. It was only after assuring myself that the book was ready that I went to the venue of the wedding in Uttarpara in the evening. Had Bandana been alive, we would also have celebrated our fiftieth wedding anniversary today. But as I said, the whims of the Almighty have always filled my personal life, intellectual life and literary life with loneliness. Not all my efforts have enabled me to exercise control over this state of affairs. But today I surrender to all of you; now that I am being held prisoner by your love, this exhausted writer is unconditionally putting his hands up after all these years.

Accept me as I am, with all my flaws and weaknesses. I beg you, do not reject me on this momentous occasion.

Parental Veto: From Binodini to the Emperor and the Beauty

IN 2015, I HAD THE OPPORTUNITY TO BE PRESENT AT THE LAUNCH of the memoir of a stage enchantress. It was after a long time that a heroine of Bengali theatre had picked up the pen. She had disappeared from view for several years before this, which was why there were a large number of people eager to catch a glimpse of her at the auditorium in Chowringhee.

The night-flowering jasmine, the precious shefali flower of the late evening who lit up the stage had originally been named Arati Das. The long-standing effect she used to have on the human pulse as the goddess who had captured the heart of the metropolis from the unique restaurant named Firpo's, just a stone's throw from the Rotary Club auditorium, is unlikely to be repeated. Before saying a few words about her, I conveyed my heartfelt welcome to Shefali the writer, and, using the words of one of the finest poets of this city, asked, 'Where were you all this time?'

Softly and pleasantly she answered, 'I have been wherever God in all his wisdom has wanted me to be.'

As a matter of fact, members of the new generation were completely unaware that the queen of cabaret in the twentieth century was still living in Calcutta despite the number of times the hemlock of humiliation had been forced down her throat.

It seems to me that this is the inevitable fate of many stage actresses in this wretched country. They light up the theatre briefly with the flame of their appealing youthfulness, providing short-lived pleasure to their audiences. Passion overflows at the bar, but the only payment made is with the eyes. Their fame is never permanent. Even the firefly has not been blessed with a long life by the whimsical creator. Clouds of forgetfulness arrive quickly to draw a shroud over all the suffering. This is the way of the pleasure-giving world of theatre in Bengal. No one expects the enchantress to be part of long-lasting happiness, nor do the enchantresses themselves expect it.

It is our fortune, however, that although Shefali, the empress of the evening dance, disappeared from the limelight, she survived the ordeal by fire that cruel life put her through, and could be present at the launch of her book. After baring her secrets night after night at Firpo's, she was driven by necessity to move to the stage, where she shook its very foundations and won the hearts of theatre-lovers.

I saw her up close during the staging of my own novel. Her booming popularity led many star actors and actresses, and even the writer, to wonder who the main attraction of the play *Chowringhee* being staged at Biswaroopa was.

That was a time when the juggernaut that was *Chowringhee* was racing towards its thousandth night on stage, leaving all past achievements by the wayside. The sight of hundreds of thousands of theatre-lovers thronging the auditorium left some people delighted, while others were distraught at the thought of the dwindling gap between the cabaret hall and the theatre hall which would ruin the nation. Seeing the continuous stream of 'full houses' no one would have guessed that the days of the theatre in Bengal, a century-old tradition, were numbered, that a time would soon come when there would be no such thing as a neighbourhood of theatre halls, once the envy of theatre-lovers all over India, in Calcutta.

The theatres have closed now, audiences are flocking to multiplexes for newer pleasures, but many of the actors and actresses from the forgotten days remain alive with all their memories. This is not an accurate description, though, for a number of them are actually struggling for survival.

As it happens, Shefali was involved with the dramatized versions of two of my novels, *Chowringhee* and *Samrat O Sundari*. A third was added to this list, thanks to the chief priest of all our joyous rituals, Satyajit Ray. Firpo's has come and gone, but the dance scene set in Firpo's in the film version of my novel *Seemabaddha—Company Limited*—is not lost. And that was how the Bengali dancer, who could neither be a mother nor a daughter to anyone, claimed a permanent spot, virtually uninvited, in the hearts of several generations of post-sundown pleasure-seekers.

In this context, let me say a few things about my family connections with the actresses, singers, dancers and enchantresses of the Bengali stage of a hundred years ago. Towards the end of the nineteenth century in Purulia district, after losing his own father at an early age, my orphaned father, Haripada Mukhopadhyay, took shelter in his maternal uncle's home in Gobordanga. Subsequently he came into the company of the renowned playwright and actor Jogeshchandra Chowdhury and was attracted to the world of theatre. The dramatist of the well-known play *Sitla*, Jogeshchandra used to teach at Gobordanga School at one time. I was still young when I learnt of my father's role as a playwright. The stories I heard then, and those that I read later about Kohinoor Theatre, embedded themselves in my mind. Even in the twilight of my life, they have not been wiped out entirely.

My father did not reveal much about these matters. Whatever I had learnt was from my mother and from my stepbrother Gaurishankar. Those old stories floated up before my eyes when I went to the launch of Shefali's book. Bangla theatre is not all that old—the National Theatre was established in 1872. Interestingly, the theatre that the British ran before this in Calcutta was named Chowringhee, and Prince Dwarakanath Tagore was personally involved with its founding and ownership. It burnt to the ground in 1839. Thoughts of Prince Dwarakanath Tagore's Chowringhee Theatre came unbidden to my mind when I was collecting information for my novel of the same name.

One of my teachers, Professor Ajitkumar Ghosh, who used to research the history of Bengali theatre assiduously, would occasionally tell us stories about Binodini and Star Theatre. The address of the original Star Theatre was 68, Beadon Street—the building was demolished during the construction of Chittaranjan Avenue. Star Theatre was founded by the wealthy Marwari Gurmukh Rai Mushardi, who was besotted after watching Binodini on stage. His offer to Girish Ghosh to set up a theatre had a difficult condition—the beautiful Binodini must become his mistress. It is said that Binodini agreed to this indecent proposition for the sake of a new theatre, which was to be named for her.

The land at 68, Beadon Street was leased and a theatre was built with Gurmukh Rai's money and under Girish Ghosh's supervision, but at the last moment the cunning authorities refused to name it for Binodini on the grounds that a public theatre could not carry the name of a prostituted woman.

Star Theatre begin its journey on 21 July 1883 with the play *Dokhhojoggo* written by Girish Ghosh. My mother knew by heart the names of all of his plays that were staged there over the next six months. Because of illness, Gurmukh Rai eventually sold Star to a group of four theatre professionals for just Rs 11,000. Star Theatre ran at its original location for four more years after this. Binodini did not sever her relationship with Star, and Girish Chandra Ghosh remained the person in charge. His new play *Chaitanyalila* was a sensation—with Binodini as Nemai and Banbiharini as Netai. On the evening of 21 September 1884, Ramakrishna Paramhansa personally went to see the play and, overwhelmed, gave his heartfelt blessings to Binodini. According to stories told by our elders, after suffering constant humiliation, Binodini abandoned theatre on New Year's Day in 1887 and was never seen on the Calcutta stage again.

Some years later, the millionaire Motilal Seal's worthy descendant Gopal Lal Seal felt he was slighted during his visit to Star Theatre and proceeded to buy the land on which it stood at 68, Beadon Street. The owners gave up the theatre for a sum of Rs 30,000, but they did not relinquish the name Star Theatre.

The theatre that Gopal Lal Seal started was named Emerald Theatre. Established in 1887, its lifespan extended to 23 February 1896. It was in this Emerald Theatre that he first made arrangements for the use of imported electric lights. It is said that Seal lured Girish Ghosh into a five-year contract with a fat salary and bonus—Rs 350 a month and Rs 20,000, respectively. Girish Ghosh took over as manager of Emerald Theatre on 19 November 1987, and occupied the post for some time.

Soon after the actor Ardhendushekhar Mustafi took over as manager of the Emerald. He was probably a favourite of my father's, who named my younger brother Ardhendu after him.

Bengali theatre has been riddled by financial crises and management problems from its birth. And, along with these, litigation of various kinds. It was thanks to legal tangles that the ownership of Emerald Theatre passed to Benarasi Das, the owner of B.D. Company. Thereafter the theatre was rented out—first to City Theatre, and then, later, to Classic Theatre.

Classic Theatre was established on 16 April 1897, and was associated with Amarendra Dutta. Despite his enormous talent, he could not hold on to Classic. In spite of creating history several times, the building went on the block, and was purchased in an auction for Rs 1,60,000 by the feudal landlord Sarat Kumar Roy, who established Kohinoor Theatre. It was this same theatre with which my father, Haripada Mukherjee, became associated at a rather tender age.

Girish Ghosh had joined Kohinoor at a monthly salary of Rs 500 and a bonus of Rs 10,000. Two of Star's actresses featured in the performance on the very first night—Tinkori and Tarasundari. Re 1 tickets were sold on the black market for Rs 3 that evening. But Sarat Kumar Roy died just four months later, in December 1907, whereupon his younger brother Sisir Kumar Roy assumed responsibility of the theatre.

According to the stories that circulated in our family, several plays were staged successfully in 1908. Among them was Khirodprasad Vidyavinod's *Ashok*, whose main attractions were the renowned Dani Babu as Ashok, Tinkori as Dharini, and Promodasundari as Kunal. Girish Chandra Ghosh was not keeping well at the time, and could not come to the theatre regularly. Irked, the owner stopped his salary, but Girish Ghosh took him to court, won the case and extracted both the salary and the bonus due to him. That same year he left Kohinoor along with Dani, his son, and joined Minerva Theatre.

I believe my father joined the fold of Kohinoor in 1909; he was still absurdly young when his play *Rani Durgaboti* was selected to be staged. Its subject was the valiant struggle waged by Queen Durgaboti of Garmandal and King Baj Bahadur of Malav to protect their kingdoms from the Mughal emperor Akbar, which ended in their defeat and Durgaboti's suicide on the battlefield. The play premiered at the 68, Beadon Street auditorium on 25 December 1909. There was tremendous excitement all over the city for Promodasundari appeared on stage astride a horse as Queen Durgaboti. The scene featuring a roaring waterfall stunned the connoisseurs among the audience.

Sisir Kumar Roy suggested that the young dramatist next write a play based on the life of the sage Dadhichi. The play was written speedily, but a sudden turn in the fortunes of the owner of Kohinoor Theatre prevented its production. Meanwhile, the great thespian Girish Chandra Ghosh died on 9 February 1912. It is said that a dispute arose between Sisir Kumar Roy and his elder brother Sarat Kumar's widow, and a growing burden of debt led to Kohinoor Theatre being auctioned off. The wealthy Manmohan Pandey purchased it for Rs 1,11,000, and renamed it Manmohan Theatre. Having squandered a good deal of time on the theatre, the impoverished Haripada Mukherjee, BSc, BL, went back to the legal profession and concentrated on making a living.

Various stories about Promodasundari and Binodini lived on in our family for many years, however, along with anecdotes about Girish Chandra Ghosh, Dwijendralal Roy and Khirodprasad Vidyavinod. A number of books bearing their signatures were carefully preserved in our home in Howrah. Strangely enough, *Rani Durgaboti* survived for many years among Bengal's sophisticated theatre circles in the form of a bestselling book with several editions.

Having wasted so many valuable years of his life on the theatre, Haripada Mukherjee was opposed to any of his children joining this field or taking up literature. But playwrights and actors had free access to our house, and numerous unpublicized stories circulated about the actresses of that era, especially Binodini and Promodasundari. The adults did not share these stories in my presence, but as I prepared their tobacco out of sight, on my father's instructions, I grew up eavesdropping on many a thrilling tale.

When I was a student of class four in 1941, the news of Binodini's death reached our drawing room too. My father used to say the theatre was not meant for those who did not have unlimited family wealth, which was why my first published piece in the school magazine did not please him at all.

My mother, however, believed in destiny, and was aware that my horoscope indicated success for me in the same field as my father's, and made frequent references to his accomplishments being repeated by his offspring. In happier times, she had assumed that I too would bring glory to the family as a lawyer. But due to a cruel turn of fate, I had to give up my education on my father's untimely death and become a lawyer's clerk, or what was, in the parlance of the Calcutta High Court, a barrister's babu. The barrister in question was Noel Frederick Barwell, the last British barrister at the Calcutta High Court.

My mockery of an existence shifted to the areas in and around the High Court in 1951. By then Noel Barwell had dispatched his wife Marianne to Ranikhet, wound up his household, and moved to the historic Spence's Hotel in Wellesley Place, north of the Raj Bhavan, at a monthly rent of Rs 700. The reputation of this hotel at the time was no less than that of the Great Eastern Hotel just a few yards away. The British still considered it the oldest hotel in the Orient, established in 1820. Wellesley Place was subsequently renamed Red Cross Place.

As I was saying, one thing leads to another. Had I not been Mr Barwell's 'babu', it wouldn't have been possible for me to have written *Kato Ajanare*. Nor would I have succeeded in writing

Chowringhee and erasing the stigma of being a one-book author had it not been for easy access to various rooms in Spence's Hotel.

Foreign cabaret dancers ruled over the evening sessions at Spence's Hotel at the time. Connoisseurs of alcohol would visit the place every evening for a brief spell of peace. Being privy to these sights was a matter of rare fortune for me. The permanent as well as temporary employees of Spence's had drawn into their fold the young man of seventeen who commuted from Howrah. I was allowed to go anywhere I wanted, from the reception desk to the kitchen, from the pantry to the dance floor.

The liftmen would unquestioningly take me up to the roof terrace where there were several wooden cubicles with asbestos roofs. Besides the employees, the musicians, crooners and dancers also lived in these rooms. After labouring all afternoon and evening, they had to gather the energy to satisfy some of the lustful guests through the night.

It was here that I had the unexpected opportunity of consorting closely with dancers and singers. Beautiful women from India and other countries sunbathed in light gowns with no desire to undress fully. To preserve their beauty, they applied all kinds of creams and lotions to their bodies while soaking in the mild sunshine, and chatted with me all the while. Their stories originated in West Asia or Egypt, Italy or Hungary. They were kindness incarnate, often breaking off slabs of imported chocolate for me, and even taking their scissors to my hair at times to save me the expense of getting a haircut.

I was young then, and inexperienced to boot, but I was fortunate enough to discover a hitherto undiscovered world. For a callow youth from a blind lane in Howrah, this was the ultimate gift. *Chowringhee* would never have seen the light of day had Mr Barwell not chosen to stay in Spence's Hotel for months on end.

What I have not dared to say all this while is that no one could have imagined that an impoverished young man who had never spent a single night in a five-star hotel would nevertheless write a novel about a hotel that would attract the attention of the world. This wondrous journey beyond India's shores began in England, and then spread to France, Italy, Spain, Russia, and elsewhere. The entire world came to love the scantily dressed dancer Connie. But no matter how many nights one watched Connie and her dwarf associate Lambreta perform in the cabaret, it was impossible to truly know who they were. For this it was necessary to visit the roof terrace of Spence's Hotel—which, of course, was forbidden to outsiders.

While a student at Vivekananda Institute, I had heard many stories of the faith that the heroines of the Bengali stage reposed in Ramakrishna. It wasn't just Girishchandra Ghosh's name that was far from unfamiliar to me when in school, but also those of, among others, Binodini, Promodasundari, Manodasundari, Tarasundari, Neerasundari, Tinkori, Kusumkumari, Golapsundari and Tukomoni.

Among them Binodini, Tinkori and Tarasundari remain alive in people's memories to some extent. Binodini is renowned for her memoir *My Story*. It appeared for the first time in the Bengali year 1319, within three years of my father's *Durgaboti* being staged. I, however, read it much later, by which time my first book, *Kato Ajanare*, had already been published. But well before this, I had heard stories in the drawing room at home about how the long-suffering Binodini had spent the final years of her life on the pavement outside Star Theatre, with not even the gatemen being aware of the extraordinary sacrifice she had made to ensure that the theatre was established.

There was a time when devotees of Ramakrishna had memorized the final words of Binodini's autobiography. 'I have no family, I am reviled, rejected by society, a woman in prostitution, there is no one I can open my heart to, no one to listen. What does the tainted woman have besides her taint?' Many nuggets about the young and lascivious Gurmukh Rai circulated afterwards. Upon his father's death he had come into enormous wealth at the age of eighteen. Binodini was dangled as a bait to extract money from him to run the theatre. Subsequently, Gurmukh Rai sold the theatre under pressure from his family and went away to Kashi to live among hermits. He died at just twenty-two in 1886.

My attention was also drawn to the considerable success enjoyed by two other women whose names were linked with Swami Vivekananda's when he was away from home. He was particularly interested in both of them, and had even immortalized them by writing about them. These two beautiful French women were Sarah Bernhardt and Emma Colvey.

It would be no exaggeration to state that Emma Colvey was the finest opera singer of modern times. As Vivekananda himself wrote, 'Her singing has earned so much appreciation that her annual income runs to three hundred thousand or four hundred thousand rupees, and all from singing.' As for Sarah Bernhardt, she was the world's most discussed empress of the stage in her era. Being French, both women were completely unfamiliar with the English language, and yet earned hundreds of thousands of dollars on their tours of England and America.

These enchantresses of the stage had the most unusual lives. Sarah Bernhardt continues to be the queen of the hearts of people around the world on account of her dedicated pursuit of her craft and her belief in God. Her figure, her voice, her divine acting skills and her superhuman work ethic had enabled her to scale the peaks of acknowledgement, respect and success. I went to great trouble to get hold of her memoir, *My Double Life*, from abroad and have read it several times, only to be astonished afresh every time.

According to *Sarah Bernhardt: The Art of High Drama*, an illustrated book published by Yale University, the name Sarah Bernhardt has become 'synonymous with acting'. 'She was an icon of French nationalism, a target of both admiration and scorn, an artist and sculptor, and a trendsetting avatar of style.' Sarah Marie Henrietta Bernhardt was an illegitimate child. The profession that her mother had taken up when seeking her fortune in Paris was technically that of a 'demi-monde'. According to the dictionary, the word doesn't exactly refer to a woman in prostitution, but to someone who is engaged in relationships with the rich, occupying the more debased rungs of society. In 1896, Swami Vivekananda watched Sarah Bernhardt perform on the stage in America and was mesmerized. I have chronicled her incredible life in my book *Ashchorjo Vivekananda*.

She did not hesitate to form sexual relationships with many an individual in the course of her conquest of the world. Among her famous lovers were the former Prince of Wales Albert Edward, the French writer Victor Hugo, and the artists Gustave Dore, Alfred Stevens and Georges Clairin.

Sara Bernhardt's slim feminine figure was a wonder of the world, but she also achieved unparalleled success playing male characters on stage. She was famous too for falling in love with the men, both on and off stage, who were besotted with her. It was said that she was the greatest actress of all time when it came to death scenes—she is believed to have died on stage at least ten thousand times. Additionally, alongside the actress Sarah Bernhardt, there was the painter and sculptor Sarah Bernhardt too. She would hold exhibitions of her art in every city she visited to act on stage.

Sarah Bernhardt died on 26 March 1923. Three days later, a million men and women walked on the avenues of Paris to pay their last respects to their favourite actress.

The other woman I mentioned was, of course, the beautiful singer Emma Colvey. She too was an admirer of Swami Vivekananda's, and went with him on a tour of several countries aboard a special train. After his death, she came to Calcutta to meet his mother and visited Vivekananda's monastery at Belur as well.

Both these women went from being ordinary individuals to extraordinary personages and became immensely wealthy, but still in their final years, they were forced to depend on others.

The lives of these enchantresses from the West, Sarah Bernhardt and Emma Colvey, will be talked about for a long time. But Shefali, our heroine of contemporary times, is no less a subject of wonder. Her memoirs have enriched Bengali literature with greater diversity. If the world of cinema here becomes more significant, Shefali of the evening will become the subject of a film one day, through which viewers around the world will learn how a young refugee girl from East Pakistan waged a war against fate to win over a heartless metropolis. This accomplishment is by no means inferior to Binodini's. If Shefali had been a foreigner, a museum would have been built to house the objects she used.

Many memorable spots in the city of Calcutta have lost their war against time and vanished in the past fifty years—the living no longer have any memories of Peliti and Firpo's restaurants, no one will remember where Biswaroopa Theatre was located or the skirmishes at Circarena Theatre for a glimpse of Miss Shefali. Nor should anyone be expected to recall how the backdrop for *Chowringhee* was provided by the affection and indulgence of Spence's Hotel.

With Uttam Kumar in the lead role, the film version of *Chowringhee* became vastly popular. I was genuinely surprised to learn that the possibility of its being turned into a play existed. But Rashbehari Sarkar, the indefatigable cornerstone of Biswaroopa Theatre was adamant and took the plunge. The first performance took place on 25 September 1971, and the final one on 1 July 1973. By a quirk of fate, I became involved with the theatre despite my father expressly forbidding it.

The clever, dexterous use of cabaret dances in the play made Rashbehari Sarkar's venture enormously successful, and brought fame to Shefali. A new phrase was coined at this time—the clothing revolution. Connie would divest herself of most of her clothing on stage, and finally dance in a bikini. This was a new experience for me—the dark side of the stage which reminded me that little had changed in the theatre in a hundred years, especially the cruelty of some men. I felt a strong urge to write about the activities of the players on and off stage.

I am frequently reminded nowadays of the horoscope that my mother had preserved, which said that her offspring would be attracted to the same profession as his father, and one thing would lead to another. Otherwise why would the irony of fate force the son of a lawyer to start his life as a legal clerk? Why would this clerk's employer choose to live in Spence's Hotel and open the doors to his clerk's writing *Chowringhee*? It didn't end there. Why would the same novel arrive at Biswaroopa Theatre and crown the dancer Shefali for a thousand performances? Why would the son of Haripada Mukherjee, the dramatist of Kohinoor Theatre, get involved with the theatre all these years later, and protest against the amassed injustice of a hundred years and speak up against corruption on the stage with the novel *Samrat O Sundari*?

Who'd have thought that my novel would elevate Shefali the dancer to Shefali the actress? She has overcome all obstacles and achieved the pinnacle of success. What had been unimaginable became real on the Circarena stage—a memorable achievement in the history of Indian theatre—1,200 consecutive performances of a single play. Shefali conquered. And then she demonstrated the courage to write about her life when she is in its twilight.

There has not been such an audacious venture in Bengali publishing since Binodini's memoir. I pray for Shefali's success with this book. As the descendant of a near-forgotten dramatist of nearly a hundred years ago, I feel unbounded joy.

Arriving at Platform No. 80

HAVING PASSED MANY A STATION, JUNCTION AND SIGNAL, THE train of my life finally entered Platform No. 80 on 7 December 2014. In terms of heredity this was a big achievement, for my father did not live to see sixty, while his father had an even shorter life, forcing his orphaned son to grow up as part of someone else's family. My father won scholarships and medals in every examination from the Entrance to BSc with his own talent and effort. The lack of money deprived me of the loving touch of a university in the first phase of my life, though, many years later, I did acquire a BA degree through the back door, thanks to Bangabasi Evening College.

I have been told there is no need to be an octogenarian to leave a mark on this world. Our Swami Vivekananda did not make it to the other side of forty. There is no cause-and-effect relationship between age and accomplishment. Later in life I did manage to evade various obstacles and overcome family tradition and cruise past the milestones of fifty and sixty. And then something interesting happened another twelve years later, at the age associated in the Bengali language with senescence. On 7 December that year, Anil Biswas, a public leader with a sense of humour, rang me from the CPI(M) head office in Alimuddin Street. 'You will have to be patient for a year, people will try to belittle you as senile, but only for a year. Everything will become normal afterwards.'

I adjusted to being seventy-two, or senile in Bangla, for an entire year, making no loose statement, and recalling what the late writer Bimal Mitra had said, 'It's not just blood pressure and diabetes, but also chattering away for no good reason and giving unending advice to young people that is the most dangerous symptom and disease of old age.'

Bimal Mitra used to say, 'Youth is the only stage of life that matters in our country, it is this age that is feted and garlanded, for old age is rare here, you will not see too many people of advanced years on the streets.' It's different in the West, although their ability to work is diminished, the power of their accumulated wealth goes a long way, and besides, the old have extracted a number of concessions from the government—bus concessions, train concessions, plane concessions, tax concessions, even laundry concessions. The more the ranks of old people swell in this country, the more the demand for such benefits will rise, and as this continues, the earth will eventually bend under the weight of the aged. The social equilibrium of the world will also come under pressure from the burden of those people who have not the ability to earn but a disproportionate ability to spend. The thinkers and intellectuals entrusted with the task of running the country have considered the arguments of those opposed to old age but still wish to provide additional benefits to senior citizens. The age of eighty is a significant milestone for them. And so, having arrived at eighty myself, I hereby declare that everyone must arrive here for maximum happiness.

Being greedy and needlessly inquisitive about the future does not suit my advanced years. It is far more becoming to look into the rear-view mirror and recall the past. I was born in the final month of 1933 in Bongram, where Bibhutibhushan Bandyopadhyay's immortal novel *Pather Panchali* is set. The country was not independent yet, but it was a glorious time for Bangla writing. It is thrilling to recount the names of those engaged in serving the goddess of literature at the time. I take some pleasure in the fact that Rabindranath Tagore himself was at his zenith; Kazi Nazrul was still a creative force. That revered figure of storytelling, Saratchandra Chattopadhyay, was busy conquering India. Across the river Ichhamati that flows past Bongram, the village where I was born, Bibhutibhushan was on his way to international recognition. Even if the golden age of Bangla literature had not begun yet, its citizens had already announced their presence on the literary stage. The other two Bandyopadhyays—Tarashankar and Manik—were in the process of assuming command of their triumphant chariots. Another Bandyopadhyay—Saradindu—had also appeared on the scene.

A grand festival of Bangla letters was about to start, graced by the presence of so many more memorable writers—Abanindranath Tagore, Bimal Mitra, Banaphool, Premendra Mitra, Sailajananda Mukhopadhyay, Shibram Chakraborty, Bibhutibhushan Mukhopadhyay, Achintya Kumar Sengupta, Parasuram. We also revere those essayists who were already born by then—Dineshchandra Sen, Sunitikumar Chattopadhyay, Jadunath Sarkar, Romesh Chandra Majumdar, Niharranjan Roy, and, undoubtedly, Acharya Prafullachandra Roy.

I was five when Saratchandra passed away. My father, a legal practitioner, had arrived with his family in search of a fortune in the very same Howrah that Saratchandra had left a few years earlier. When 'Rabi the sun' set forever, I was a student of class four in Howrah District School. The masses streamed towards his home in Jorasanko that day, but I was not able to find my way to Calcutta all by myself that day. It is my lifelong regret that only a small miscalculation has kept me from saying I have seen Rabindranath Tagore.

The Second World War and the presence of the military made it a difficult time. Many schools were shut down so they could be converted into barracks for the military and the paramilitary. I was forced to leave the district school and join Vivekananda Institution nearby. Even though Rabindranath Tagore had slipped out of my grasp, I found Swami Vivekananda within reach, for many of the teachers were bachelors and completely taken with him. My father, initially the playwright and later the lawyer for Kohinoor Theatre still held Girish Ghosh and Michael Madhusudan Dutt close to his heart. He did not remotely encourage his eldest son by his second wife to participate in literary activities. When I was in class eight, he expressed his annoyance at one of my pieces appearing in the school magazine, telling me to focus on mathematics instead of wasting my time on useless things.

There was, admittedly, plenty of reason for this. Despite having acquired some fame in his youth as the playwright for Kohinoor Theatre on Beadon Street, my father considered it a waste of time that had delayed progress in his legal career. He did not wish any of his children to be afflicted with literary fever. However, the headmaster of my school, Sudhangshushekhar Bhattacharya, was singing a different tune. His invitation and encouragement led me to compose a belles lettre in secret. At that time my only enthusiastic fellow traveller in Chowdhurybagan on my literary journey was my next-door neighbour Badal Chandra Bose, a committed bachelor who was devoted to his mother, and who worked as a stenographer at Kalamazoo & Co. He had secretly written the opening paragraph of my essay 'Race of Penpushers'. I did not care for it at all; I had meant to begin with a glittering quotation from Rabi Thakur himself, but Badal Kaku had not read much of

Tagore. A firm believer in taking a dip in the Ganga every day, he began the essay thus. 'Smearing his body with oil by the Ganga, the head clerk of Gillander & Co. exclaimed one day, "This race of penpushers will never amount to anything."' Strangely, everyone at the literary society meeting in school liked the essay very much. The headmaster said, 'Write boldly what you have seen for yourself without bothering about anyone. It is far better to be original than to be polished.'

This advice stood me in good stead later in life. It was how, in my first novel, I was able to give equal space to the British barrister and the grim-faced judge as well as the barrister's and lawyers' clerks who occupied the benches in front of the bar library at the High Court. My headmaster used to say, 'When plain muri is converted into spicy moshlamuri in the seller's tin container, its price increases manifold. Read Vivekananda, you will not only grasp all there is to know, but also find a path for yourself through the inaccessible forest of literature.'

Swami Vivekananda repeatedly prescribed holding your head high all the time. Why then have I had to pass so much of my life with my eyes on the ground? The reason is possibly my mother Abhayarani's father, Khirode Banerjee. He used to have a reasonably good job at a British merchant firm in Dalhousie, but when a young Englishman tried to humiliate him, my grandfather delivered a stinging slap on his face and resigned. Many praised him for holding his head high, but my mother's father and his daughter were cast adrift. My mother was extraordinarily beautiful, but her father's poverty meant she had to become the second wife of a man whose eldest daughter by his first wife—deceased by then—was already married. It wasn't only her fate that was changed by her wedding but also her name—Gauri—for it was what her husband's eldest son by his first wife was named. She was renamed Abhaya—I do not know who chose the new name, but whoever it was seemed to have accurately anticipated her new role as a dispenser of courage.

Khirode Banerjee of Nokphool village visited his daughter Abhaya's newborn son in Bongram. His dearest daughter was sobbing her heart out in the labour room. Everyone was ruing the birth of such a dark-skinned boy from the womb of such a fair-skinned mother. Her father had brought pink German powder to lighten the complexion of the newborn. He told his daughter, 'Don't be upset, Abi, your son will grow up to be another Ashutosh Mukhujje.'

My mother took her father's prediction very seriously. Ashutosh Mukherjee was a fount of knowledge, a judge, the recipient of a knighthood, the vice chancellor of Calcutta University. I realized at a very early age that amidst all her suffering my mother was building her hopes around me. In time I discovered that Ashutosh Mukherjee was a redoubtable mathematician. After I had taken my mathematics test in the half-yearly examination that year, my father complied with my mother's insistent request to estimate my marks, and concluded that I was likely to score between 80 and 86. When the results came out, I had scored 12. The identity of the person responsible for this catastrophic evaluation of my mathematical prowess is still wrapped in mystery. But to be honest my embarrassing performance in mathematics every year was a source of great anguish for my mother.

Still, the affectionate headmaster Sudhangshushekhar Bhattacharya reposed great faith in me. He advised me to come up with and write about things that would stun readers. But none of this materialized, for about five months before India became independent, my father passed away on a curfewed night, casting my mother and his eight children adrift on the high seas, as it were. I still do not entirely understand how my mother saved all of us, living in a rented house with nothing but a couple of life insurance payouts as her resources. When I was sixteen, my mother informed me that unless I could start earning some money in two or three months, starvation was inevitable.

I knew no one in Calcutta, and I was a minor to boot. I wandered about in Dalhousie all day near the merchant offices, but the longer I wandered, the hungrier I got. At that time the old man in charge of dispensing drinking water on behalf of the Kashi Vishwanath Seva Samiti in Curzon Park near Dharmatala sometimes handed out pieces of batasha if he was genially disposed towards you. A stranger gave me useful advice—drinking enormous quantities of free water along with batasha or some muri could effectively kill hunger pangs.

Such priceless learnings courtesy of strangers proved greatly beneficial later, during my literary life. 'Keep going, do not stop,' great men have advised. This is especially valuable counsel. Unexpected encounters lead to friendships and, sometimes, small opportunities for earning too. They also provide repeated evidence that this world is not yet devoid of love. Still, whenever I was assailed by doubts, I would go up to the statues of famous men—the Maharaja of Darbhanga, the founder of Chartered Bank, James Wilson, Sir Hariram Goenka, and many others. If you spoke to them with reverence, they responded in their own languages to penniless young jobseekers. All of this proved immensely useful.

I was tempted to believe much of the things they said, but many warned me that times had changed. One's own efforts alone could no longer change one's fortunes; a change of politics was also necessary. But I had no time to ponder over any of this, I had to earn money.

Did that mean I couldn't afford any personal luxuries? Not at all.

Books and chilled water were freely available in the former USIS Library in Esplanade Mansion. Arriving there one day with a parched throat, I leafed through an English book and wrote an article about what I had read. Then, to save on postage, I trudged northwards to the old office of *Anandabazar Patrika* on Burman Street near the fruit market of Chitpore. And, how strange, the article was published in the Sunday section of *Anandabazar Patrika*. I even received a payment of Rs 10 by money order. All of this occurred more than six decades ago, when the possibility of earning so much on the strength of my pen kept me awake at night.

Later, though, I had to toss my dreams of being a writer in the wastepaper basket, and learn shorthand. The headmaster of Vivekananda School at the time took pity on me and gave me a job as a teacher. Eventually I acquired the rare honour of being the last clerk to the last English barrister of the Calcutta Hight Court, Noel Frederick Barwell.

The time I spent in Barwell's company is the most memorable of my life. Under the loving protection of an extraordinary man, I found the keys to an incredible world, without which my tragic life would have remained incomplete. There was a time when his health had become a matter of concern for us. Knowing full well that I couldn't afford a single day of unemployment, it was he who found me a job with the Bengal Chamber of Commerce on the understanding that I would work for him every evening. But those pleasant days did not last long. In 1953 Mr Barwell went to Madras on a case and fell ill in the courtroom. And the final horrifying telegram arrived in Calcutta: He had died in Madras.

But even the memories of such a man are bound to fade one day. Perhaps a day will come when I myself will not believe that this compassionate foreigner had told me, 'Never forget that you're an exceptional person.'

Unable to find any other way to preserve his memory, I tried to arrange for a road in Calcutta to be named after him. I didn't succeed, for no one in independent India was enthusiastic about honouring an Englishman. In the end I remembered that I had inherited from my father the right to be a writer, and writing involved no expenditure. So one day I got down in secret to recording my remarkable experiences with Mr Barwell. Of course, the piece already published in *Anandabazar Patrika* gave me the courage to embark on this journey.

I have passed a long time in the field of literature since then. Bimal Mitra used to say that this line of work is most unreasonable; once you have written something good, there's no escape. Unless you can write progressively better, disgrace is inevitable. The more readers get, the more they want. What he also said in addition to this is unforgettable. 'The Bengali writer's life is like a life-insurance policy, what is owed will not be calculated before death. The real money only comes posthumously; in their lifetime the writer receives nothing but a food allowance. Writing is the only profession that revives the creator after their death. Look around you: It is the dead who have reigned imperiously over most of Bangla literature since the beginning of the twentieth century.'

To learn how painful and agonizing it is to start early and live a long time, all you have to do is ask a writer who has had a long life. And yet to arrive able-bodied at eighty with a pen in hand, having overcome obstacles, fame, criticism, expectations and disappointments is a unique experience. It might even cause unmitigated happiness.

If you were to ask what the writer's greatest joy is, I would have no hesitation in stating that it is the love of readers. No writer has as yet succeeded in discovering how this bounty arrives and, equally, why it departs suddenly. And so I wish to reserve the final goodbye of this lifetime for all my readers, known and unknown, present and absent.

We were told in Vivekananda School that life is nothing but the effort to bud and then bloom in the face of constantly hostile circumstances. During my working days in the legal arena of the High Court, the English barrister had told me that all the joys of life are doubled if they are shared, and the sorrows halved the same way. At a time of extreme suffering, as she read by the light of a lantern, my mother would say, 'A mind that is lit up gives the greatest illumination.' My stepbrother Shibshankar would sing, 'Victory shall be ours, the world is made for human beings, it is not for demons.' My begging bowl overflows today with everyone's offerings. Coming face to face with 7 December in my eighties fills my heart with wonder.

Eighty-One and Alone

AND NOW THE SAME TRAIN HAS FOLLOWED THE UNPREDICTABLE Almighty's equally unpredictable timetable and entered Platform No. 81. Having begun the journey back in 1933 and found myself exhausted at the sight of the crowd on the platform every year since then, I never imagined being so very alone on scaling the Himalayan peak of age. Neither my parents nor my wife is with me, each of them adhered to the timetable that was assigned to them and left punctually, sometimes after serving notice and sometimes unexpectedly. At one time I used to believe in another life on the opposite bank of the river of death; I even had the firm conviction that I would be reunited with those who had left, but at the doorstep of eighty-one I felt suddenly afraid that the much-publicized idea of rebirth is nothing but a bedtime story, that those who are gone are gone forever, and all the things they say in the Upanishads on the subject are nothing but false consolation offered by a lying master poet, a Vedic prescription for protecting the hopelessly grief-stricken from complete collapse.

One of my favourite writers used to criticize his contemporaries constantly and hand out advice which another favourite writer from the same period did not approve of. This second person would say, 'Great writers do not wield their pens to become whole-time auditors or vigilance officers. Had that been the case the officers in charge of police stations would have been the most revered authors in the country.' Reports of this observation had reached the first writer, and irked him so much that he instructed me not to spend much time in Saradindu Bandyopadhyay's company, for when the body is home to too many Brahminical qualities it is not possible to be a man of letters.

It is my great fortune never to have been deprived of the loving indulgence of Bengal's star writers. It was one of them who had said to me as he was having a drink, 'There used to be violent riots between Bengali Brahmins and Bengali Kayasthas at one time here in Kidderpore. Anglo-Indian police sergeants quelled those riots after great effort, Swami Vivekananda himself encouraged Kayasthas to don the sacred thread of Brahmins. I believe Bengali-Muslim writers will eventually earn the mantle of being the best novelists. The basic truth I have arrived at after perusing the Chandi and Gita and Bible and Koran is that you, O God, might be infinitely compassionate, but you have no grasp over time, which is why you give young wives to old men, and it is also why you give those who have no teeth left in the twilight of their lives the affluence to consume mutton curry in restaurants.' The writer in question was Syed Mujtaba Ali.

I have basked in the company of one star writer after another here in Boipaara, believing this to be the due of any writer, something I can enjoy as long as I live. But who would have known that the boss upstairs would take them away one day, making me beg for their company once more?

Yet another brilliant writer, Banaphool or Balaichand Mukhopadhyay, used to say that no one is born a writer. 'You have to go to a great deal of trouble; it needs tremendous dedication and effort.' At which another writer born under a bright star, Shibram

Chakraborty, said, 'Let me tell you, it all boils down to the piety of your parents. No matter how much chemical fertilizer you add, a cauliflower plant will never yield flowers.'

The greatest writer from the place where I was born, Bongram, was Bibhutibhushan Bandyopadhyay. He smoked bidis, his clothes were not always spotless, and he wrote copiously on the afterlife. There was a rumour on College Street that he and his friend Parimal Goswami had made a verbal pact that whichever of them died first would somehow find a way to send a message to the survivor confirming the existence of the hereafter. When Bibhutibhushan passed away unexpectedly, Parimal Goswami waited a long time for a message before concluding with certainty that there's no such thing as an afterlife. On losing his wife, it was natural for this writer to not be particularly interested in conducting the rituals pertaining to the afterlife. There was some criticism of this in Boipaara, but I didn't add my voice to it.

But I digress. This is the problem with octogenarians. It is the law of old age to forget addresses, lose one's way, and arrive unknowingly at Gariahat from Howrah Station when the plan was to take the bus to Bagbazar. Bimal Mitra was extremely critical of such slackness. 'You must decide before leaving home where you're going. Writers who don't do this cheat both themselves and readers.' He would often warn me, 'The reader is your master. If I were being poetic I'd say they're the lord of your life, their time is valuable, they must never be cheated, the rickshaw-puller must take the passenger exactly where they want to go.'

And so, back to the main thread: How did I happen to turn up at eighty-one all by myself? Why do I not see any familiar faces on this remote mountain peak?

I should not by rights have any memories of the day I was born eighty-one years ago. My father, Haripada Mukhopadhyay, was a reticent man, seldom revealing anything. What I have heard is almost entirely from my mother, Abhayarani. It was she who told me about Noni Babu's house in Bongram where the family lived on rent. The house was still intact when I visited my birthplace many years later, though I don't know whether that is still the case. We were on very good terms with our neighbours, the jeweller Panchu and his family.

As I have already mentioned, my mother was originally named Gauri. Her hot-tempered father Khirode Banerjee had lost his job suddenly and was floundering with three extremely beautiful unmarried daughters. This was the time Haripada Mukhopadhyay the lawyer lost his first wife, who left behind a daughter and two sons. I think he was forty-three when he married a second time. Since his son was also named Gauri, there was social objection to stepmother and stepson having the same name, and so my luckless mother had to give up hers. True to the goddess she had been named after in terms of her beauty, Gauri became Abhaya thanks to a cruel turn of fate.

Seeking a fortune in the practice of law, my father transported the entire family to Howrah. Not all my siblings had been born yet, but with my two stepbrothers thrown in, the two rooms were awfully crowded. I still remember the problem I created once. My stepbrothers had dressed up for a visit to their sister's house across the river in Bowbazar on the occasion of Bhaiphonta, observed as brothers' day. I threw a tantrum, asking to go with them; my mother was deeply embarrassed, for I had not been invited. Eventually my favourite among my two stepbrothers, the younger one, did not go to his sister's house either—seeing which my mother beat me up in annoyance.

The company of neighbours brought me joy that ended my loneliness temporarily. In particular I depended greatly on the unmarried Badal Kaku and his younger brother Pochu Kaku. Our house was too crowded for my parents to pay any attention to me. That was the time there was a development without which I would have been in deep difficulties afterwards. Pochu Kaku was friends with Satish Babu of Howrah District School. Out for a walk with me one day, he dropped in on his friend at the school and realized that admission tests were going on. In 1940 it wasn't as difficult to secure admission in a school as it is nowadays. On a whim Pochu Kaku made me take the admission test with the intention of surprising my mother. Entering the exam hall a little later, he found me sitting quietly with the arithmetic questions, unable to answer any of them. Pochu Kaku promptly answered the questions himself. They results came out immediately, but it turned out that the District School had no class one or class two, the lowest level was class three. I, however, was only seven. Undeterred, Pochu Kaku enrolled me, precocious as I was, in class three, paying the fees from his own pocket, and returned triumphantly to Chowdhurybagan. I remained eternally weak in mathematics, besides having to face the calumny of being much shorter than my classmates, since I was two whole years younger. But Pochu Kaku had unknowingly done me a great favour, for although I was only thirteen when my father died unexpectedly in 1947, I was already in class ten.

The free tiffin at the District School was enough to wipe out all my daily disappointments. Even after all these years I recall the taste of the luchi and slow-cooked potatoes we were given. But the unbridled happiness of this midday meal did not last long, for, as I have mentioned earlier, the school was closed for months during the Second World War to operate as billets for foreign soldiers. After a perfunctory promotion to class six, word spread that the school wouldn't reopen until after the war ended. And no one knew when the war would end. Many in Howrah were already learning Japanese in secret. No one was worried about school, with a large number of people fleeing in fear of being bombed by the Japanese, and the word 'evacuation' had been appended to the Bangla language.

The Mukherjee family of Howrah had returned to Bongram, but on Badal Kaku's advice I had stayed back with my father. Despite being so young, I went off on my own in search of a new school. Sudhangshushekhar Bhattacharya, the headmaster of Vivekananda Institution on what was then named Khurut Road, was so delighted to see a little boy turn up at the school all on his own to be admitted that he waived the admission test. I am still terrified at the thought of what might have happened had there been a mathematics test.

One reason for my personal disappointment with Vivekananda Institution was the absence of the free tiffin. A bearer sold snacks from a basket during the break, while servants from the homes of my affluent schoolmates brought specially prepared food from home, which the lucky boys, too embarrassed to eat alone, consumed rapidly as they sat facing the walls. The headmaster would tell us stories about Swami Vivekananda's penchant for food and for cooking, about how he publicized the Vedanta and biriyani simultaneously in America, and how his childhood friend Rakhal used to eat a kilogram of kochuri for breakfast before becoming Swami Brahmananda.

Having weathered the evacuation from Bongram, my mother returned to Chowdhurybagan. She was still willing to bear all her hardships in the hope that her eldest son would become another Ashutosh Mukherjee. My enquiries had revealed that Sir Ashutosh was a mathematical genius, had been one since childhood. I was consumed by embarrassment after scoring twelve in my mathematics exam—I still don't know why—despite my father's prediction of eighty or so. But the disappointment on my mother's face was enough to make me downcast.

Thus I concluded, following much deliberation, that there was nothing to say every famous person in the world had to be an expert in mathematics. I decided to make my mother proud by becoming a renowned artist. I bought paints, brushes and paper and, taking the entry fee from her, took part in a sit-and-draw competition. We were told to draw a human face. I submitted my artwork with great enthusiasm. The eternally resourceful Pochu Kaku went to ferret out advance information and came back with a glum face to inform us that what awaited me was not a prize but a surprise. Because I had drawn a ripe papaya in the shape of a human face. The fault of course was not mine, for great artists are alone even in a crowd, and although I was young I had already observed that every human does in fact resemble a jackfruit or wood apple or gourd or coconut. I realized I was ahead of my times; if Picasso were asked to paint a face, the pumpkin painted on his canvas would be worth millions of dollars. The concept of artistic freedom had not reached Howrah yet.

But my mother's tears made me miserable. I could not fathom how to be worthy of her expectations. After trying various options, what finally came my way was not something I had imagined.

At that age it was unbearable to have so many people living at home. I preferred the atmosphere in the Basu family next door. Badal Kaku's younger brother, my favourite Pochu Kaku, had left home after quarrelling with his brother; their grandmother wept alone in her room; and in another room Badal Kaku gazed at a photograph of Mr Livingstone, the all-in-all of the Kalamazoo Looseleaf Company to hide his tears, muttering that unless England won this war the world would go to hell.

Calcutta had been largely emptied out at the time by evacuation. My father put the pot on the stove himself to make boiled rice and potatoes for the two of us before leaving for the courts. In the evening some of his lawyer friends came to chat with him about his life in the theatre—especially about his association with Kohinoor Theatre on Beadon Street, which had vanished by then, and about Girish Ghosh. My father told his friends how he had needlessly frittered away much of his youth because of his obsession with the theatre—a facet of his life that was completely unknown to me—and he did not want his children to become besotted with the world of theatre. And all this time, unknown to him, I was dreaming of becoming a writer with my headmaster's encouragement.

Unable to make a reasonable living in the theatre, my father had begun practising law in Bongram. When that first attempt proved a failure, he moved to Howrah. You cannot be successful at law in a new place when you have to cook in the morning. My father relied on a judge of Howrah district who liked him. This gentlemen told my father on meeting him unexpectedly in Bongram, 'Move to Howrah at once, I can give you the responsibility of being the receiver of a landowner's estate. You will have a fixed income of one hundred and fifty rupees a month for a few years. You can use that time to establish your practice.'

Many years later a court officer had reminded my father, 'Remember the trouble you ran into?' My father had been waiting impatiently after submitting the papers for the receivership in the court of the judge, but there was no response. So he had had no choice but to force his way into the presence of the judge, who said, 'What! But Haripada Mukhopadhyay has already signed the appointment letter.' The court officer was sent for, and he realized that the appointment letter had been handed over to the wrong Hari, not the one with the moustache. Fortunately the other Hari turned out to be a gentleman. On being told that the officer had a made a mistake, he returned the 'life-saving papers', which finally found their way to the Hari with the moustache. There was much laughter when my father recounted this incident to his friends, and I got to hear it too as I prepared their tobacco.

In school I asked Hadu Da, 'Aren't lawyers good people?' Hadu Da said, 'Thakur Ramakrishna used to make fun of doctors and lawyers, but his favourite disciple Vivekananda belonged to a family with several generations of lawyers, Swami-ji himself had purchased lawyers' robes from Dharmatala and begun his working life in the attorneys' offices near the High Court.'

Hadu Da would sometimes tell the younger students too about Vivekananda. Even during the worst period in his life he did not accept defeat, always keeping his faith, we shall overcome, we shall overcome. That was when I learnt that Naren Dutta's father had died suddenly. Not that there was any sign that the same fate would soon overtake me as well.

The house was much too crowded at the time. A dozen people had to sleep in two small rooms on beds made on the floor. From setting the mattresses to putting up the mosquito nets and taking up our respective sleeping positions, it was a most troublesome affair.

One day my father and I went to Bongram to watch a performance of the play *Rani Durgaboti*, which he had written. Evening had fallen by the time we were returning; the train was not particularly crowded. I loved that someone who normally maintained a distance was so close to me that day in the moving train. Suddenly I blurted out, 'I am afraid of being alone.' Instead of scolding me, he said, 'Look at me, I am alone too, my father left me long ago. Eventually everyone finds the strength to live alone, it no longer seems hard.'

He alone knew whether he was hinting at a future yet to come. Very late one night I heard the sound of people sobbing in the other room. By the time I rushed in, my father had left eight young children and my mother to depart to an unknown land from where return is impossible.

That was the beginning of one of the strangest periods in my life. Thanks to Pochu Kaku's far-sightedness years earlier, I was able to take the matriculation examination rather young. By way of friends there was my neighbour Badal Kaku, and, at the school, Hadu Da, who had passed on Vivekananda's mantra to me, which had helped me keep my self-identity alive even in the face of extreme adversity.

I had not expected these unbearable circumstances to be eased. But by a stroke of luck a series of incidents took place. The lawyer's son met the English barrister Barwell, but death snatched him away too. Still, none of the conspiracies proved successful in the end. I finally wrote my first book as a tribute to his memory. Even if I didn't turn out to be the Ashutosh Mukherjee that Khirode Banerjee had promised his daughter, my mother was probably pleased to see her son walk in his father's shoes. As she used to say herself from time to time, half a loaf is better than no bread.

As for me, I went from lonely to lonelier. It had become my habit during a particular phase of my life to recite two particular lines of Rabindranath Tagore's—'If they don't come when you call, just walk alone.'

Many years later I discovered to my surprise that my father's untimely death had dispatched me from childhood to old age directly, the locomotive of my life had not made even the shortest of stops at the junction of youth. My mother used to say I had ripened too early, and later, my wife, Bandana, found this line in something I had written, 'Youth in its whimsy knocks on some people's doors but a few times and goes back rebuffed.' In my defence I was citing Bankim Chandra Chatterjee—we are the slaves of circumstances, when will circumstances be our slaves?

I can admit after all these years that with the blessings of Bankim Chandra, Rabindranath and Vivekananda, I have succeeded in enduring all the pain of loneliness and arrived at this distant location of eighty-one. None of those who have been beacons to me on this desolate, often unendurable, journey—Baba, Ma, Badal Kaku, Pochu Kaku, Hadu Da, Bibhuti Da, Mr Barwell, and my companion on the last stretch, Bandana—are alive to greet me. Still I can say to them that I have reached the age of eighty-one today because you were there once.

Dear Reader

I HAVE FACED MANY QUESTIONS FROM MANY PEOPLE ABOUT THE writer–publisher–reader relationship. Taking on the mantle of well-wishers, some have asked, why do you not publish your books yourself? Janakinath Sinha Roy of New Age, my very first publisher, taught me the answer.

His advice was, 'Tell anyone who asks, not even the best barber in the world can cut his own hair. Everyone must be allowed to do what they are best at.'

On another occasion, a gentleman with a droll sense of humour had introduced his wife to me as his publisher. When I asked him which book he had written, he said, 'Me and a book? I'm just a workman, this lady has "published" our only child, hence a publisher.'

In truth publishing is a hundred times more arduous than writing a book—compose the text, check the proofs, do the layouts, check the proofs again, get the index made if necessary, get the cover designed, print the book, chase the binder, before that fast at the damp and dark altar of the printer, then bring the printed books home, keeping an eagle eye on the transportation, whether it is a pushcart or a rickshaw—both the responsibilities and the risks are endless. And then, after all this, there may be no sign of buyers. The publisher's sales counter is patronized by flies in the daytime and mosquitoes at night, but still the author must strut about with a smile, claiming that sales are soaring, that copies are flying off the shelves.

Writing is a laborious task to begin with, every thick book that is produced shaves five years of its writer's lifespan. On top of this, if the writer also had to pay the bills of the paper-seller, the binder and the landlord, that is the end of that. Novelists are not long-lived in this land. Bankim Chandra Chattopadhyay left us at fifty-six, Saratchandra Chattopadhyay at sixty-two, Bibhutibhushan Bandyopadhyay at fifty-six, and Manik Bandyopadhyay at only forty-eight. To stay healthy Bimal Mitra avoided fried food and lived on bitter leaves, boiled vegetables and light fish curry with rice. Writing with your heart and mind takes an enormous toll on the brain and the body, your insides are hollowed out. So please do not impose any additional responsibility on writers besides writing.

It can be said with certainty that the first book written in the world had no publisher. Humans did not know of printing, for it did not exist, therefore nobody had any dreams of a bestseller. When the practice of printing books was introduced, handwritten manuscripts became a thing of the past, but what the writer acquired was financial responsibility. It wasn't enough to write a book, you had to spend your own money to buy paper and meet the printer's bill. Not all writers could stomach this, but avoiding the pain did not necessarily lead to pleasure. And so the writer effectively became a well-dressed beggar. Put on some garments and off you go to the king's palace or the landowner's mansion or the merchant's residence, chanting your poetry. If they are pleased with your flattery they will give you permission to dedicate the book to them, which means, in plain language, 'I will give you a hundred rupees to print this.' Far from making any money from the sales proceeds, it is a matter of great fortune not to be chastised by the moneylender. In those days nobody became a writer in order to have a comfortable, happy existence.

Then the market deteriorated further. The kings and emperors grew wise to the game of the writers. When the landowner was told that a writer was sitting patiently in the drawing room to extract permission to dedicate their book to him, not only he but also his manager and cashier would be furious. Keep them waiting as long as possible, let hours go by. Why all this subterfuge when you're actually here to beg?

Finally someone's patience snapped, and though history doesn't tell us who this writer was, we bow to them a thousand times, for they secured independence for the tribe. No more presenting oneself at the royal court for financial patronage, they declared, the offering will now go directly to the people. If the writer must bow to someone in deference, let it be to the reader and nobody else.

Thus began the democracy of writers. Freedom, truth and honour secured victory. From now on it was only the reader who would win.

Time propelled the writers' democracy another step forward. People began to dream of libraries outside palaces and monasteries—millions were eager to be part of the world of delight created by writers. The rich lock away their money only in banks and in the form of gold, but the people also have savings in the form of knowledge, pleasures, ideas and thoughts.

People did not rest after this taste of freedom, now they began to dream of small collections of books in their own homes. At the same time, they wanted to give the writer the right to survive. An empty stomach is conducive neither to religious practices nor to devoting yourself to the goddess of learning. What a writer can give you after a hearty meal is incomparable. They are not just analysts of the past and the present, they are also as constant as the North Star, painting all of human life in an ethereal glow. An endless array of choices will lie in front of you, select only what you want, do not worry about what you don't want, time is eternal, shaped as it is by the varying tastes of individuals. Nothing will remain unsold in the grand carnival of printed books. Someone or the other will pick it up, perhaps today, perhaps tomorrow or the day after, or in another era, in another time.

It was a revolutionary time in the lives of writers—of transformation, of radical change. The writer was no longer alone in the struggle for rupees and paise, they had a new companion named the publisher. If the writer is the god of creation, the publisher is Mother Earth—taking the seeds of creation into her womb, she weaves dreams with ever-widening expanses for the author; freeing them from the responsibility of nurture, she gives them the freedom to create anew. This is why the far-sighted writer never considers the publisher inferior, nor does the experienced publisher think that life would have been easier without the writer.

We have an answer to the first question, then. Where the match between the writer and the publisher is made in heaven, spring can reign eternal.

'But what about me?' someone seems to be screaming. 'Your love would have been barren without me, O god of the three worlds!' Indeed, what is the purpose of writers being born in a readerless world? Some writers have stated with great indignation, who's this reader anyway, I don't write for anyone, I don't dress myself up and wait at the door with the evening lamp for anyone. I write for myself, for my own satisfaction.

Were they lying?

I have been confronted by this question time and again in my writerly life. They weren't lying, possibly it was a harsh expression of their pain, for who would willingly bear the labour pain of delivering a book had the world been devoid of readers? I don't believe such a writer has been born yet, and I say this from the experience of consorting with writers all my life. What about the declaration of pride then: I fulfil myself, I depend on no one, I am no one's slave. Take it easy, my friend. Reader, do you hear only the words the poet utters, do you not hear what their heart says?

In that heart lies the thirst of the desert. This love–hate relationship is inevitable, for after all this is not a mere transaction between buyer and seller. The value of what the writer creates in their madness cannot be measured by price, and they expect something more than the price of a book from readers.

What is it that they expect? In Urdu, it is known as 'taarif'. This word, it's far too difficult, its meaning far too wide-ranging, it goes too deep into the core. The spurned lover knows only too well that recognition is not always forthcoming in this merciless world, nor is honour. What is is condemnation, criticism, and, even worse, neglect. Still the writer cannot stop marching, though the path is littered with thorns. Why, even the bloodied, wounded foot composes music. Those who walk on this path, those who have felt the embrace of their beloved reader even once, cannot turn back; the more their feet bleed the louder they echo the poet's lyrics: *This is best, O cruel one, this is best.*

And so the writer is the heroine and the reader the lord of her life, the one for whom she has assumed human form in wakefulness, in sleep, in her dreams. But the question is, who came first, the writer or the reader? Which of them is to be found at the beginning of this eternal game? A very difficult question. Which came first, the seed or the tree, the chicken or the egg?

Readers and writers alike will have to immerse themselves in an ocean of cogitation to find the answer, they will have to discover one another over and over, a thousand times, in the light of new feelings. When I was young, I used to get books from the local library for my eternally suffering mother. She used to say, 'The writer is great, so great, the reader stands nowhere in comparison.'

But when, several years later, thanks to a turn of fate and the ironic sense of humour of adversity, I entered the field of literature myself, her happiness knew no bounds. The sense of deprivation was wiped out—she was now a writer's mother. That was when I asked her: Who is greater, the writer or the reader?

She smiled and withdrew her earlier claim. Without a moment's hesitation she said, 'Of course it's the reader. For it is the reader who becomes a writer one day. Someone who has never been a reader will never be a writer.'

I had interpreted this to mean the reader is the lord of the three worlds, that the great carnival of literature exists for the reader's entertainment alone.

I salute this reader. It is for this reader that the writer lives and dreams.

FIN

Sankar is one of the top-selling Bengali writers of all times, with a literary career spanning over seventy years. His novel *Chowringhee* continues to be a bestseller sixty years after publication.

Arunava Sinha translates fiction, non-fiction and poetry from Bengali to English and from other languages into Bengali. Over seventy of his translations have been published so far.

30 Years *of*

HarperCollins *Publishers* India

At HarperCollins, we believe in telling the best stories and finding the widest possible readership for our books in every format possible. We started publishing 30 years ago; a great deal has changed since then, but what has remained constant is the passion with which our authors write their books, the love with which readers receive them, and the sheer joy and excitement that we as publishers feel in being a part of the publishing process.

Over the years, we've had the pleasure of publishing some of the finest writing from the subcontinent and around the world, and some of the biggest bestsellers in India's publishing history. Our books and authors have won a phenomenal range of awards, and we ourselves have been named Publisher of the Year the greatest number of times. But nothing has meant more to us than the fact that millions of people have read the books we published, and somewhere, a book of ours might have made a difference.

As we step into our fourth decade, we go back to that one word – a word which has been a driving force for us all these years.

Read.

Harper Collins
4th
HARPER PERENNIAL
HARPER BUSINESS
HARPER BLACK
हार्पर हिन्दी
HarperCollins *Children'sBooks*
HARPER DESIGN
HARPER VANTAGE
Harper Sport

